A Publication of the Economic Growth Center, Yale University

THE TRANSITION IN
OPEN DUALISTIC ECONOMIES

Theory and Southeast Asian Experience

DOUGLAS S. PAAUW
and
JOHN C. H. FEI

New Haven and London, Yale University Press

Copyright © 1973 by Yale University.
Second printing, 1977.
All rights reserved. This book may not be
reproduced, in whole or in part, in any form
(except by reviewers for the public press),
without written permission from the publishers.
Library of Congress catalog card number: 73–77163
International standard book number: 0–300–01641–7

Designed by Sally Sullivan
and set in Times Roman type.
Printed in the United States of America by
The Murray Printing Company,
Westford, Massachusetts.

Published in Great Britain, Europe, Africa, and Asia
(except Japan) by Yale University Press, Ltd., London.
Distributed in Latin America by Kaiman & Polon, Inc.,
New York City; in Australia and New Zealand by
Book & Film Services, Artarmon, N.S.W., Australia;
and in Japan by Harper & Row, Publishers,
Tokyo Office.

Contents

List of Diagrams and Tables

DIAGRAMS

TABLES IN THE TEXT

TABLES IN THE STATISTICAL APPENDIX

Foreword

This volume is one in a series of studies supported by the Economic Growth Center, an activity of the Yale Department of Economics since 1961. The Center is a research organization with worldwide activities and interests. Its research interests are defined in terms of both method of approach and subject matter. In terms of method, the Center sponsors studies which are designed to test significant general hypotheses concerning the problem of economic growth and which draw on quantitative information from national economic accounts and other sources. In terms of subject matter, the Center's research interests include theoretical analysis of economic structure and growth, quantitative analysis of a national economy as an integral whole, comparative cross-sectional studies using data from a number of countries, and efforts to improve the techniques of national economic measurement. The research program includes field investigation of recent economic growth in twenty-five developing countries of Asia, Africa, and Latin America.

The Center administers, jointly with the Department of Economics, the Yale training program in International and Foreign Economic Administration. It presents a regular series of seminar and workshop meetings and includes among its publications both book-length studies and journal reprints by staff members, the latter circulated as Center Papers.

Gustav Ranis, Director

Preface

This book is a study of development in a particular type of less developed country with an open dualistic economy. Much contemporary development theory has focused upon the closed dualistic economy, emphasizing interaction between the two domestic sectors, agriculture and industry. In this book an effort is made to take the next logical step by analyzing the role of foreign trade in the development of a dualistic economy. Such an effort is more than justified by the prevalence of a colonial heritage among less developed countries. In the colonial economy, activity centered upon foreign trade, especially in regard to primary product exports. Thus this study of open dualism attempts to move development theory in the direction of greater realism.

Colonialism was a long era of growth enduring in many less developed countries, typically for a period of centuries, prior to World War II. In this historical perspective, the period of postwar growth (1950 to 1970) is a brief interim of transition growth which marks the end of colonialism and which, it is hoped, will usher in an era of modern growth. Our book is explicitly concerned with this first generation of transition growth, with special emphasis upon the relevance of the transitional economy's historical background.

Methodology appropriate for the study of less developed countries involves a combination of economic theory, institutional economics, and statistical data. In our present study of open dualism the theoretical aspect emphasizes a triangular pattern of interaction among agriculture, industry, and the foreign sector. The empirical aspect is based upon four Southeast Asian countries (Taiwan, Malaysia, the Philippines and Thailand) for which statistical data

have been collected in a statistical appendix at the back of the
book to corroborate theoretical findings.

The data presented conform to our design of analysis which emphasizes macroeconomics. Professor Kuznets has raised the very
legitimate question of the specific commodity content of aggregate
magnitudes employed, e.g., "imported industrial consumer goods,
imported capital goods," "agricultural exports, and nonagricultural exports." These magnitudes are derived from classification
and aggregation of detailed data from the countries in question at
the industry level. Derivation of these aggregate estimates has required extensive empirical work in the four countries over a period
of five or six years. Details on methods and data sources have been
presented in several intermediate studies. Ultimately, the empirical
validity of our work rests upon this statistical foundation. We re-
gret that this basic work is too bulky to produce in this volume.
References to the data studies are found throughout the chapters
on specific countries.

The institutional aspect in our study is interpreted as the political and economic-geographic factors that influence government
policy and thus shape the course of transition growth. Since the
background factors inherited from colonialism are intrinsically
heterogeneous, considerable diversity of actual growth experience
is found in the four Southeast Asian countries. The implication is
that realistic development theory must be typological in nature.
The selection of four countries for application of our analysis
allows us to demonstrate the relevance of the typological approach
for these "small," open, dualistic economies.

The typological approach to development is a pragmatic compromise between an all-inclusive general theory of universal ap-
plicability and mere individual country case studies. At various
points in our work we refer to comparable experience in countries
beyond our specific empirical focus on the four countries we have
studied intensively. These references suggest the possibility of
transferability of our conclusions. It should be borne in mind,
however, that references to other countries are heuristic, intended
to stimulate further research in the typological approach to transition growth.

Much of the original research and data work behind this study was conducted at the National Planning Association under a research contract with the Agency for International Development. We are grateful for this sponsorship of our work as well as for more recent assistance from the Southeast Asia Development Advisory Group (SEADAG) of the Asia Society, New York, which allowed us to extend our empirical work and to complete the study in its present form.

At the National Planning Association, we received continuous encouragement from the Chief of International Studies, Theodore Geiger, and the Executive Secretary, John Miller. Our colleagues in the Center for Development Planning were available for evaluating and criticizing our developing ideas. We acknowledge an intellectual debt to Eliezer Ayal, Forrest Cookson, George Hicks, Richard Hooley, Alek Rozental, and Joseph Tryon, all closely familiar with Southeast Asian economies.

The empirical research for the study was conducted in several Southeast Asian countries. The National Planning Association maintained a cooperative relationship with the School of Economics, University of the Philippines, and with the Faculty of Economics, Thammasat University (Thailand). We wish to acknowledge with thanks significant contributions by both institutions. We are especially grateful to Dean Amado Castro of the University of the Philippines and to former Dean Puey Ungphakorn of Thammasat University for their constant interest and cooperation in our work. Colleagues at both institutions offered stimulating help and counsel. We acknowledge our debt to José Encarnacion, Agustin Kintanar, Gerardo Sicat, and others at the University of the Philippines and in Thailand to Laurence Stifel of Thammasat University and to Snoh Unakol. We are grateful for research assistance provided by Casimiro Miranda (Philippines), Medhi Krongkaew (Thailand), and Marcia Brewster (Thailand). In Singapore we received cooperation from Dean Lim Chong Yah of the University of Singapore, who graciously arranged seminars for testing our ideas at the Economic Research Centre. Similar arrangements were made for us in Taiwan through the courtesy of Huang Chin-Mao of the National University of Taiwan. Without the cooperation of these and many other Southeast Asian scholars, this book could not have been written.

In the preparation of drafts of this book we have received competent and conscientious help from Mrs. Jennie Payne, Mrs. Dolores Hildebrandt, and Mrs. Adele Bogdan. Most recently we have received very penetrating comments based on careful reading of our manuscript from Simon Kuznets, Gustav Ranis, and Lloyd Reynolds. These comments have been particularly helpful in improving the final draft of the manuscript. The Economic Growth Center, with which these scholars and the authors of the present study have been associated, is the source of many ideas in this book. We acknowledge with gratitude the stimulation, criticism, and support received from colleagues in the Center. We assume sole responsibility, however, for the analysis and conclusions of the study.

D. S. P.

J. C. H. F.

March 1973

Part I

GENERAL PRINCIPLES OF TRANSITION GROWTH

1

Transition Growth in Historical Perspective

This book analyzes a generation (1950 to 1970) of growth experience in open dualistic economies in Southeast Asia. From a long-run historical perspective the postwar growth of these and many other less developed countries represents a unique growth process, which may be referred to as transition growth.

The notion of transition growth is based on the idea of long-run growth epochs. Kuznets defines an economic epoch as "a relatively long period (extending well over a century) possessing distinctive characteristics that give it unity and differentiate it from epochs that precede or follow it." [1] Before World War II, Southeast Asian countries shared a common epoch of colonialism, i.e., a primarily agricultural economy containing an enclave dedicated to the export of primary products. Decolonization after World War II has led toward the emergence of a new epoch of modern economic growth. The postwar generation is a unique historical experience of transition from the colonial epoch to the epoch of modern growth. [2]

I. The Colonial Economy

The study of transition growth obviously must begin from an understanding of the colonial epoch from which the transition evolves. The colonial epoch may be interpreted as the superimposition of

1. Simon Kuznets, *Modern Economic Growth: Rate, Structure and Spread* (New Haven: Yale University Press, 1966), p. 2.
2. The major event of the transition from colonialism has received attention from political scientists, historians, and scholars from other disciplines as well as economists. For an example of the economist's approach see John C. H. Fei and Gustav Ranis, "Economic Development in Historical Perspective," *American Economic Review* 59, no. 2 (May 1969): 386–400.

3

foreign political control upon an agrarian economy, enforcing upon this economy a very special mode of operation relying upon primary product exports. The colonial economy's structure and its mode of operation may be pictured in terms of intersectoral relationships among its key economic sectors.

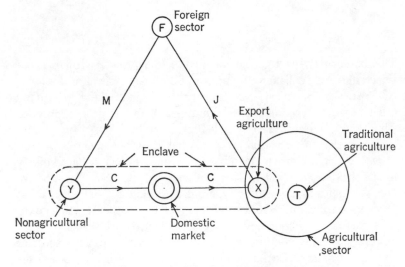

Diagram 1.1. The Colonial Economy

The operational outline of the colonial economy is depicted in diagram 1.1. Domestically the economy is characterized by sectoral dualism between a nonagricultural sector, Y,[3] and an agricultural sector. The latter is subdivided into a commercialized agricultural sector, X, and a traditional agricultural sector, T, which is large, noncommercialized, and backward. Sectors X and Y form an enclave which is involved in a triangular pattern of resource utilization with the foreign sector, F.

The economy's operation may be visualized in terms of the basic resource flows (shown in *real* terms) among the three sectors. Primary product exports, *J* (e.g. jute or sugar), flow from the com-

3. Roman capital letters will consistently be used in the text to refer to economic sectors, which are denoted in diagrams by encircled capital letters.

mercial agricultural sector, X, to the foreign sector, F.[4] This leads to the importation of manufactured goods, M, by the nonagricultural sector, Y. There is a domestic market in which purchasing power is generated by primary product exports, J. To complete the triangularism, the nonagricultural sector, Y, sells goods and services, C (industrial consumer goods and commercial services), to the domestic market serving commercialized agriculture, X.

This triangular mode of the economy's operation serves to achieve colonialism's fundamental goal, the realization of profits through production and export of primary products. Export surplus may be defined as the surplus from exports over and above imports required to maintain the existing level of production. In diagram 1.2a, where flows are now shown as *monetary* payments, suppose primary product export earnings J equal 100 and imports necessary to sustain this level of exports are $M = 80$. Then an export surplus, $J - M = 20$ emerges, initially flowing to the domestic finance sector, Z.

The economic goal of colonialism was to extract from the colony a tangible gain in the form of this export surplus, $J - M$. Institutional arrangements facilitated the conversion of this export surplus into export profits, π, accruing to alien entrepreneurs. These colonial profits were either employed to expand export production through reinvestment in the enclave or transferred abroad.

The long epoch of colonialism alternated between active and passive growth phases, depending on the state of foreign demand for primary product exports. In periods of rising demand, export profits, $\pi = 20$, were reinvested, leading to import of capital goods, $M_i = 20$ (see diagram 1.2b). This induced expansion of export capacity is the key phenomenon in the active phase of the colonial economy epoch. Conversely, during periods of falling world demand, export profits, $\pi = 20$, were repatriated to the mother coun-

---

4. Primary product exports may include "extractive products" (e.g. minerals and lumber) as well as agricultural goods. The essential characteristic of all primary product exports is that they are land-based, i.e. that they require specific natural resource content. The technique of production of these primary product exports may be either traditional technology (e.g., rice in Thailand) or more modern technology (e.g., rubber and palm oil in Malaysia). The economic significance of this distinction will be introduced later in the analysis (see chapter 2 and introduction to chapter 8).

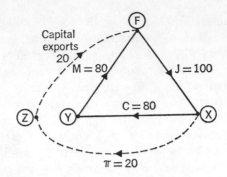

a.

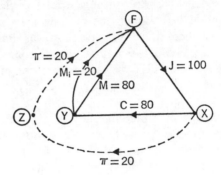

b.

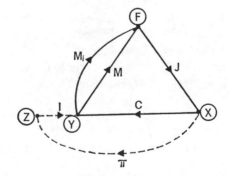

c.

Diagram 1.2. Colonial Finance and Decolonization
  a. Colonialism: passive phase
  b. Colonialism: active phase
  c. Redirection of saving after decolonization

try (as in diagram 1.2a), tantamount to capital export and causing stagnation of domestic export capacity.

To sum up, colonialism had a particular trade pattern which generated colonial export profits. These two economic characteristics of colonialism are significant in the analysis of the transition growth process because export profits are employed to modify production and trade structure. Subsequent chapters show, however, that the use of export profits to modify production and trade is not uniform among countries during the transition process. We identify two major types of experience. Under economic nationalism trade-related profits are employed to drastically alter production and trade patterns. Under neocolonialism, by contrast, trade-related profits are employed to strengthen the rural infrastructure and to expand and diversify the colonial trade pattern.

2. IMPLICATIONS FOR TRANSITION GROWTH

The colonial heritage left behind certain conditions which profoundly affect the nature and course of transition growth. Structurally, the economy was compartmentalized into two insulated parts: a modern, export-oriented enclave and a large, backward, traditional, agricultural sector. A primary task of transition growth is to integrate these two insulated parts into a national economy through the promotion of sectoral interaction. Integration contributes to the modernization of agriculture as well as to the diversification of industrial (nonagricultural) activities.

Income generation in the colonial economy was dominated by the export of land-based resources. The development of other domestic primary resources (i.e. entrepreneurship, skilled labor, and capital) was discouraged. Thus, shifting from the land base through the promotion of growth and development of these other domestic resources becomes a basic goal of transition growth.

Under colonialism the nonagricultural sector was characterized by provision of commercial services to facilitate land-based exports. Because of the land-based profit orientation of colonialism, investment was concentrated in these export services and the pace of investment was controlled by foreign market demand. Hence, the industrial sector developed no internal growth momentum of its own. A purpose of transition growth is to overcome this deficiency through industrialization, in which continuous development of manufacturing plays a major role.

Traditional agriculture, isolated from the enclave, remained a stagnant and backward sector under colonialism. Typically, low labor productivity was caused by primitive technology, an unfavorable land-labor ratio, and noncommercial attitudes. During a successful transition, these conditions must be overcome through the modernization of traditional agriculture as integration with the industrial sector evolves.

To summarize, transition growth requires the integration of the agricultural and industrial sectors, the growth and development of indigenous factors of production (entrepreneurship, skilled labor, and capital), industrialization, and the modernization of traditional agriculture. The focal point of transition growth analysis is to investigate the process through which these interrelated changes occur as modern growth is gradually initiated.

3. Design of Analysis

A theory of transition growth requires designing an analytical framework to incorporate major growth phenomena. From the above discussion, a number of distinct methodological issues suggest themselves. First, the theory must be short-run in nature. The major growth phenomena exhibit characteristics observable within a fifteen to twenty-five year time span. For purposes of the present study, the major theoretical content will be verified by statistical data collected from Southeast Asian countries for the period 1950–70.

In diagram 1.3, the transition is shown as an overlapping period between the long preceding epoch of colonialism and the subsequent epoch of modern growth. The shortness of the transition implies that the theoretical content is very different from phenomena occurring within a growth epoch.[5] During transition, the economy moves through radical changes resembling a process of evolution.

5. Thus the study of transition growth differs markedly from classical (Ricardo) and neoclassical (Solow, Kaldor) growth theory, both of which are addressed to epochal growth rather than to growth between epochs.

This feature of transition growth suggests the need for identifying transitional phases, shown as S_1, S_2, and S_3 in diagram 1.3, each lasting five to ten years. The sequence of phases means that the economy is not only growing in the quantitative sense, but also that its basic rules of growth are being gradually modified.

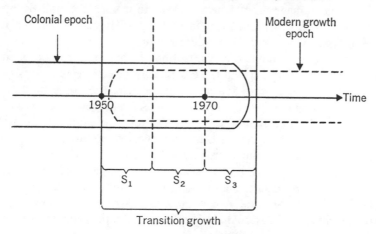

Diagram 1.3. Growth Epochs and the Transition

There are two quite different types of growth phenomena in this evolutionary view of the transition growth process, those having to do with the economy's mode of operation and those concerning the economy's mode of organization. The economy's mode of operation under colonialism is shown in diagram 1.1 by the triangular pattern of resource flows. This example emphasizes that an economy's mode of operation involves a holistic and intersectoral pattern of resource utilization. The holistic perspective embraces the whole economy rather than a part. The intersectoral approach focuses upon the relatedness of the major economic functions — production, consumption, saving, investment, export, import, etc. — that must be performed by transactions among the key sectors of the economy. The sequence of steps through which the economy's mode of operation changes is central to transition growth analysis, and, as such, will represent a major focus of this study.

The choice of a holistic, intersectoral approach for a comparative study of several countries circumscribes the analytical content of our book. This approach places our study in the macroeconomic tradition, which necessarily deemphasizes detailed intrasectoral analysis. In this connection, we may mention differences among regions, crops, and internal infrastructures of the traditional agricultural sector. Similar internal characteristics may be identified within the nonagricultural sector. We hope that the holistic approach of this study will provide useful guidelines for research in the internal issues of the individual sectors.

The economy's mode of organization refers to the method of social decision through which the essential intersectoral functions are carried out. Under colonialism economic decisions were made by alien entrepreneurs, and these decisions were coordinated by a foreign trade related market system. Typically, after decolonization, organization during the transition evolves into a mixed system. On the one hand, reliance on private entrepreneurial decisions under free markets is continued while, on the other hand, newly independent governments may modify this system through the introduction of a large variety of control policies (e.g. exchange controls, tariffs, subsidies). Analysis of changes in the economy's mode of organization and their implications for the course of transition growth is another major task of this study.

Less developed countries emerging from a colonial background inherit an open, dualistic economy, i.e. an economy characterized by coexistence of agricultural and industrial sectors domestically and by dominance of foreign trade (primary product exports) externally. Even within this type of economy, however, patterns of transition differ. Variations appear in the sequence of phases, producing different patterns of alteration in the economy's mode of operation and mode of organization.

The diversity in transition growth of contemporary less developed countries with open dualistic economies requires a typological approach. A first problem is the identification of alternative patterns of transition growth. A further question in this typological approach concerns the causation of the diversity. Economic and political backgrounds are dominant in explaining the emergence of different growth patterns. The economic background refers to economic-geographic factors, i.e., the supply of indigenous entrepreneurship, the relative backwardness of the agricultural sector, and the supply of natural resources for primary product exports. The political background refers to the society's composition in terms of economic interest groups such as remaining aliens, landlords, indigenous entrepreneurs, and ethnic groups, all of which contend for political power. Compromise among these contending groups leads to adoption of a particular method of organization for transition growth.

Typological differences are basic for understanding the reasons behind variations in growth and structural change in contemporary less developed countries. These variations signify that progress in transforming the inherited colonial economy to a modern growth economy is far from uniform. During the post–World War II generation (1950–70), performance varied from rapid transition in a few countries to very modest change in others.

To summarize, transition growth analysis focuses upon the sequence of phases occurring as a country terminates the colonial epoch and moves toward the epoch of modern growth. The central growth phenomena are changes in the economy's mode of operation (pattern of resource utilization) and in mode of organization. Diversity of transition growth, even within the family of open dualistic economies, calls for a typological approach.

4. TRANSITION GROWTH IN SOUTHEAST ASIAN COUNTRIES

The framework of analysis just described will be applied to a group of Southeast Asian countries: China (Taiwan), Malaysia, the Philippines, and Thailand. These countries share a common heritage of economic colonialism characterized by reliance upon primary product exports, backward traditional agriculture, and an undeveloped industrial sector. Transition experience during the first generation (1950–70) has centered upon attempts to modify this colonial heritage.[6] In broad outline, these countries show the common characteristics of transition growth within the family of open dualistic economies.

6. Throughout this book, the historical period 1950 to 1970 will be referred to as the "first generation" of transition growth. From a long-run perspective, this generation represents the initial period of transition growth. During this initial period, one or more phases of transition growth may occur.

It should be noted that these Southeast Asian countries are all relatively small, which causes foreign trade to be particularly vital in their transition growth. This means that the empirical conclusions from our study are directly relevant to small open economies, although the basic analytical framework is appropriate to open dualism generally.

Despite these common characteristics, however, differences in economic and political backgrounds lead to the emergence of two major types of transition experience, neocolonialism and economic nationalism. Malaysia and Thailand are examples of neocolonial transition growth while the Philippines and Taiwan exemplify growth under economic nationalism.

Growth under neocolonialism maintains considerable continuity with colonialism by continuing reliance upon primary product exports as the major growth force. Its chief organizational feature is retention of the free market system with little modification through use of government controls. In contrast, growth under economic nationalism represents a sharper break from the colonial heritage by emphasizing the development of domestic manufacturing industry. Organizationally, this is accomplished by government intervention in the free market system through import substitution policies. These typological differences, and variations in the course of transition growth within each major type, will be examined by analyzing the underlying background factors inherited from colonialism.

The empirical aspects of our work consist of both descriptive material and statistical data (1950–70) collected from the four Southeast Asian countries. This empirical evidence will be employed to show typological contrasts among the four countries as well as to show the sequencing of transition growth phases within countries. The statistical data that we will employ are consistent with our aggregate view of the economy, emphasizing intersectoral relationships through time.

5. OUTLINE OF STUDY

Subsequent chapters will expound the analytical framework presented in this chapter. Chapter 2 will introduce the economic aspect of transition growth by presenting the alternative modes of

operation occurring during the transition of open dualistic economies. Alternative patterns of resource utilization are analyzed in
terms of relationships among the key economic sectors. Three contrasting modes of operation will be analyzed: import substitution,
export promotion, and export substitution.

Chapters 3 and 4 deal with the issue of mode of organization for
transition growth. Chapter 3 is addressed to the control system of
economic nationalism appropriate for import substitution growth.
Chapter 4 analyzes the mechanism of the free market system of
neocolonialism as adopted for export promotion growth.

Chapter 5, which is concerned with the general issue of the
typology of transition growth, will investigate the reasons why a
country embarks upon a particular course of transition growth as
identified in chapter 2. Economic and political background factors
as they appear in the Southeast Asian countries will be relevant in
explaining the emergence of contrasting systems in different countries.

Part 1 (chapters 1 through 5) is thus devoted to the general
principles of transition growth in open dualistic economies. Part 2
will apply these general principles to the analysis of transition
growth in the four specific Southeast Asian countries mentioned.
The final chapter summarizes development strategy and policy conclusions which follow from the analysis of our study.

2

Economic Aspects of Transition Growth

During the transition in open dualistic economies, industrialization and modernization of agriculture must be accomplished through development of the society's primary factors of production (entrepreneurship, skilled labor, and capital). As these resources are augmented and improved qualitatively, their utilization will permit changes in the economy's mode of operation engendering growing integration between the agricultural and industrial sectors of the dualistic economy. These general transition tasks may, however, be achieved through alternative routes and processes. The alternatives are limited by the common properties which open dualistic economies inherit from colonialism.

1. THE COLONIAL HERITAGE AND TRANSITION GROWTH

The colonial heritage of a triangular pattern of resource utilization based on primary product exports is the foundation for transition growth. Since the industrial sector is undeveloped, the country must rely upon the agricultural sector, especially upon the agricultural export component, as a base for industrialization. Development of the industrial sector from this base necessitates a choice of orientation for its growth, i.e., what products it will produce and to what markets it will sell. Thus, the means for industrialization and its orientation are the two main determinants of alternative transition growth types.

1.1. Interaction Between Industry and Export Agriculture

At the outset of the transition the agricultural export sector forms the base for industrialization by providing foreign exchange, markets, and finance. Referring to diagram 1.1, the nonagricultural sector Y of the colonial enclave becomes the embryo for industrial growth during the transition.[1] Development of this nascent industrial sector requires the introduction of modern technology and capital goods from abroad. Foreign aid aside, the only way the country can acquire these resources is through the foreign exchange made available by primary product exports. Thus, the major resource role of the agricultural export sector is to provide imported capital goods, *M*, through primary product exports, *J*. This is a natural consequence of the colonial heritage.

The lack of indigenous entrepreneurship is a major bottleneck to the development of the industrial sector. An adequate market for industrial goods is essential to induce new entrepreneurs to invest in industrial production. It may be seen from diagram 1.1 that the domestic market is the traditional market outlet for the industrial sector's output. Purchasing power in this market is generated by income from primary product exports, *J*. Thus, industrial investment incentives are directly tied to income generated from this source.

The agricultural export sector is also the foundation for industrialization in the financial sense. From diagram 1.2 we recall that under colonialism, profits, *π*, from primary exports could be used either to finance capital goods imports (as in the active phase shown in diagram 1.2b) or for capital export (as in the passive phase shown in diagram 1.2a). After decolonialization, this agricultural export surplus continues to be the major source of the economy's saving fund. However, now through nationalization or other measures, these profits are removed from alien control and they may be devoted exclusively to the finance of domestic industrial investment. This redirection of export profits is shown in diagram 1.2c, where

---

1. It should be noted that the nonagricultural sector Y under colonialism included several types of services which accommodated primary product exports. The sector frequently also had a nascent manufacturing component producing physical inputs for agricultural production and, in some cases, also producing consumer goods. This mixture of service and manufacturing functions is elaborated upon in chapters 8 and 9 where we show that the nonagricultural sector plays different roles in transition growth, depending on which component is dominant.

these profits, π, are used to finance domestic investment, I, accommodated by capital goods imports, M_i.

To summarize, in countries with a colonial heritage, the agricultural export sector tends naturally to provide an integral package of functions for industrialization during the initial phase of the transition. Consistent with this mode of operation, the orientation of the industrial sector is necessarily toward the internal market. This pattern of resource utilization will occur under a market system, but it may be accelerated by government measures as in the case of an import substitution strategy.

1.2. Interaction Between Industry and Traditional Agriculture

The mode of operation which evolves in the earliest stage of the transition involves interaction between the industrial sector, Y, and export agriculture, X (see diagram 1.1). The colonial heritage also left a large traditional agricultural sector, T, outside the enclave. This latter sector continues to resist modernization impulses. Depending on its degree of backwardness, integration with the other sectors and modernization tendencies appear only later in the transition process.

When interaction between the traditional agricultural sector and the rest of the economy evolves, a new mode of operation is created in the transitional economy. Increasing productivity in this sector permits it to play a new role in the industrial sector's growth, supplementing and eventually displacing the agricultural export sector base.

The nature of interaction between traditional agriculture and industry is well developed in the theory of growth of the dualistic economy.[2] In addition to the intersectoral functions of providing markets and finance (as described above), the traditional sector may become the source for rapid labor transfers to the industrial sector. These labor transfers are significant in eventually changing the input composition in the industrial sector. This lays the basis for evolution of a new mode of operation in the transition process,

2. See, for example, John C. H. Fei and Gustav Ranis, *Development of the Labor Surplus Economy: Theory and Policy* (Homewood, Illinois: Richard D. Irwin, Inc., 1964).

built upon the export of labor-intensive industrial goods. The industrial sector's orientation now shifts to producing export manufactures for the foreign market.

Thus, it is in interaction among the key sectors of the economy that the means of industrialization as well as the industrial sector's orientation are determined. Initially, the major interaction is between the industrial sector and the export agriculture sector. In this early phase, the country relies upon land based export as the means of industrialization. In a later phase, the focus shifts to interaction between the industrial sector and the traditional agriculture sector. In both phases, agriculture provides market outlets and savings for industrialization. However, in the early phase, land-based exports provide imported resources as the key input into the industrial sector. In the second phase, labor transferred from traditional agriculture becomes the crucial input. Thus, in the second phase of the transition, the growth system changes from a land base to a labor base.

1.3. Alternative Modes of Operation

Historical perspective leads to identification of three major modes of operation for transition growth in open dualistic economies: *import substitution, export promotion* and *export substitution*. Each of these alternative growth types offers a holistic view of resource utilization among the economy's key sectors. The industrial sector's orientation is the dominant criterion for distinguishing these three alternative modes of operation.

In import substitution the industrial sector is oriented toward the domestic market to replace traditionally imported consumer goods. An existing and visible market for industrial output is conducive to the easy launching of this growth type. Import substitution growth is normally facilitated by nationalistic trade policy designed to exclude competitive foreign imports.

In export promotion growth the industrial sector is oriented toward the domestic market, but output consists of goods and services for stimulating the expansion of primary product exports. This growth type is feasible only where the country's natural resources base is adequate for continued reliance upon land-based exports. In this sense, export promotion resembles the colonial mode of operation, and is likewise typically supported by a perpetuation of the free market system.

In export substitution growth, the industrial sector is oriented toward the foreign market, and output consists of labor-intensive manufactures in which the country enjoys comparative advantage. The very term export substitution signifies that in this mode of operation the country succeeds in substituting industrial exports for its traditional primary products. The emergence of this phase represents a dramatic departure from the internal industrial orientations of the past, based upon the acquisition of sufficient entrepreneurial skills to penetrate export markets.

Only import substitution and export promotion are sufficiently close to the colonial heritage to serve as initial transition growth systems. In the Philippines and Taiwan, the transition was begun through import substitution, while in Malaysia and Thailand, export promotion was adopted. Taiwan is the only country among these four in which the initial transition growth system has led to the more advanced system of export substitution.

2. IMPORT SUBSTITUTION GROWTH

2.1. The Model of Import Substitution Growth

The model of import substitution growth is based upon a slight modification of the colonial structure (diagram 1.1). Total imports, M, are now differentiated into two types, industrial consumer goods, M_y, and producer goods, M_p. Industrial consumer goods were regularly imported under colonialism, while the importation of producer goods on a regular and growing basis is a phenomenon of import substitution growth. In practice M_p contains two types of producer goods, raw materials, M_R, and capital goods, M_i. For the time being, this distinction is neglected and the analysis is conducted in terms of the general category of producer goods, M_p.[3]

Producer goods imports, M_p, are employed to build up domestic industrial capital stock, K, thereby creating capacity for production

3. The differentiation between imported raw materials and imported capital goods is essential for "backward-linkage import substitution" (see chapter 6).

of manufactured consumer goods, y. This output is supplied to the domestic market which now absorbs industrial consumer goods from two sources, imported, M_y, and domestic, y. Since the industrial sector is still undeveloped, purchasing power in this market is largely generated by income from primary product exports, J. The major phenomenon of import substitution growth is diversion of primary product export earnings, J, to importation of producer goods, M_p, in order to create domestic industrial capacity, K, enabling production of consumer goods, y, to replace gradually imported goods, M_y, in the domestic market where purchasing power is generated by exports, J. It may be noted that import substitution growth is a mode of operation involving resource flows among all the key sectors of the open dualistic economy.

Suppose the prices of the internationally traded commodities (P_y for M_y, P_p for M_p, and $P_J = 1$ treated as a numeraire) are determined internationally and are fixed. In diagram 2.1, let M_y and y be measured on the horizontal axis and M_p on the vertical axis. Let us assume that the volume of primary product exports, J, is fixed. When the foreign exchange earnings are spent entirely on imports of M_y and M_p all alternative combinations of M_y and M_p are shown by the fixed import frontier line *ab*.

The import frontier shows, first, that the agricultural export sector provides the means for industrialization, i.e., the alternative amounts of producer goods imports. Second, the import frontier shows that the agricultural sector also provides the market outlet for industrial consumer goods by generating income from J. This income is measured in terms of consumer goods as the distance *Oa* on the horizontal axis.

Third, the agricultural export sector provides savings to finance industrialization. The agricultural surplus is shown as the distance *ad* on the horizontal axis, representing that part of income not spent on industrial consumer goods. Under these assumptions the consumption demand for industrial goods generated by export income is *Od*. During the passive phase of colonialism, the export surplus (profit) was repatriated (see diagram 1.2). We see that it is now redirected consistently to finance domestic industrialization.

Let us assume that the domestic industrial capacity is zero when

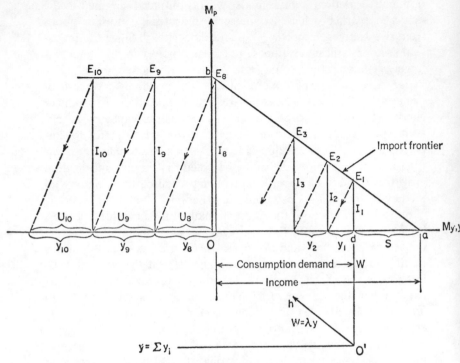

Diagram 2.1. Import Substitution Growth

the country emerges from colonialism. Since the entire consumption demand, Od, must be imported, the equilibrium point on the import frontier is E_1. Initial producer good imports, I_1, lead to the emergence of domestic industrial capacity, y_1, indicated on the horizontal axis. The slope of the dotted line drawn from E_1 is the capital-output ratio, k. Since income, Oa, and consumption demand, Od, remain unchanged, emergence of domestic industrial capacity releases foreign exchange for larger capital imports, I_2, and hence the equilibrium point is shifted to E_2. This leads to further expansion of output, y_2, and a cumulative output capacity of $y_1 + y_2$. In the next period capacity for capital imports is raised to I_3, and in this way the import substitution process is determined dynamically, as seen from the sequence of equilibrium points, E_1, E_2, E_3, ...

This import substitution model may now be formulated in algebraic terms with the aid of the following equations:

(2.1a) $J = P_y M_y + P_p M_p$ (Import frontier, with $P_J = 1$)

(2.1b) $y = K/k$ (Production function, where k is the capital-output ratio)

(2.1c) $dK/dt = M_p$ (Capital accumulation)

(2.1d) $M_y + y = J/P_y - S$ (Demand for industrial consumer goods)

Equation 2.1a is the import frontier where the fixed world price for exports, P_J, is taken to be the numeraire. Equation 2.1b is the production function, based on a constant capital-output ratio, k. Equation 2.1c asserts that the increase of the capital stock is determined by, and equal in magnitude to, producer goods imports, M_p. Equation 2.1d specifies that the demand for industrial consumer goods, imported plus domestically produced, is determined by domestic income from primary product exports, J/P_y, less savings, S.

For solution of the system, we have:

(2.2a) $dy/dt = M_p/k$ (by 2.1b, c)

(2.2b) $M_p = ry + .rS$ where

(2.2c) $r = P_y/P_p$ (by 2.1a, d)

(2.2d) $dy/dt = dM_p/dt = (r/k)y + G$ where

(2.2e) $G = rS/k$ (by 2.2a, c)

From equation 2.2d we see that domestic output capacity, dy/dt, and imported producer goods grow by the same amount through time as described by a linear differential equation. (Notice that G is a constant determined by the import price ratio, r, savings, S, and the capital-output ratio, k.) The solution for the time path of domestic production of industrial consumer goods, y, is given by:

(2.3a) $y = (y_0 + S)e^{(r/k)t} - S$ or

(2.3b) $y = S(e^{(r/k)t} - 1)$ for $y_0 = 0$

If the initial domestic industrial capacity for producing consumer goods, y_0, is zero, the time path for industrial capacity is given by

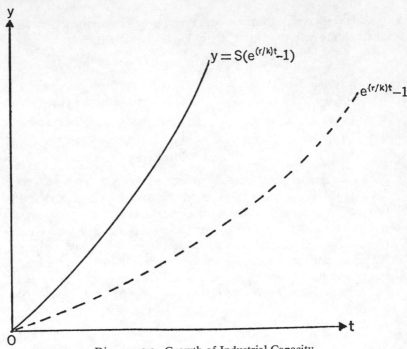

Diagram 2.2. Growth of Industrial Capacity

equation 2.3b. In diagram 2.2, the term $e^{(r/k)t} - 1$ is represented by the dotted curve rising from the origin. The time path of y is indicated by the solid curve which is obtained by multiplying the dotted curve by savings, S. Domestic industrial capacity, y, eventually grows at a constant rate, r/k. Thus, y expands at a higher rate the lower the value of the capital-output ratio, k. A higher value of $r = P_y/P_p$ also contributes to a higher growth rate for y because reductions in consumer goods imports will release foreign exchange (the high P_y effect), enabling the country to import more producer goods (the low P_p effect). The magnitude of y is also seen to be proportional to S, the amount of savings from agricultural export income.

2.2. Features of Import Substitution Growth

The analysis shows that import substitution, as a transition growth type, exhibits certain distinctive characteristics. Import substitution growth both builds on the colonial heritage and modifies that heritage. While retaining triangularism based on primary product exports, import substitution departs from the colonial pattern by adopting an internal orientation for growth through the creation of a domestic industrial sector.

Agricultural exports constitute the foundation for industrialization. First, they provide the means of expansion in terms of savings and foreign exchange resources. Second, they provide the market outlet and, hence, the incentive for industrial investment. Agricultural exports dominate these growth roles because the industrial sector is still embryonic and modernization of the traditional agricultural sector has not yet occurred.

Import substitution growth involves two basic substitution phenomena. On the one hand, there is substitution in the foreign exchange allocation sense as producer goods imports, M_p, displace consumer goods imports, M_y. This may be seen from the movement of the equilibrium points, $E_1, E_2, E_3, \ldots$ upward along the frontier in diagram 2.1. On the other hand, there is substitution in the domestic market sense as domestic output, y, replaces imported consumer goods, M_y. These two phenomena can be statistically measured, and their simultaneous occurrence comprises the major empirical criterion for the identification of import substitution.

Import substitution represents an early transition growth phase inasmuch as the country's lack of productive capacity for producer goods causes reliance upon importation. As a result, producer goods eventually become a substantial share of total imports. This sets the stage for backward linkage import substitution which occurs later in the transition, as the country begins to substitute domestic production for imports of producer goods.

Import substitution is a cumulative and self-reinforcing growth mechanism. Diagram 2.1 shows why an initially small amount of substitution leads to larger amounts in subsequent periods. Even when the volume of primary product exports is constant, the growth of industrial capacity can be sustained at a high rate, r/k (equations 2.3).

Expansion of capital stock and output capacity in the industrial sector provides growing employment opportunities. Under the assumption of a constant capital-labor ratio, the expansion of employment, W, is shown by the $W = \lambda y$ curve in diagram 2.1.[4] Given the colonial heritage, this growing labor force will be recruited from the traditional agricultural sector. Hence, import substitution growth not only begins a process of interaction between industry and the traditional agricultural sector, but it also initiates a pump-priming process toward generation of income, purchasing power, and savings from expanding industrial employment.[5]

There is a logical necessity for the termination of import substitution growth through exhaustion of the domestic market. In diagram 2.1 this occurs after the substitution process has reached E_8, when all imports are producer goods, or, equivalently, the entire domestic market is supplied by domestic output. This termination tendency may, however, be postponed by the pump-priming effect on demand and savings created by industrial employment.

Import substitution is appropriate as an initial or early transition growth system because it requires execution of only elementary growth functions at a time when a society is not yet ready for more complex growth tasks. In particular, entrepreneurial requirements are limited to those needed for producing in an existing and highly visible domestic market. In addition, import substitution is normally accompanied by government controls which protect the domestic market from foreign competition. Thus, high standards of efficiency are not needed for competition with foreign producers either domestically or in foreign (export) markets.

3. Export Promotion Growth

Export promotion represents an alternative to import substitution during the initial transition phase after decolonization. In both

4. The horizontal axis $O'y$ (measuring leftward from O') is total industrial output (i.e., $y = y_1 + y_2 \ldots + y_n$). Suppose the labor-output coefficient, λ, is constant, then the amount of labor, W, absorbed by the industrial sector is given by the radial line $O'h$ (i.e., $W = \lambda y$).

5. This analysis recognizes that the domestic market for absorbing output emanates from two sources: income generated from primary product exports and income paid to the labor employed in import substituting industries. Our formal analysis concentrates on the former because labor employment typically grows slowly given the capital bias of these industries. Inclusion of the second demand source would somewhat soften the termination conclusion stated in the text.

cases primary product exports provide the means (i.e., savings and imported resources) and the market inducement for industrial sector expansion. The major characteristic which distinguishes export promotion from import substitution is the industrial sector's orientation. Under export promotion growth, the industrial sector output consists mainly of productive inputs required for expansion of primary product exports. For this reason, growth of primary product exports becomes a dominant phenomenon in this growth system.

3.1. The Model of Export Promotion Growth

Diagram 1.1, which shows the colonial economy in the previous chapter, may be used to describe the basic mode of operation of export promotion. Primary product exports, J, provide the imported resources, M, for expansion of output capacity in the industrial sector, Y. The output of this sector, C, which is supplied to the domestic market, now consists of commercial services and physical inputs to stimulate the growth of primary product exports. This leads to expansion of primary product exports through time.

The growth of primary product exports leads to the expansion of the import frontier through time. This may be seen in diagram 2.3 by the system of parallel lines, indexed by $J(0)$, $J(1)$, $J(2)$, and representing growing volumes of primary product exports. Initially, a typical point E_0 on the import frontier $J(0)O'$, denotes a combination of imports of consumer goods, OM_0, and producer goods, M_0E_0. Importation of producer goods results in capital accumulation and expansion of output capacity in the industrial sector. This output capacity is not devoted to production replacing consumer good imports, OM_0. Instead, it is used to stimulate primary product export production, causing exports to expand to $J(1)$ and leading to a new import frontier, $J(1)O''$, in the next period.

There are two basic growth promotion forces under export promotion. The first is the propensity to save out of agricultural export income (OO', OO'', OOO''' in diagram 2.3). The propensity to save determines the allocation of foreign exchange on the import frontiers through time. The case of a constant propensity to save is shown as the straight radial line, OS, with the equilibrium points E_0, E_1, E_2. The volumes of imported producer goods (M_0E_0,

M_1E_1, M_2E_2) as determined by the propensity to save are seen to be a constant proportion of the income generated. These imported producer goods constitute investment which brings about expansion of output capacity in the industrial sector.

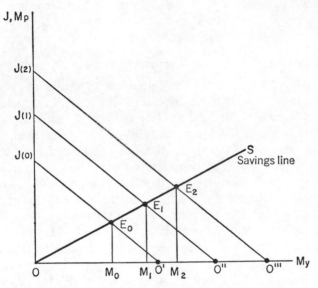

Diagram 2.3. Export Promotion Growth

The second basic growth promotion force is the response of primary product exports to the stimulus given by growing industrial inputs. This response may take alternative forms, depending on the nature of the primary products. One typical case takes the form of diversification of traditional primary products (e.g., rice, corn, jute) in which traditional technology is employed. In this case, the inputs supplied by the industrial sector are mainly commercial services to accommodate the growth of exports. A common alternative is the modern export case (e.g., rubber, sugar) where primary product export growth is based upon the introduction of modern technology. In this case, industrial inputs are mainly modern intermediate goods such as fertilizer and industrial processing services.

The deterministic aspects of export promotion growth may be summarized by the following system of equations:

(2.4a) $J = P_y M_y + P_p M_p$ (Import frontier)

(2.4b) $y = K/k$ (Production function)

(2.4c) $dK/dt = M_p$ (Capital accumulation)

(2.4d) $M_p = S(J)$ (Saving function)

(2.4e) $dJ/dt = F(y, dy/dt, t)$ (Export expansion function)

Equations 2.4a, b, c are reproductions of 2.1a, b, c for the import substitution model. Equation 2.4d is a saving function which states that imported producer goods, M_p, are a function of primary product export income, J.[6]

Equation 2.4e is the export expansion function which states that the amount of increase of primary product exports through time, dJ/dt, is traced to several factors. In case the industrial goods, y, are intermediate inputs (e.g., fertilizer), then dJ/dt is positively related to the increment dy/dt. In case the industrial good is a capital good (irrigation or agricultural equipment) then dJ/dt is positively related to the magnitude of y (i.e., J is positively related to the cumulative value of y). Finally, J can grow autonomously through time, independently of the stimulation from industrial inputs, as indicated by the time variable, t. This general formulation of the export expansion function stresses the heterogeneity of the forces affecting primary product export growth.

From equation 2.4 we deduce the following pair of equations:

(2.5a) $dy/dt = S(J)/k$ (by 2.4b, c, d)

(2.5b) $dJ/dt = F(y, S(J)/k)$ (by 2.4e, 2.5a)

These two simultaneous differential equations in J and y determine the system through time. This formal deterministic aspect is consistent with a variety of export growth patterns, depending on the emphasis given to particular components in the export expansion function. Some of these possibilities will be investigated in later chapters.

---

6. This function could be stated even more simply if it were assumed that savings are a constant proportion of export income.

To summarize, export promotion growth is a transition growth type in which industrial expansion is fostered by primary product export expansion, while industrial growth, supplemented by imports, in turn stimulates primary product export production. This mutual interaction between primary product exports and industry (as specified in equations 2.5) dominates the economy's mode of operation under export promotion growth.

3.2. Features of Export Promotion Growth

Countries with a colonial heritage may initiate transition growth through either import substitution or export promotion. In both, land-based exports remain the dominant growth feature, providing imported resources, savings, and market demand for industrial expansion. Growth continues to involve a triangular pattern of resource utilization between the inherited enclave and the foreign sector.

Export promotion differs from import substitution in the industrial sector's orientation toward producing inputs to stimulate primary product export growth rather than toward replacing consumer goods imports. In export promotion, the economy continues its external orientation toward foreign markets instead of shifting to an internal orientation as in the case of import substitution.

The external orientation of export promotion growth produces several observable characteristics which differ from those under import substitution. First, foreign trade as a fraction of national income will remain at a high level and it may even grow in contrast to a falling fraction in import substitution growth. This reflects the economy's openness under export promotion. Second, the share of foreign exchange allocated to imported consumer goods will continue to be important, signifying the absence of an import substitution process. In the domestic market the supply of industrial consumer goods is predominantly imported, reflecting the underdevelopment of domestic capacity.

Export promotion growth represents a more gradual transition toward a modern economy than in the case of import substitution. Whether export promotion relies upon diversification of traditional exports or modernization of exports, there is no attempt to abruptly terminate dependence on imported consumer goods. Thus, the departure from the colonial economy's mode of operation is gradual. The feature of gradualism, which is characterized by a continuation of the economy's openness, implies an emphasis upon productive efficiency. Externally, export producers must compete successfully in the world market to expand primary product exports. Domestically, import competition constitutes a disciplining force upon the efficiency of indigenous manufacturing industry. In short export promotion is a market-oriented system in which productive efficiency is assured by competition.

Consistent with the economy's openness and efficiency, organization under export promotion emphasizes a free market system. In the context of an open economy the free market refers essentially to non-intervention in foreign trade and exchange. Foreign trade controls and protection are absent, and the exchange rate is determined by market forces. These organizational features contrast sharply with the control system of import substitution.

Export promotion requires a favorable land-labor ratio so that the natural resource base is capable of supporting a diversified pattern of exports. Diversification is normally essential to offset unfavorable changes in world demand for a particular commodity.[7] Where this condition is not present, export promotion growth is not a feasible way to begin the transition and import substitution is likely to arise. Few less developed countries possess a land surplus, but where a suitable land supply exists — as in Thailand and Malaysia — export promotion growth may remain viable for a generation or more of initial transition growth.

Primary product export expansion is the key phenomenon in export promotion growth. The causes of export growth differ—as we have seen in the export expansion function. Moreover, the government may assume varying roles in expanding exports through infrastructure investment. For these reasons, several variants of export promotion growth may appear during the transition. In later chapters we shall differentiate the two cases of Thailand and Malaysia. Although both initiated transition growth through export promotion, Thailand focused upon diversification and expansion of

7. An exception that comes to mind is countries producing a particular commodity that remains in strong demand on the world market for a long period of time. Petroleum-producing countries are the leading examples.

indigenous export products while Malaysia emphasized modern
export products.

3.3. Import Substitution and Export Promotion

Import substitution and export promotion have been presented as
two sharply contrasting transition growth types. In the case of import substitution, it has been assumed that industrial output is devoted exclusively to consumer goods import substitution, and in
the case of export promotion it has been assumed that industry
only produces inputs for export production. In actual transition
experience, a mixture of these two processes is likely to be found.
Hence, realistically, import substitution means a case where import substitution dominates the growth process, but it may be accompanied by some export promotion. Similarly, export promotion
growth may be used to describe a case where this growth process is
dominant but where some import substitution occurs.

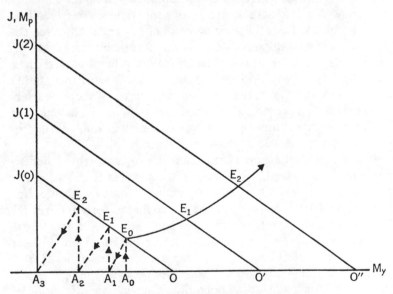

Diagram 2.4. Prolongation of Import Substitution

Diagram 2.4 shows an example of such a mixture of the two
growth processes. Suppose that there is an initial fixed import fron-

tier $J(0)O$ corresponding to initial exports $J(0)$. The import substitution process associated with this initial frontier is shown as the zigzag path A_0E_0, A_1E_1, . . . As this process nears termination at A_3, it is likely that a part of the growing industrial output will be diverted to export promotion, raising the import frontier to $J(1)O'$. The new income associated with exports of $J(1)$ enables the import substitution process to proceed further. Such a mixture of import substitution with export promotion will be referred to as prolonged import substitution and will be considered as a realistic interpretation of Philippine transition growth during the postwar generation.

Conversely, suppose the case depicted in diagram 2.3 represents pure export promotion. It is quite conceivable that the expansion of domestic income from growing primary product exports will serve to stimulate domestic manufacture of consumer goods. Then export promotion will become mixed with at least a modicum of import substitution. Such a tendency has appeared in both Thailand and Malaysia in recent years, and this tendency will be analyzed in later chapters.

4. Export Substitution Growth

A third transition growth type will be referred to as export substitution, denoting the fact that for the first time in the country's history manufactured goods displace primary products as the dominant exports. As a more advanced growth system than import substitution or export promotion, export substitution occurs somewhat later in the transition. Only a handful of less developed countries have entered a phase of export substitution growth during the postwar generation. The experience of such countries as Taiwan and South Korea indicates that approximately ten years of import substitution growth preceded the rise of export substitution.

An outline of the economy's operation under export substitution is shown in diagram 2.5. The industrial sector, Y, now has an external orientation as output, E, is exported to the foreign market, F, in exchange for imports, M. While the traditional agricultural sector is neglected in both import substitution and export promotion, export substitution leads to internal integration between industry and the traditional agricultural sector. This is reflected in flows

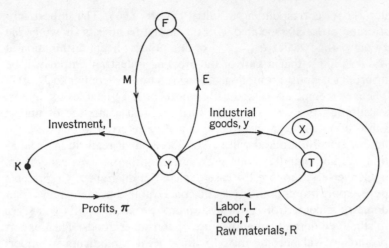

Diagram 2.5. Export Substitution Economy

of labor, *L*, food, *f*, and raw materials, *R*, to the industrial sector in exchange for industrial products, *y*. Additions to capital stock, *K*, through industrial sector investment, *I*, come to be financed by new sources of savings, mainly industrial profits, π, supplemented by savings from the agricultural sector.

This "three leaf clover" structure of export substitution emphasizes external orientation of the industrial sector, integration of traditional agriculture with the rest of the economy, and a new basis for financing industrialization. This structure is superimposed upon and gradually replaces the triangularism of import substitution. Export substitution is thus a considerably more complex and advanced growth type than its predecessors.

The economy's mode of operation under export substitution hinges on the intersectoral allocation of labor through which the abundant supply of surplus labor in the traditional agricultural sector is made available to industry. This enables the industrial sector to develop the capacity to export labor-intensive goods to the foreign market. Thus, export substitution growth is a phenomenon unique to the labor-surplus type of open dualistic economy. The appearance of labor-intensive industrial exports during the transition signifies a shift from land-based to labor-based growth.

Export substitution emerges from the natural termination of import substitution growth and the fulfillment of two more positive growth conditions. The first condition is the development of market-oriented and efficiency-conscious entrepreneurship. Such entrepreneurship can exploit the economy's labor surplus through labor-intensive innovations and effective competition in the international market. The second condition is modernization of traditional agriculture. Growth of agricultural productivity is essential for the release of labor and food. This enables the industrial sector to acquire labor at a low real cost, i.e., at favorable internal terms of trade.

When these preconditions are fulfilled during the import substitution phase, the emergence of export substitution is a natural consequence in a labor-surplus economy. Such a sequence occurred in Taiwan during the postwar generation. Conversely, when one or both of these conditions is not fulfilled, prolonged import substitution or stagnation occur. In the Philippines, the failure of traditional agriculture to modernize led to prolonged import substitution while in Indonesia the lack of entrepreneurial development led to stagnation.

Export substitution raises two types of analytical issues. First, the process by which import substitution growth promotes or impedes the rise of export substitution must be investigated. Second, the set of forces which interact to determine the dynamic course of export substitution growth must be identified and analyzed. These tasks as well as statistical verification will be undertaken in the chapter addressed to Taiwan's experience.

3

Organization under Economic Nationalism

We have interpreted the development experience of contemporary less developed countries as a period of transition growth between the colonial epoch and the epoch of modern growth. Among the three modal growth types identified in the last chapter, import substitution growth is the most common type found during the postwar generation. In this type, primary product exports finance the importation of producer goods by the industrial sector, and the industrial capacity created thereby is oriented toward selling in the domestic market, gradually replacing imported consumer goods.

In this chapter, we consider two issues relating to the political economy of import substitution growth. The first issue is the political rationality of the system. We shall argue that import substitution growth is a by-product of economic nationalism, itself a political response to decolonization.[1] The goal of economic nationalism is creation of an indigenous entrepreneurial class to replace the aliens who controlled the economy during the colonial epoch. This is accomplished through a forced industrialization strategy that favors indigenous entrepreneurs by artificially augmenting their profits through a system of political controls.

The second issue concerns the efficacy of particular policy instruments for achieving the basic objective of forced industrialization. A matrix of trade-related policies — exchange rate, inflation,

---

1. The concept of economic nationalism was chosen partly to contrast with the system of neocolonialism discussed in the next chapter. The political climate of nationalism is one major cause for the choice of policies leading to the growth type considered in this chapter. The political milieu of neocolonialism leads to quite different policy choices with important consequences for transition growth.

tariff, etc. — will be analyzed to demonstrate that they are consistent with the basic strategy of transferring trade-related profits to the indigenous entrepreneurial class.

Organization for import substitution relies upon a control system rather than free markets. The windfall profits which accrue to entrepreneurs are not commensurate with their efficiency. Given an initial lack of indigenous industrial entrepreneurs, a country may choose to suffer this cost of inefficiency in the short run to create an entrepreneurial class. If the import substitution strategy is successful, entrepreneurs will eventually become more oriented toward efficiency and relaxation of control policies will then be possible.

1. ECONOMIC NATIONALISM AND IMPORT SUBSTITUTION

1.1. The Historical Background

The end of World War II ushered in a process of political decolonization in colonial countries throughout the world. In Southeast Asia, political independence was achieved by some countries immediately after the termination of the war (e.g., the Philippines in 1946) while it was delayed in others (e.g., Malaysia in 1957). This wave of decolonization ended political and economic relationships between colonies and mother countries which had, in most cases, existed for several centuries. Decolonization is primarily a political phenomenon involving the displacement of foreign agents from positions of political and economic power in which they had been entrenched throughout the long colonial epoch.

Decolonization produced a paradoxical driving force in many newly independent countries in that former colonies strove to erect societies patterned after those of the foreigners being displaced. Despite a search for national identity, the pursuit of Western political and economic institutions, of Western technology and consumption habits, has been a dominant feature of the first generation of independence. This imitation drive may be examined from an economic as well as a political viewpoint.

In economic terms, importation of Western resources and technology was sought to close the consumption gap between the former colonies and advanced countries. Less developed countries soon grasped the possibilities for industrialization provided by the expanding inflow of new technology and resources from more advanced countries. Politically, the imitation drive led to cultivation of Western-style nationalism, emphasizing national sovereignty and unification. The almost instinctive urge to eradicate aliens from positions of power and control was merely a negative expression of this new nationalism. The more positive expression was found in the adoption of a national strategy of forced industrialization instituted with little regard for cost or efficiency and supported by the use of political controls.

After this process of nationalistic decolonization, shortage of indigenous entrepreneurs was the most critical bottleneck to industrial development. The forced industrialization strategy was seized upon to overcome this bottleneck. Opportunities for indigenous entrepreneurs to participate in decision making and to learn by doing were created through guaranteed profits in new industrial activities. This strategy necessitated identifying a source of surplus for transfer to the new entrepreneurs.

1.2. The Strategy of Forced Industrialization

At the time of decolonization the most important source of savings is the export profits which traditionally accrued to aliens under the colonial system. Historically, these profits were repatriated during the phase of unfavorable world demand conditions, while they were reinvested to expand primary product output during the active phase of rising world demand. This pattern of utilization of export profits had both political and economic disadvantages from the viewpoint of the less developed country. The economic disadvantages lay in the fluctuating nature of reinvestment and its concentration in the primary product export sector. Politically, alien control of export profits perpetuated foreign control of the nonagricultural sector, preventing the development of indigenous entrepreneurship. Foreign economic domination would have been politically odious even if export profits had been consistently used to develop the entire economy.

As a response to these disadvantages, the strategy of forced industrialization has economic and political dimensions. Economically, it seeks to assure regular investment of export profits in the industrial sector. Politically, it seeks to remove export profits from alien control and to use these resources for fostering the development of indigenous entrepreneurs to replace foreigners. The strategy is usually carried out by initial measures of nationalization or confiscation to displace aliens from position of control. These are followed by more positive import substitution policies.

A central feature of import substitution policy is that it favors indigenous industrial entrepreneurs at the expense of primary product export producers. This is true because the essence of the policy is to transfer export profits to the industrial class. The political feasibility of this policy hinges upon the distribution of political power between export and industrial interest groups. An import substitution policy will not be pursued unless the government represents the interest of the indigenous entrepreneurial class.

The political feasibility of import substitution varied among the four countries of our empirical focus. Import substitution was adopted in the Philippines and Taiwan because industrial interests dominated the central government. In Malaysia and Thailand, however, there was a special problem in that the Chinese minorities were the dominant groups with demonstrated entrepreneurial capabilities. Indigenous government largely represented the agricultural export interests, and hence import substitution was not politically feasible.

Under forced industrialization, the new industries selected for development naturally tend to be of the import substituting variety. In practice this refers to manufactured consumer goods which were traditionally imported. These industries are appropriate for inexperienced entrepreneurs because the market already exists and is highly visible. Furthermore, with purchasing power for consumer goods generated by primary product exports, the market risks confronted by the new entrepreneurs are minimized. For these reasons, industries that produce import substituting consumer goods are favored under economic nationalism.

Forced industrialization usually leads to tangible progress in creating domestic productive capacity in these selected industries. This progress, however, is accompanied by serious shortcomings. Because profits are artificially transferred by political force, they are of a windfall nature and not related to entrepreneurial efficiency. The industries created are of a hothouse variety, biased in favor of imported capital-intensive technology. This bias is inappropriate to the prevailing capital-scarcity in less developed countries and conflicts with raising industrial employment in a labor-surplus economy. Moreover, discrimination against the agricultural sector discourages improvements in agricultural productivity. The long-run success of the import substitution strategy depends upon overcoming these disadvantages.

To summarize, under the aegis of economic nationalism, an import substitution strategy is adopted to foster the development of indigenous entrepreneurs to replace foreign ones. The crux of the strategy is the transfer of export profits to the industrial entrepreneurial class at the expense of agricultural interests. This policy is feasible only where the central government represents the industrialists' interest. Although progress may be made in industrialization, the resulting industries tend to be inefficient by international standards and agricultural productivity suffers.

2. The Instruments for Import Substitution Growth

In launching the transition through an import substitution growth process, a country relies upon the basic strategy of forcing industrial growth by transfer of profits from the agricultural export surplus to nascent industrial entrepreneurs. A large arsenal of policy instruments is available for implementing this basic strategy. Three policy devices, however, may be identified as primary measures associated with the stategy: exchange rate policy, price inflation, and tariff policy. We begin by investigating these primary policy instruments, after which other ancillary measures will be considered.

2.1. Foreign Exchange Rate Policy

The essential feature of exchange rate policy under import substitution growth is its use as a mechanism to facilitate profit transfers. The basic mechanism consists of an exchange rate system which overvalues the domestic currency, thus subsidizing the importer (the industrial sector) at the expense of the exporter (the agricultural sector). This is accomplished by stipulation of an official exchange rate (e.g., $r = 4$ rupees per dollar) substantially below the equilibrium or free market rate (e.g., $b = 8$ rupees per dollar). The divergence between the official rate, r, and the free market rate, b, may be measured in terms of either their multiple or their difference:

(3.1a) $\Theta = r/b \leqq 1$ (e.g., $\Theta = 4/8 = .5$)

(3.1b) $b - r \geqq 0$ (Exploitation profit rate
                                 e.g., $b - r = 8 - 4$)

While b is determined by market forces and reflects purchasing power parity, we may think of r as a policy instrument to exploit the agricultural sector. The lower the value of r and, hence Θ, the greater is the degree of discrimination against agriculture and the higher the exploitation profit rate, $b - r$.

To examine how the system works, let us refer back to diagram 1.2 of chapter 1. Suppose the country exports J units of jute, while importing M units of machines and C units of consumer goods. If the dollar (foreign market) prices of these commodities are, respectively, P_J, P_M, and P_C, then by simple purchasing power parity, the domestic (rupee) prices are bP_J, bP_M, and bP_C.

Notice that at the discriminatory official rate, r, rupee income to the agricultural producer is $E_x = rJP_J$, which equals total rupee costs to the importers, $M^* = r(MP_M + CP_C)$. After the imported goods are brought into the country, their value appreciates to that corresponding to the free market rate, $b(MP_M + CP_C)$. Thus, a trade profit, π, emerges:

(3.2a) $\pi = b(MP_M + CP_C)$
$\qquad\qquad - r(MP_M + CP_C)$ (Trade profit)
$\qquad = (b - r)(MP_M + CP_C)$

(3.2b) $E_x = M^*$ where   (Currency balance)
$\qquad E_x = rJP_J$ (Export income)
$\qquad M^* = r(MP_M + CP_C)$ (Importer's cost)

(3.2c) $JP_J = MP_M + CP_C$ (by 3.2b)   (Import frontier)

(3.2d) $\pi = (b - r)JP_J$ (by 3.2a, c)   (Source of profit)

The "currency balance" condition (equation 3.2b) logically implies the import frontier (introduced in chapter 2) since both conditions state that all foreign exchange earnings are spent on imports. In other words, it is assumed that there is no trade deficit or surplus. Equation 3.2d states that trade profit, π, originates from agricultural exports, JP_J, and is directly proportional to the volume of exports, J, their price, P_J, and the exploitation profit rate, $b - r$. In view of the windfall nature of π, such an exchange rate policy must be accompanied by auxiliary measures (e.g., import quotas and licensing) to ration foreign exchange among potential importers.

Notice that $E_x = rJP_J$ (3.2b) is the agricultural export income in rupees, based on the official rate, r. When E_x is spent for the purchase of imported consumer goods, C, the buyer pays the higher domestic price computed at the free market rate, b. Hence, this overvaluation of domestic currency by the official exchange rate constitutes discrimination against producers of export goods. Assuming that export producers spend the entire rupee export income, E_x, on imported consumer goods, C, we can determine the imported volume of these goods. We can then also determine, with the aid of the import frontier line, capital goods imports, M. Thus:

(3.3a) $E_x = bCP_C$ or   (Export income equals im-
            $rJP_J = bCP_C$ ported consumer goods)

(3.3b) $C = \Theta(P_J/P_C)J$
            (by 3.3a, 3.1a)   (Imported consumer goods)

(3.3c) $M = (1 - \Theta)(P_J/P_M)J$
            (by 3.3b, 3.2c)   (Imported capital goods)

From equation 3.3b we see that the welfare of the agricultural export producer, measured in terms of imported consumer goods, C, is proportional to the volume of his jute exports, J, the international terms of trade P_J/P_C, and the ratio of the official to the free market exchange rate, Θ. A similar interpretation can be given to M in equation 3.3c. Notice that a lower value of Θ or r (a more discriminatory exchange rate policy) represents a greater squeeze upon the welfare of agricultural exporters while providing greater profit to industrial entrepreneurs (equation 3.2d), leading to a larger volume of imported capital goods (equation 3.3c). Assuming that the value of industrial investment, I, equals imported capital goods at domestic market prices,

(3.4a) $I = bMP_M$ (Investment equals capital imports)

(3.4b) $\pi = I$ (by 3.4a, 3.3c, 3.2d) (Trade profit equals investment)

Equation 3.4b asserts that trade profits are used to finance, and are equal in magnitude to, investment. From this we see that the significance of a lower more discriminatory official exchange rate, r, as a policy instrument lies in, (1) squeezing the agricultural export sector, (2) augmenting profits of industrialists, and (3) promoting growth of the industrial sector through capital accumulation. The model thus portrays the organizational principles adopted by a country just emerging from colonialism which relies upon primary product exports to finance industrial capital formation.

To explore the profit transfer mechanism as an integral part of import substitution growth, let the import frontier of equation 3.2c be reproduced in diagram 3.1. At a typical point, E, the elasticity, ϵ, of the import frontier is:

(3.5a) $\epsilon = (\Delta M/M)/(\Delta C/C)$ (Elasticity of import frontier)
$= (P_C/P_M)(C/M)$ (by 3.2c)
$= \Theta/(1 - \Theta)$ (by 3.3b, c)

(3.5b) $\Theta = \epsilon/(1 + \epsilon) = BE/AB$ (by $\epsilon = BE/EA$)

Thus, when an import frontier AB is given (see diagram 3.1), the equilibrium import point E is determined by the value of Θ, the policy variable, according to equation 3.5b. A more discriminatory (or growth-oriented) policy which corresponds to a lower value of Θ leads to an upward movement of the equilibrium point on the frontier (e.g., from E to E'). Conversely, if the official exchange rate is nondiscriminatory and coincides with the free market value (i.e., $r = b$ and $\Theta = 1$), then the equilibrium point is established at A, indicating that all imports are consumer goods. At the equilibrium point E, with a discriminatory official rate, CA units of agricultural export income are converted to windfall profits leading to CE units of imported capital goods purchased at the official rate, r.

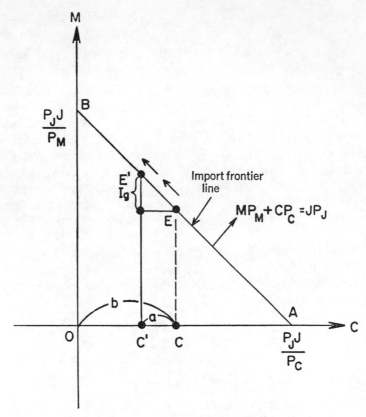

Diagram 3.1. Exchange Rate Policy

Since obtaining foreign exchange at the official rate is a sufficient condition for gaining windfall profits, demand pressure is great. This implies the necessity for government controls to ration foreign exchange and to assure that it is used only for productive (capital goods) imports (e.g., by means of import licensing). Normally, during early transition growth, there is little assurance that these scarce foreign exchange resources will be rationed with economic efficiency, which, indeed, is a somewhat irrelevant criterion during this phase.

2.2. Inflation Policy

Forced industrialization is frequently accompanied by price inflation, which lowers the purchasing power parity of domestic currency and increases the free market exchange rate, b. Assuming the official exchange rate, r, remains the same, inflation will automatically lower the value of Θ, resulting in greater discrimination against the agricultural export sector. A policy of domestic price inflation is thus consistent with the forced industrialization strategy through profit transfer, and, for this reason, is often found as a concomitant of import substitution growth.

Inflation is a politically practical method to achieve profit transfer, to induce greater austerity, and presumably to foster rapid industrialization. As a means of exploiting the agricultural export sector, inflation is more covert and less provocative then exchange rate appreciation (i.e., decreasing r). In fact, the latter is seldom used where inflation accompanies forced industrialization, because mere abstention from devaluation during inflation can achieve the same result.

2.3. Tariff Policy

In an open dualistic economy with a colonial background, import duties are typically the most important source of government revenue—both because exports of primary products are the major source of the economy's surplus and because of the administrative ease with which such taxes may be collected. Tariff duties provide a reliable source of revenue and for this reason they are an important policy instrument.

In the context of the forced industrialization strategy, tariff policy may be used for a number of purposes: (1) as a supplement to exchange-rate policy in forcing *profit transfers;* (2) as a *protective device* to foster domestic infant entrepreneurship by reducing foreign (import) competition; (3) as a *selective device* to discriminate among types of import goods on the basis of presumed differences in their contribution to industrialization; and (4) as a *revenue instrument* to channel resources to the government for public investment or transfer expenditures. In analyzing these potential roles, it is useful to consider tariffs in conjunction with the exchange rate mechanism. The two are complementary in principle, and in practice they are frequently used together.

Tariffs and profit transfer. Let T be government revenue (in rupees) collected from a selective tariff imposed only on the import of consumer goods. Then the buyers of these goods (i.e., the agricultural export sector) must bear the full burden of the incidence of the tariff duties. We see that the essential economic logic of the tariff is to impose an additional squeeze on the agricultural export sector. To illustrate, let us assume that revenue collected from the tariff is spent entirely on public investment.

Notice that trade profit, π (in equation 3.2a), remains valid since the imposition of the tariff leads to an equal increase in both the cost and the revenue associated with consumer goods imports. Domestic price increases of these goods will shift the burden of the tariff to the ultimate consumers. The only difference is that now trade profits, π, finance private investment while tariff revenue, T, finances public investment.

Let us assume that the ad valorem tariff rate, t, is imposed on the free market value of imported consumer goods (bCP_C). We can then calculate the value of T, and we find the burden falling entirely upon export income (rJP_J). The amounts of imported consumer goods, C, and imported capital goods, M, can also be determined:

(3.6a) $T = tbCP_C$ (Tariff revenue)

(3.6b) $T + bCP_C = rJP_J$ (Tariff burden)

(3.6c) $C = \Theta Jq$ where   (Consumer goods imports)

$q = (P_J/P_C)/(1 + t)$

(by 3.6a, b)   (Net terms of trade)

(3.6d) $M = [1 - \Theta/(1 + t)]J(P_J/P_M)$

(by 3.6c and 3.2c)   (Capital goods imports)

In equation 3.6c, q is the net terms of trade, i.e., the "gross" terms of trade, P_J/P_C, adjusted by the tariff effect, $1/(1 + t)$. A higher ad valorem tariff rate, t, results in less consumer goods imports and more capital goods imports. This adds to the squeeze upon the agricultural export sector, supplementing the effect of discriminatory exchange rate. Notice that if $t = 0$, equations 3.6c and d reduce to the special case of 3.3b and c.

In diagram 3.1, when $t = 0$ let the import point be E, with private investment financed by trade profits of CA units. With imposition of a positive tariff rate, t, the import of capital goods will be raised from CE to $C'E'$, leading to I_g units of public investment. In this diagram, the following ratio describes the "tariff" effect on allocation:

(3.7) $OC'/OC = BE'/BE = 1/(1 + t)$ (by 3.6c, 3.3b)

To show the economic interpretation of this ratio, suppose OC' units of textiles are imported and the tariff revenue is $tOC' = \overline{CC'}$. Their sum, $(1 + t)\underline{OC'} = OC$, represents the total amount of foreign exchange (measured on the C axis) used to purchase imported consumer goods (of OC' units) and to purchase capital goods (of I_g units) from the government's tariff revenue ($tOC' = \overline{CC'}$ units). A higher tariff rate, t, leads to lower consumption by agricultural export producers, since more of the foreign exchange earned will be absorbed by the government and used for public investment.

Policy alternatives. Let us now apply the above analysis to the specific issue of the public-private composition of investment finance.[2] In diagram 3.1, suppose E' is the equilibrium point when the government chooses a particular combination of the policy variables comprising the official exchange rate, r, inflation, b, and tariff, t. Then the following geometrical ratio represents the average propensity to consume out of export income:

(3.8) $BE'/BA = (BE'/BE) \ (BE/BA) = OC'/OA$
$= \Theta/(1 + t)$ (by 3.5b and 3.7)

We see that in a controlled system, this propensity is not a matter of volition on the part of income recipients. Instead it is determined

2. The analysis in this section assumes that only tariffs are employed to generate government revenue. In fact, in many less developed countries, exchange rate policy and inflation are also used to produce government revenue, an aspect neglected in this analysis. We are grateful to Professors Lloyd Reynolds and Gustav Ranis for suggesting the possibility of further research to absorb these additional aspects of public finance in the development process.

by a political force expressed through policy decisions. We may now compute public (T), private (π), and total (I) investment, and the public-private investment ratio (T/π) as follows:

(3.9a) $T = [t/(1 + t)]rP_JJ$
                                    (by 3.6a, b, c)   (Public investment)

(3.9b) $\pi = (b - r)P_JJ$ (by 3.2d)   (Private investment)

(3.9c) $I = T + \pi = [b - r/(1 + t)]JP_J$
                                    (by 3.9a, b)   (Total investment)

(3.9d) $T/\pi = [t/(1 + t)][\Theta/(1 - \Theta)]$ (Public-Private
                                    (by 3.9a, b)   investment ratio)

With the aid of these equations, the impact of alternative growth-oriented policies (i.e., those leading to increased total investment, I) may be examined. The three alternative growth-oriented policy instruments are the official exchange rate, r, the tariff rate, t, and the free market rate, b (which reflects price inflation). Table 3.1

Table 3.1. Impact of Growth-Oriented Policies on Investment

	Investment		
Policy	Public (T)	Private (π)	Public-Private ratio (T/π)
Exchange appreciation (r decreases)	decreases	increases	decreases
Increasing tariffs (t increases)	increases	nil	increases
Price inflation (b increases)	nil	increases	decreases

shows the effects of adjustments in these policies upon the level of public investment, T, private investment, π, and the public-private investment ratio, T/π.

Although all the growth-oriented policy changes lead to an increase in total investment, they produce different effects upon public and/or private investment. Exchange rate appreciation will increase private investment while causing a drop in public investment. (In diagram 3.1, this would be shown as an upward shift of both E and E' by the same proportion so that T will decrease as imports of capital goods, *M*, increase.) Raising the tariff rate, *t*, will cause public investment to increase while leaving private investment unchanged. (In diagram 3.1, this may be seen as an upward movement of point *E′* alone on the import frontier line.) Price inflation will increase private investment with no effect on public investment (shown in diagram 3.1 as an upward movement of both points *E* and *E′* by the same amounts). The effect of each of these policy changes on the public-private investment mix (T/π) is shown in the last column.

The rational combination of these policy instruments depends upon the availability of entrepreneurship and its distribution between the public and private sectors. For a country with an adequate supply of potential private entrepreneurship and an underdeveloped public sector (e.g., the Philippines and several Latin American countries), price inflation is a natural means of financing forced industrialization. For countries with a relatively efficient public sector and inadequate or politically unacceptable private entrepreneurship (e.g., Malaysia), tariff financing will be more appropriate.

The combination of the three policy instruments (*r*, *b*, and *t*) implemented through political decisions determines the amount of consumption (or forced saving) from export income. This, in turn, leads to a growth process which we referred to in chapter 2 as import substitution growth, which may now be briefly recapitulated.

In diagram 3.2, let the import frontier *AB* be reproduced corresponding to a fixed volume of primary product exports and export-generated income. Suppose the government chooses a combination of the policy variables (*r*, *b*, and *t*) so that the initial equilibrium import point is indicated by *E*, with an average propensity to consume *BE/AB* (see equation 3.8). The dynamic process of import substitution is indicated by the zigzag path *CE*, C_1E_1, $C_2 E_2$, . . . as described in the previous chapter. During the second period, for example, domestic output capacity is CC_1 (generated by capital import of *EC* in the first period). Since the export income *OA* and the average propensity to consume remain unchanged, *CA* is saved while *OC* constitutes consumption expenditure (of which OC_1 is spent on imported goods and CC_1 on domestic goods). Thus, AC_1 is that portion of income used to purchase imported capital

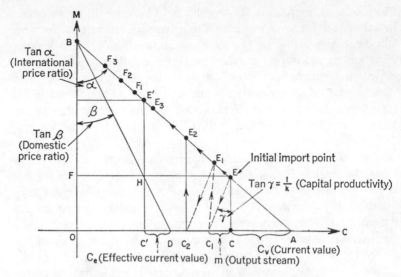

Diagram 3.2. Import Substitution and Protection

goods (of C_1E_1 units) of which CA is "forced saving" and CC_1 is consumption expenditure on domestic output paid to industrial producers. Thus, through time, while the import equilibrium points are represented by the sequence $E, E_1, E_2, \ldots$ the consumption equilibrium point remains at the initial position E, as determined by government policy.

Tariffs as a protective device.   Import substitution growth arises from the favorable treatment given the industrial sector under the forced industrialization strategy. The entrepreneurial tasks involved in supplying the domestic market are relatively undemanding, precisely because the market already exists and is highly visible. When the import substitution phase terminates and industrial expansion requires a new orientation (e.g., selling in the foreign market), the tasks confronting industrial entrepreneurship become more difficult. Thus, the import substitution phase may be conceived of as a period in which entrepreneurs, through learning by doing, may gain experience to prepare them for more demanding tasks in subsequent growth phases. Viewed in this context, the significance of the imposition of tariffs lies in their *protective effect*, quite independently

from the public investment effect analyzed above. By offering protection, tariffs provide an opportunity for gradual development of
human agents to assume the increasingly difficult roles of the future.
The fact that the protective effect is quite separate from the public
investment effect may be emphasized by assuming that all tariff
revenue is spent for nondevelopment purposes. We proceed to
analyze the protection effect on this assumption.

The economic rationale of protection may be seen from diagram
3.2. When the initial import point is E, imported capital goods CE
have an exchange value of $C_v = \underline{CA}$ units of current value in terms
of imported consumer goods, as determined in the world market.
Since $m(=CC_1)$ is the value of the perpetual output stream deriv-
able from these capital goods, we may define m/C_v as a rate of
return to capital. A domestic entrepreneur with investible capital of
C_v units (measured in terms of C) can purchase $\underline{CE}$ units of capital
(through imports) and thus be assured of a perpetual stream of
m units of output (also measured in terms of C.) In this situation,
investment will not take place unless the rate of return on capital,
m/C_v, is significantly higher than the rate of interest.[3]

The logic of an import tariff as a protective device is to increase
the expected rate of return to capital (m/C_v), making investment
more attractive. If, for example, a consumer goods import tariff
rate, t, were imposed, the import point shifts from point E to E' in
diagram 3.2. Let the straight line BH be drawn from point B to
point H. The net result of an import tariff on consumer goods is to
increase their exchange value relative to capital goods. Thus, the
domestic price ratio between consumer goods, C, and capital goods,
M, is now given by the slope of BH[4] and shows an increase of the
relative price of C compared to the international price ratio (represented by the slope of BA, the import frontier line).

3. Realistically, the rate of return to capital should be written as gm/C_v,
where $g > 1$ shows the effects of current (e.g., wage) costs of operating the
capital equipment.
4. In diagram 3.2, BF units of capital goods can be converted into FE
units of consumer goods in the world market. The latter, when brought into
the country subject to the tariff, will appreciate in exchange value relative
to capital goods. Suppose x units of consumer goods have an exchange value
equal to BF units of capital goods after imposition of a tariff. Then xP_C
$(1 + t) = BFP_M$ or $x/BF = (P_M/P_C)/(1 + t)$. This implies that $x = FH$ in
diagram 3.2 by equation 3.7.

At the effective domestic price ratio (the slope BH), a domestic entrepreneur wishing to acquire $\underline{EC} = \underline{HC'}$ units of capital goods will now have to invest only $C_e = \overline{C'D}$ units (in terms of consumer goods) rather than C_v, which he would have had to invest in the absence of the import tariff. Thus, the rate of return to capital is now raised to the level of m/C_e (rather than m/C_v) and represents a substantial investment incentive to the domestic entrepreneur. This clearly represents the protection effect of a selective tariff on consumer goods.

The protection effect of import tariffs is quite different from the profit transfer effect analyzed earlier. Tariff revenue accrues to the government and does not benefit private entrepreneurs directly unless the government chooses to subsidize them out of tariff revenue. However, the private entrepreneur does benefit from the protection effect, as we have just shown, even when the government does not undertake subsidies. The benefits associated with protection arise from price distortion which make capital goods cheaper relative to consumer goods.

2.4. Ancillary Policies

The primary policy instruments for forced import substitution growth, exchange rate, price inflation, and tariffs, are often supplemented by ancillary policy measures. We shall briefly discuss several of these ancillary measures to show their consistency with the underlying profit transfer rationale of forced industrialization. The following will be discussed in turn: foreign aid, export promotion, and interest rate subsidies.

Foreign aid. Foreign aid policy may be analyzed with the aid of diagram 3.3, in which the import frontier line, AB (before foreign aid), is reproduced. Suppose D units of foreign aid (valued in terms of capital goods imports) are made available, shifting the import frontier to $A'B'$. Suppose that the initial import point, without aid, is at point E'. Several alternative cases may now be considered, depending on the use to which the foreign aid resources are put.

In the simplest case, the foreign aid fund, D, is directly used by the government to purchase capital goods for public investment. The new equilibrium import point will be at Q, and the additional

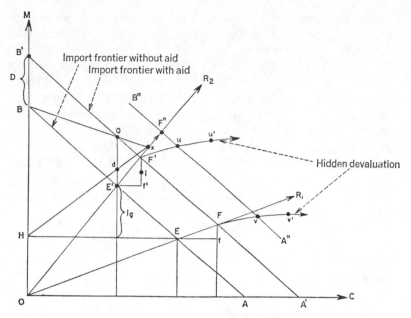

Diagram 3.3. Foreign Aid and Export Promotion

(aid-financed) capital goods imports, $E'Q$, are used entirely for public investment.

Suppose, instead, that the government uses the aid fund, D, to provide incentives for agricultural exports, making export producers the aid beneficiaries. Given the official exchange rate, r, and the tariff rate, t, the positions of E and E' on the original import frontier line will be determined; i.e., $BE/AB = \Theta$ and $BE'/BE = 1/(1 + t)$. Assuming Θ and t are unchanged, these points are projected on the new frontier line at point F and F' by the radial lines, OR_1 and OR_2. Under our assumption of the pre-aid import point at E', consumer goods imports will increase by $E'f'$, benefitting agricultural export producers; and total investment will increase by $f'F'$, of which the increase in private investment is fF ($=iF'$) and the increase in public investment is $f'i$. Thus, all pre-aid magnitudes of both consumer goods and capital goods imports are raised proportionately when aid directly benefits the export sector.

As a third possibility, the government may adopt a more growth-oriented approach of selling (at the official rate) the entire amount of foreign exchange from aid, D, to private industrial entrepreneurs for import of capital goods. The equilibrium import point will now fall at Q. The government is the beneficiary of the foreign aid in its local currency receipts from the sale of foreign exchange (equal to rP_MD) — ordinarily referred to as "counterpart funds." The government may now purchase from importers an equivalent amount of imported capital goods at the free market (domestic) price. The aid-financed capital goods imports will then be shared between the government, as the original aid beneficiary, and the private importers, whose share as indirect beneficiaries will be equivalent to the windfall foreign exchange profit bestowed upon them. This results from the overvalued exchange rate.

To provide a general equilibrium solution, let the straight line, BQ, intersect the radial line OR_2 at point x. Let a straight line Hx intersect the line segment $E'Q$ at point d. Then dE' represents the gain in private investment and dQ, the gain in public investment.[5]

It is evident that a given volume of foreign aid may have different effects upon consumption and investment, depending on the government's policy with regard to aid beneficiaries. These complexities should not obscure the fact that, where primary forced industrialization policies (e.g., exchange rate, tariffs, inflation) are in effect, foreign aid is likely to add to windfall profits distributed to industrial entrepreneurs.

Promotion of primary product exports. Export promotion policies to stimulate export volume (e.g. multiple exchange rates and export certificate voucher systems) are occasionally pursued during forced industrialization to ameliorate the basic strategy of squeezing

---

5. To see why this is true, let us assume that foreign aid is OB units (as measured on the vertical axis), the same as the agricultural export earnings on the import frontier, AB. Under this assumption the calculation of windfall profit and the ratio of public to private capital imports would be indicated by E, i.e., representing private imports of OH units and public imports of BH units. This is true because such a division implies that private investment, OH, corresponds to the windfall profit determined by Θ. The assertion in the text is based upon the equality, by construction, $OB/E'Q = OH/E'd = HB/dQ$.

the traditional export sector. These policies amount to hidden devaluation of the official exchange rate.

The logic of export promotion is shown in diagram 3.3 by the successive outward expansion of the import frontiers AB, $A'B'$, and $A''B''$, each corresponding to an increased volume of exports, J, or more favorable external terms of trade. If the ratio of the official to the free market rate, Θ, and the tariff rate, t, are unchanged, the equilibrium import points through time are given by E', F', F'' on the radial line OR_2. The case of hidden devluation is represented by the sequence E', F', u, u', falling on a path which bends downward as Θ increases. Such an export promotion policy is based on the expectation that the induced dynamic export expansion effect (increasing J) is sufficient to compensate for the depressing effect of hidden devaluation on capital goods imports. For example, the export expansion effect may be measured by $F'F''$, and the depressing effect, by the downward movement $F''u$. The net result, consistent with the policy aim, is shown by the greater height of u compared with F'.

In a dynamic context, such export promotion policies complement the basic forced industrialization strategy by prolonging the import substitution phase.[6] These policies, if effective, not only provide greater supplies of foreign exchange to import capital goods but they also expand the domestic market for industrial goods as income from agricultural exports increases.

Interest rate policy. Consistent with the general strategy of profit transfer, the government may divert its revenue, T, to stimulate private industrial investment by providing loans at artificially low interest rates. This offers an inducement to investment which is complementary to the protection afforded import substitution through tariff policy (see diagram 3.2). Interest rate subsidies operate to stimulate investment by affording the entrepreneur a favorable rate of return on capital compared with his cost of capital, i.e., compared with the interest rate. This policy leads to a dichotomy between the official and free market interest rate (similar to

---

6. In chapter 2 this was referred to as prolongation of import substitution growth.

the foreign exchange rate spread), necessitating government controls and credit allocation.

In summarizing our discussion of organization under economic nationalism, we see that once a society adopts a forced industrialization strategy, a large variety of primary and ancillary control measures are available to carry out this strategy. These measures are all consistent with the basic objective of profit transfer. The goal of developing indigenous entrepreneurship is gradually achieved as these policies are effective in building up domestic industrial capacity.[7]

3. TERMINATION OF IMPORT SUBSTITUTION GROWTH

Organization for import substitution growth under economic nationalism is characterized by a system of pervasive economic controls. Under an umbrella of protection and profit transfer measures, new entrepreneurs are offered opportunities for decision-making experience. After several years of accumulated exprience, growing maturity of entrepreneurs may precipitate a search for an organizational system more conducive to efficiency in production. As entrepreneurs become able to compete through growth of efficiency, a free market system will be gradually instituted. Import substitution growth is arrested as liberalization measures are adopted to end the control system.

Termination of import substitution as a transition growth phase is caused by exhaustion of the domestic market. The purchasing power generated by primary product exports is gradually shifted from the purchase of imported consumer goods to domestic output of the import substituting industries. Unless domestic purchasing power can be increased by expansion of primary product exports, the import substitution process will inevitably terminate (see chap-

7. The purpose of the analysis of policy instruments has been to demonstrate their consistency with the basic profit transfer strategy and to show that this strategy is relevant to import substitution growth. This emphasis reflects our view that policy consideration must be sensitive to the typology of transition growth, a viewpoint we elaborate in the concluding chapter. This viewpoint explains our avoiding exhaustive treatment of every policy measure cited in this chapter, each of which might indeed require a separate volume.

ter 2). The experience of Taiwan, Korea, and the Philippines indicates that import substitution runs its course in about ten years. The length of time required for developing entrepreneurial maturity is thus of crucial importance. Specifically, entrepreneurship may or may not be sufficiently developed to undertake new growth tasks. If entrepreneurial maturity is achieved by the time import substitution has run its full course of approximately a decade, the necessary condition for liberalization of controls is present (e.g., Taiwan, Philippines, South Korea). If, however, entrepreneurial development is inadequate, liberalization cannot be undertaken.

Import substitution growth is dominated by interaction between export agriculture and the industrial sector. The economy also inherits from colonialism a large traditional agricultural sector which is backward and where subsistence agriculture is practiced (i.e., sector T in diagram 1.1 of chapter 1). This traditional agricultural sector is not involved in the dynamics of import substitution growth. However, a part of the surplus being squeezed from export agriculture may be used to develop traditional agriculture, as when government revenue, T, is employed to create agricultural infrastructure (e.g., Taiwan). More frequently, the traditional agriculture is completely neglected (e.g. the Philippines and Indonesia).

Where primary product exports are relatively stagnant, the initial phase of transition growth under import substitution lasts about ten years (on the basis of experience in Taiwan, South Korea and the Philippines.) This is a period in which industrialization tasks are easy since available markets can be reserved for indigenous entrepreneurs by excluding imports. However, this brief time must be used to attack more difficult problems, i.e., the development of entrepreneurship and modernization of traditional agriculture. Since inherited entrepreneurial capabilities and the degree of agricultural backwardness differ among countries, the termination of import substitution will lead to variations in subsequent transition experience.

Taiwan, South Korea, the Philippines and Indonesia all began transition growth through import substitution under economic nationalism. Taiwan's and South Korea's heritage was favorable in regard to both a supply of experienced entrepreneurs and preconditioning of the traditional agricultural sector. For this reason the termination of import substitution led to the liberalization of controls and the emergence of export substitution growth. Entrepreneurs, making use of the abundance of labor cheaply supplied by the agricultural sector, were capable of producing labor-intensive exports for foreign markets. The Philippines inherited from colonialism an adequate supply of private entrepreneurs and a backward traditional agricultural sector which continued to be neglected by the government. For this reason the initial phase of import substitution was followed by prolonged import substitution growth in which private entrepreneurs were relied upon to expand primary product exports under a partially controlled system. In Indonesia, where both the entrepreneurial and agricultural heritage was least favorable, ten years of import substitution terminated in chaotic growth. These typological differences and their empirical verification are the subject of chapter 5.

This chapter has interpreted the process of import substitution growth as a particular transition growth process encompassing three interrelated facets of the society: (1) the mode of operation of the entire economy crucially involving the inherited primary product export base; (2) the method of organization employed to foster this growth regime; and (3) the historical background from which the growth type emerges. The term "import substitution" in contemporary literature tends, however, to stress only limited aspects of this holistic process, frequently emphasizing only the industrial sector.[8]

8. This partial equilibrium approach to import substitution is found, inter alia, in Ian Little, Tibor Scitovsky, and Maurice Scott, *Industry and Trade in Some Developing Countries: A Comparative Study* (London: Oxford University Press, 1970); and in Albert O. Hirschman, "The Political Economy of Import-Substituting Industrialization in Latin America," *Quarterly Journal of Economics* 82, no. 1 (February 1968): 1–32.

4

Organization under Neocolonialism

In this chapter we analyze an alternative organizational system for transition growth which will be referred to as neocolonialism to emphasize its continuity with the colonial past in both the economic and political aspect. From the economic standpoint, a more gradual termination of colonialism is evident because the colonial precedent of reliance upon primary product exports as the main growth force is continued, with industry playing a supporting rather than a leading role. Politically, the system is characterized by the retention of dominant alien[1] influence in the nonagricultural sector of the economy. Among Southeast Asian countries, Malaysia and Thailand may be cited as examples of neocolonialism in this sense.

While economic nationalism is associated with import substitution growth, neocolonialism fosters export promotion growth. Since continued expansion of primary product exports in foreign markets must be relied upon, neocolonial organization is based upon a free market system, which constitutes the focal point of analysis (section 2 in this chapter). The government maintains a relatively neutral and noninterventionist position in the international trade market. The development focus of the government is on infrastructure expenditure in the agricultural sector, consistent with the basic objective of the expansion of export production.

The causes behind the emergence of neocolonialism consist of a

---

1. We use the term "alien" to refer to the nonindigenous population (e.g., the non-Malays in Malaysia and non-Thai in Thailand). Such usage is customary in Southeast Asia. See, for example, J. D. Caldwell, "The Demographic Background," in T. H. Silcock and E. K. Fisk, *The Political Economy of Independent Malaya* (Berkeley: University of California Press, 1963), p. 60.

combination of unique political conditions and relatively favorable natural resource endowments. This same set of factors influences the long-run prospects of transition growth under neocolonialism. We shall see in the final section of this chapter that availability of land resources for exports and the political acceptability of industrial entrepreneurs determine neocolonialism's long-run outlook.

1. Emergence of the Neocolonial System

1.1. Neocolonialism as a Compromise

From the economic viewpoint, colonialism was characterized by an externally oriented commercial enclave which engaged in the export of land-based primary products, with the tempo of economic activity exclusively controlled by the forces of foreign market demand. Transition growth under a neocolonial system retains these characteristics. It is sensitive to foreign demand and it tolerates transfer of capital abroad. The industrial sector continues to stimulate the expansion of primary product exports. For these reasons, the economy's mode of operation may be characterized as export promotion growth.

In Southeast Asia, the politics of neocolonialism are dominated by the multiracial nature of the society and the necessity to maintain balance among ethnic groups. There are two contending groups in these countries. One includes the indigenous people (e.g., Malays in Malaysia and Thai in Thailand) who represent agrarian interests and control the political power structure. The other group consists of alien minorities (e.g., Chinese and Indians) as well as former Western colonialists (e.g., the British in Malaysia) who dominate industry and commerce. With the indigenous group formally in control of government, a compromise in power-sharing between the indigenous majority and the alien minority is an essential condition for emergence of neocolonialism.

The free market system is accepted as a fundamental condition of this political compromise. The government remains neutral, abstaining from aggressive interference in foreign trade and domestic markets. Alien and indigenous economic agents are free to participate in the economy on equal terms, regulated by competitive and impartial market forces. This neutrality on the part of the government in actuality represents a concession to alien and minority groups whose domination of commerce and industry is thereby not threatened.

Active government development policy emphasizes productivity gains in the agricultural sector through public investment in rural infrastructure. This policy serves political and economic objectives. Politically it mollifies the indigenous majority in the rural sector, while economically it is consistent with land-based export promotion. A compromise of this nature has existed in Malaysia since independence (1957) and in Thailand since the mid-1950s.

Where this particular organizational system (i.e., government neutrality in the economy) arises as a necessary compromise among contending ethnic groups, its viability ultimately depends upon the degree of cultural affinity among these groups. In the case of Thailand, a common heritage of Buddhism and racial intermarriage render the compromise workable. In Malaysia, however, sharp religious and cultural differences exist between the Islamic Malay and the Buddhist Chinese, causing worsening stresses in the organizational system.

1.2. The Economic Geography of Neocolonialism

An adequate natural resource base is essential for the viability of neocolonialism since land-based exports remain the primary growth promotion force. The supply of natural resources must be adequate to sustain continued increases in per capita income from this export base. Quantitatively, the economy must be land-abundant, endowed with a favorable land-labor ratio. This allows new land to be brought under cultivation as the population increases so that export production need not encounter increasing costs due to diminishing returns.

Qualitatively, a varied natural resource base favorable for diversification of agriculture is conducive to neocolonialism. This allows an expanding stream of secondary agricultural and mineral products (e.g., maize, palm oil, tin) to supplement the main export crop (e.g., rice, rubber). Such diversification of export products affords protection against both long-run worsening of the terms of trade and short-run fluctuations in world demand, two problems from which a primary product export economy is likely to suffer.

These favorable resource endowments are found in both Malaysia and Thailand, which are often referred to as "land-surplus economies." Since land resources are so crucial for export promotion growth under neocolonialism, the management and development of these resources are typically a major focus of government policy.

Given a favorable natural resource base, the rate at which primary product exports grow depends upon the stimulation received from the nonagricultural sector. Stimulation may take alternative forms. In one case, nonagricultural inputs are predominantly commercial services to accommodate the diversification of traditional primary product exports. In an alternative case, inputs are mainly of the modern intermediate goods type, leading to the introduction of modern processed export goods. While Thailand represents the first case, Malaysia exemplifies the second.

Neocolonialism, as a continuation of the colonial economic heritage, represents a compromise between indigenous and alien economic interests. Organizationally, this political compromise is rooted in the perpetuation of a relatively free market system, with little government interference. Since a favorable natural resource base is a prerequisite for continued reliance upon primary product exports, the government's major growth-promoting function consists of developing the land base.

Some perceptive readers of our manuscript have raised questions about the usefulness and precision of the term "neocolonialism." To avoid futile semantic debate, we wish to define unequivocally our usage of this term (which we admit may connote emotional overtones). In the absence of a more appropriate term, we have retained "neocolonialism" for three reasons: (1) From the economic viewpoint, these transition systems closely resemble the colonial heritage in maintaining reliance upon primary product exports as the major growth force. The "neo" characteristic is reflected in national control over infrastructure investment which is typically used, at least in part, to foster the growth of the traditional agricultural sector, a public function typically ignored under colonialism. (2) From the political viewpoint, these systems resemble colonialism in their tolerance of the continued dominance of indigenous aliens in the entrepreneurship of the nonagricultural sector, this tolerance sustained while new features of compromise between indigenous political control and alien entrepreneurship emerge. (3) Typologically, this term is selected to highlight the contrast of the preceding two aspects with the alternative system of economic nationalism in which a sharper break with colonialism occurs.

2. THE MARKET SYSTEM

2.1. Export Promotion under a Market System

Under neocolonialism, expansion of primary product exports is carried out in the context of a market system. The organizational features of this system are thus very different from the controlled system of economic nationalism analyzed in the last chapter. Under the free market system, prices are determined as guidelines to co-ordinate economic activities and to subject economic agents to the discipline of competition. In the remainder of this chapter, we investigate export promotion growth under this free market mechanism.

In diagram 4.1, the pattern of *real* resource flows in an open dualistic economy is reproduced. Under neocolonialism, primary products, J, are exported from the agricultural sector X, and these exports finance imports of consumer goods, M_c or capital goods, M_i. Capital goods imports, M_i, lead to investment, I, adding to the growth of capital stock, K, in the industiral sector Y permitting expansion of output, y. This output, as well as imported industrial consumer goods, M_c, are, in turn, delivered to the agricultural export sector X. From this description, we see that the overall pattern of real resource utilization under neocolonialism superficially resembles that of import substitution growth under economic nationalism.

There are, however, several features which distinguish growth under neocolonialism from growth under economic nationalism. First, expansion of primary product exports, J, is the dominant growth promotion force. Second, import substitution (i.e., the substitution of M_c by y) proceeds at a much slower pace since the growth of domestic industrial capacity, y, is constantly threatened by import competition, M. Third, as under colonialism, export profits, π, are allowed to migrate abroad as capital exports during periods of unfavorable world demand, and foreign capital is welcomed

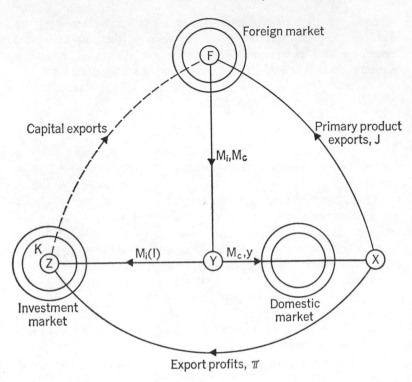

Flows: M_i = Imported capital goods   I = Domestic investment
           M_c = Imported industrial   y = Domestic output of
               consumer goods   industrial goods

Sectors: Ⓕ = Foreign sector   Ⓨ = Nonagricultural sector
         Ⓧ = Agricultural export sector   Ⓩ = Finance sector

Diagram 4.1. Structure of the Neocolonial Economy

to accommodate an import surplus when world demand is favorable. Fourth, political force is not used to transfer export profits to industrialists, in this case, the alien minority. Under the free market system, in fact, government tends to encourage the use of export profits to promote primary product export growth.

    Neocolonialism relies upon the system of three markets shown in diagram 4.1: (1) the foreign market where primary product exports are exchanged for current and capital imports, (2) the domestic market where imports and domestic output compete and (3) the investment goods market which determines whether export profits will be used for domestic investment or transferred abroad (capital flight). We begin by analyzing the operation of these markets at a point in time, then proceeding to their consequences for growth through time.

2.2. The Market Mechanism

Forces of demand and supply operate in the domestic commodity market. For demand, we have

(4.1) $y = D(p, J)$ (Demand for domestic industrial goods)

which emphasizes that demand for domestically produced industrial goods, y, is a function of their price, p, and export income, J. In diagram 4.2a, let price, p, be measured on the vertical axis and quantity demanded, y, on the horizontal axis. The demand function (equation 4.1) is represented by a system of negatively sloped demand curves, each indexed by an export income index, i.e., $J_0 < J_1 < J_2$ . . . , showing that higher export income causes the curve to shift upward.

We assume that the part of export income not spent on domestically produced industrial goods will be spent on imported consumer goods. Hence:

(4.1a) $P_M M_c = P_J J - py$ (Demand for imported consumer goods)

Once the demand function of equation 4.1 is given, the consumption pattern from export income (i.e., its distribution between y and M_C) is determined as functions of domestic price, p, export income, $P_J J$, and price of imported consumer goods, P_M.

Turning to the supply side, short-run supply of domestically produced industrial goods is determined mainly by productive capacity, i.e., capital stock, K, the short-run bottleneck factor. This supply force is shown in diagram 4.2b, in which the vertical axis (pointing downward) measures capital stock, K. The radial line pictures a production function

(4.2) $y = K/k$ (Production and supply of domestic industrial goods)

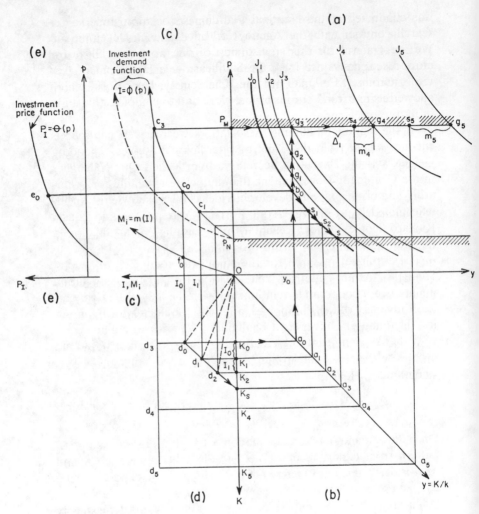

Diagram 4.2. Market Dynamics: The Neocolonial System

where k is a constant capital-output ratio. If the initial capital stock is K_0 units, then output of Oy_0 units will be generated and reach the commodity market. In short, both capital stock, K, and output, y, are fixed in the short run; they can be increased only through growth and capital accumulation.

The next link in the market system is the stimulation of investment demand, I, by the commodity price, p, and, possibly, by many other factors in the investment market. Formally, we may write the investment demand and the investment price functions as:

(4.3) $I = \phi(p, P_M, k, i, w_n)$ (Investment demand function)

(4.4) $P_I = \theta(p)$ (Investment goods price function)

Equation 4.3 states that entrepreneurial demand for investment goods depends upon the commodity price, p, the price of imported capital goods, P_M, the productivity of capital, $1/k$, the interest rate, i, and the wage cost, w_n. Equation 4.4 shows that the price of investment goods, P_I, is determined simultaneously and consistently with equation 4.3. Thus, given p, both I and P_I are simultaneously determined by equations 4.3 and 4.4.[2] It is obvious that the investment demand function is highly complex since, in fact, it can be deduced only from the "optimizing behavior" of the entrepreneur, based upon his anticipations of future profits — as will be explained in the appendix.

In diagram 4.2c let investment, I, be measured leftwise on the horizontal axis. Treating other variables in equation 4.3 as parameters, the investment function, $I = \phi(p)$, is then represented by the positively sloped solid curve. A more favorable investment climate reflecting changes in the "other" parameters in equation 4.3 will cause the curve to shift to the left and become more price elastic, as shown by the dotted curve. Notice that there is a floor commodity price, p_N, below which no investment will take place (i.e., investment occurs only when $p > p_N$). The existence of such a floor is explained by the fact that there is a positive real cost associated with new investment projects, and the commodity price will have to be significantly above zero to cover these costs and induce investment.

In diagram 4.2e, let the horizontal axis, leftwise, be the price of investment goods. The investment price function, $P_i = \theta(p)$, is

2. The determinants of industrial investment, I, are analyzed in the appendix to this chapter, where P_M, k, i, and w_n are treated as parameters of the investment demand function. As in the Keynesian tradition, this function explains the forces determining the magnitude of investment which entrepreneurs are willing to undertake.

shown as a positively sloped curve. Higher commodity prices, p, lead to higher prices of investment goods, P_I, consistent with the increased demand for investment goods in the investment market.

Demand for investment goods, I, induces the production of new capital goods. The production of capital goods requires mainly an imported capital component, M_i:

$$(4.5) \quad M_i = m(I) \qquad \text{(Capital goods import function)}$$

This function is shown in diagram 4.2c by a positively sloped curve, indicating that higher investment leads to increased capital goods imports.

We are now in a position to analyze the operation of the market system at a particular point in time. Two magnitudes, $K = K_0$ (capital stock) and $J = J_0$ (agricultural exports), are initially taken as given and fixed. This fixes the point K_0 on the vertical axis of diagram 4.2b as well as the position of the "J-curve" as J_0 in diagram 4.2a. From the point K_0 we may now determine, in succession, (1) output (point a_0 on the production function in diagram 4.2b), (2) the commodity price (point b_0 on the demand function in diagram 4.2a), (3) the volume of investment (point c_0 on the investment demand function of diagram 4.2c), (4) the price of investment goods (point e_0 on the investment price function in diagram 4.2e), and (5) the volume of capital imports (point f_0 on the import function of diagram 4.2c). The short-run equilibrium is described by the equilibrium rectangle, K_0, a_0, y_0, b_0, c_0, f_0, I_0, d_0 (and the point e_0). Combined, these equilibrium points show the interactions of the forces of production, supply, demand, investment, and imports.

We can also determine imports on current account, M_c, by equation 4.1a and, hence, the magnitudes of capital flight, A, and profits, π, can be determined at the closed end of the model, i.e.:

$$(4.6) \quad A = P_J J - P_M (M_c + M_i) \qquad \text{(Capital flight)}$$

$$(4.7) \quad \pi = P_I I + A \qquad \text{(Industrial profits)}$$

Capital flight, A, equals the export surplus, while industrial profits lead to investment, $P_I I$, and/or capital flight, A.

Notice that capital stock, K, and primary products exports, J, are both exogenous variables in the short run. Once their values are given, every other variable in the system can be determined for a point in time. Analysis of the dynamics of growth must thus focus upon the rules of growth determining changes of K and J through time.

As a summary, the equations introduced in this section are:

(4.1) $y = D(p, J)$ (Demand for domestic industrial goods)

(4.1a) $P_M M_c = P_J J - py$ (Demand for imported consumer goods)

(4.2) $y = K/k$ (Production and supply of domestic industrial goods)

(4.3) $I = \phi(p, P_M, k, i, w_n)$ (Investment demand function)

(4.4) $P_I = \theta(p)$ (Investment goods price function)

(4.5) $M_i = m(I)$ (Capital goods import function)

(4.6) $A = P_J J - P_M(M_c + M_i)$ (Capital flight)

(4.7) $\pi = P_I I + A$ (Industrial profits)

In essence, these equations depict the central logic of a market system, where the income generated by primary product exports determines, through income and price effects, the volume of consumption and commodity prices in the commodity market. The commodity prices, when favorable, in turn stimulate investment in import substituting industries. Capital flight may occur when investment demand cannot fully absorb the profits of the industrial sector.

3. Growth Prospects under Neocolonialism

The growth potential of the neocolonial economy depends upon the behavior of J (primary product exports) and K (industrial capital stock) through time. Hence, two issues suggest themselves: (1) the rapidity of growth of J and K, and (2) the balance between the growth of J and K. Since the accumulation of capital through time is given by the accounting relation,

$$(4.8) \quad dK/dt = I \quad \text{(Investment and augmentation of } K)$$

the growth potential of the economy may be investigated in terms of two alternative behavior patterns for primary product exports J: stagnation and continuous expansion.

3.1. Export Stagnation

Let us begin by analyzing industrialization prospects under the assumption that agricultural exports are stagnant, as represented by a fixed demand curve, e.g., curve J_0 in diagram 4.2a. Let the J_0 curve intersect the horizontal line extending from p_N (the floor price) at a point s. Starting from the initial capital stock, K_0, and the market equilibrium point, b_0 (in diagram 4.2a), successive investment will lead to capital stock of $K_1, K_2, \ldots$ determining market equilibrium points, $s_1, s_2, \ldots$ on the J_0 curve. Notice that the process of industrialization comes to an end as point s is approached, at which point investment ceases. The equilibrium points, $d_0, d_1, d_2, \ldots$ of diagram 4.2d, approach the point K_s, the maximum capital stock.

This case is properly described as industrial stagnation. Any temporary expansion of investment from the K_s equilibrium point will depress industrial commodity prices (diagram 4.2a), reducing investment incentives (diagram 4.2e) and causing disinvestment (diagram 4.2c) until capital stock is reduced to the K_s equilibrium amount (diagram 4.2d). This case reminds us of colonialism since industrial growth is, indeed, pushed by agricultural exports in this system. Continuous expansion of industrial output is only assured by expansion of primary product exports. Conversely, when primary product exports are stagnant, investment in import substituting industries will lead to market saturation and unfavorable price trends discouraging further investment. In this case industrial profits will be diverted to capital flight.

3.2. Continuous Export Expansion

Let us now consider the case in which agricultural exports expand continuously as the J curve shifts from J_0 to $J_1, J_2, \ldots$ We note, first, the consequences in the short run, with capital stock fixed at K_0. As the demand curve shifts progressively upward in diagram 4.2a, successive increases in the price of industrial goods occur — from b_0 to g_1, g_2, g_3.

Note, however, that because of the eventual effect of import competition in an open economy, domestic price increases are not unlimited. In diagram 4.2a, the height of the horizontal line through the point P_M (on the vertical axis) represents the price of imported industrial goods. As agricultural exports exceed the J_3 level, the domestic industrial goods price remains at the P_M level because of import competition. At the export level, shown by J_4 for example, the incremental quantity of the industrial goods demand of Δ_1 units will be met entirely from imports (the domestic supply being fixed at the level g_3).

The existence of a ceiling price (set by the import price in an open, free trade economy) constitutes a serious limitation to domestic industrialization. While economic nationalism seeks to eliminate this handicap by protection, this control policy is impossible under neocolonialism because of the necessity for political compromise between industrial and agrarian interests. As long as this ceiling price prevails, the volume of investment will remain constant in each succeeding period (at the amount shown by point C_3 in diagram 4.2c). The resulting capital growth path is shown by points d_3, d_4, d_5, in diagram 4.2d, indicating that both capital stock and output increase by a constant amount through time:

(4.9a) $\quad K = K_0 + \bar{I}t$

(4.9b) $\quad y = y_0 + (\bar{I}/k)t$

Industrial growth of this kind is slow, in fact, too slow to effect positive import substitution, even when expansion of agricultural exports proceeds at a satisfactory rate, i. At the constant price level, P_M in diagram 4.2a, we may reasonably assume that demand for industrial output, C, will also expand at approximately the same rate:

(4.10a) $\quad J = J_0 e^{it}$

(4.10b) $\quad C = C_0 e^{it}$

It follows that imported industrial consumer goods, M_c, will occupy an increasing share of the domestic market and that domestic output, y, will represent an ever decreasing share, while capital stock will not grow as rapidly as exports:

(4.11a) $$y/C = \frac{y_0 + (I/k)t}{C_0 e^{it}}$$

(4.11b) $$K/J = \frac{K_0 + It}{J_0 e^{it}}$$

Domestic output of y grows slowly because the force of import competition holds down price and thus investment incentives are discouraged.

Thus, we see that domestic industrial output lags behind imports and the growth of industrial capital stock lags behind exports. This case may be referred to as reversion to enclavism. The economy's openness (in the sense of lack of protection) produces a situation in which the agricultural (export) sector becomes increasingly linked with the outside world. The domestic industrial sector, although not absolutely stagnant, grows too slowly to achieve import substitution. This reminds us of the enclavism of the colonial epoch, which many less developed countries try to overcome by avoiding import competition. Reversion to enclavism is seen to be a realistic possibility where the country deliberately chooses a relatively free trade system. The country will remain specialized in primary product exports as development of domestic manufacturing is thwarted by foreign competition.

Both of the extreme cases just discussed (industrial stagnation and reversion to enclavism) contain undesirable features. Industrialization will founder whether or not primary product exports expand.[3] This dilemma is easy to explain; for, after all, neocolonialism is merely a new variant of the old colonial system which we know from experience is not a growth type conducive to industrialization.

---

3. Slow growth of domestic manufacturing in the neocolonial countries of Thailand and Malaysia stands out in sharp contrast to rapid import substitution in the Philippines and Taiwan. (See diagram 8.7 in chapter 8.)

3.3. Viability of Neocolonialism

Neocolonialism emerged in Malaysia and Thailand from both political and economic background factors. While these countries were
favored by relatively abundant endowments of natural resources,
the ethnic composition of the population and their specialized roles
in the economy rendered necessary a compromise organizational
solution under a free market system. The viability of neocolonialism, as a transition growth type toward modernization, must be
explained in terms of these geographic and political factors.

From the economic viewpoint, neocolonialism is viable in the
short run, i.e., within our time horizon of one generation. This is
true because natural resources are abundant enough to allow the
country to rely on primary product exports to sustain an adequate
rate of increase of per capita income. From the economic standpoint, the duration of this growth type could conceivably last as
long as the supply of natural resources is adequate.

The major disadvantage of neocolonialism is that it does not
offer a significant departure from colonial land-based growth nor
the prospect of rapid labor-based industrialization. Even where primary product exports grow at a satisfactory rate, momentum toward
industrialization is impeded by import competition and freedom
for capital flight. This reminds us of colonialism in which similar
openness of the economy relegated the industrial sector to a subsidiary role in accommodating primary product exports.

The long-run prospects of neocolonialism hinge upon the interaction between these economic consequences and the background
factors which led to its emergence. There are two alternatives. If
the political compromise of the free market system remains necessary to preserve racial harmony, the country will continue to pay
the price of slow industrialization through reliance on land-based
export growth — at least as long as land resources are adequate.
Where, however, the ethnic problem begins to recede as indigenous
entrepreneurs appear, the country may choose to abandon the slow
industrialization of neocolonialism, particularly if land resources are
becoming exhausted. In this case, a more controlled organizational
system will be adopted to favor industrial entrepreneurs (as in the

case of import substitution, analyzed in the previous chapter). Such tendencies have recently begun to appear in both Malaysia and Thailand, although they may continue to be hampered by racial strife, particularly in Malaysia.

Before concluding our examination of the neocolonial organization for transition growth, let us briefly recapitulate our discussion up to this point. The method of organization under neocolonialism relies heavily on the free market system (in export markets, investment goods markets, and commodity markets) to coordinate and regulate economic activities. This method of organizing the economy during transition growth stands in sharp contrast to the control system adopted under economic nationalism, and analyzed in the preceding chapter.

The choice of an organizational system for transition growth is not an accidental matter. The emergence of a particular system is related to both the specific growth functions to be performed and the institutional background of a country. The free market system was adopted in Malaysia and Thailand to promote externally oriented growth through the expansion of primary product exports, while the control system which emerged in the Philippines and Taiwan was adopted to promote internally oriented growth through import substitution. The free market system in Malaysia and Thailand was compatible with government neutrality in the economy to foster ethnic harmony. In the Philippines and Taiwan, controls were consistent with transferring export profits to indigenous entrepreneurs.

It should be observed, to avoid misunderstanding, that both economic nationalism and neocolonialism rely upon a mixed organizational system combining government intervention and free markets. This mixture, in fact, is a feature of the colonial heritage. Despite this common feature, however, the contrast between the two systems has not been overdrawn. Though tariffs and interest rate subsidies have been employed in Thailand and Malaysia, for example, their impact has been modest. More important, we must look behind the use of specific policies to identify the governing strategy of each country. In this connection, there can be no doubt that the strategic intent in the Philippines and Taiwan was to transfer export-related profits to industrialists for import substitution while this has not been true in Thailand and Malaysia. This chapter has emphasized some major features of growth potential under a neocolonial organization. Under this system, the economy's openness and tolerance of import competition lead to tendencies toward an unbalanced, slow growth and a reversion to colonial type enclavism.[4] These ideas will provide the initial guidelines for construction of more rigorous models to analyze transition growth in Malaysia and Thailand in later chapters.

APPENDIX: DETERMINANTS OF INDUSTRIAL INVESTMENT

Under neocolonialism inducements to invest are basically oriented toward profit expectations in the free market system. This underlying assumption was built into the investment demand function (equation 4.3) and the investment goods price function (equation 4.4) postulated in the text. In this appendix we investigate what lies behind the two functions. In diagram 4.3 capital is measured on the horizontal axis, and the production function, $y = K/k$ (equation 4.2), is represented by the radial line, OR. Let us assume that initial capital stock is K_0. Let point N (on the radial line directly above K_0) be a new origin relative to which investment, I, is measured on the horizontal axis. Let the following increasing functions of investment be postulated:

1. the radial line, py, representing the anticipated gross revenue stream obtained by multiplying output, y, and price, p (as determined in the commodity market);
2. the gap between py and the radial line, Nn, representing current costs of operation (e.g., labor and raw materials for new output capacity);

4. When a country has already developed adequate entrepreneurship, import competition may be expected to serve as a stimulus toward greater productive efficiency. This phenomenon is largely irrelevant, however, to a less developed country just escaping from colonialism in which deficiency of indigenous entrepreneurs is the most crucial bottleneck to development. As we saw in chapter 3, the major purpose of the import substitution strategy is to promote the development of entrepreneurship. Neocolonial countries are deprived of this strategy because of the necessity for government neutrality. Hence, our model emphasizes the negative effect of import competition.

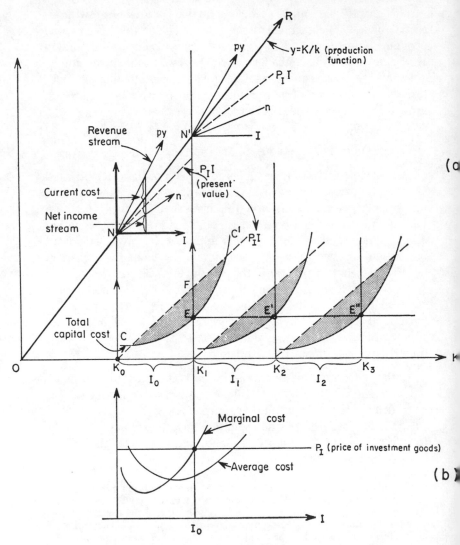

Diagram 4.3. Investment Determination

3. the height of the radial line, Nn, representing the anticipated net income stream (i.e., the difference between gross revenue and current costs);

4. the radial line, $P_I I$, representing the present value of the anticipated net income stream (obtained by discounting number 3 in this list by the market rate of interest, r).[5]

The last function (4) is now shifted down to the main part of diagram 4.3 as the $P_I I$ function beginning from a new origin, K_0, and is construed as the present value of investment. The curve CC' represents total costs of investment (i.e., all costs associated with construction of new capital goods). The shaded vertical distances are then profits under the free market system. Industrial entrepreneurs will choose that level of investment, I_0, which will maximize profits, shown as the vertical distance, FE. This maximizing principle is shown in the lower (b) deck of diagram 4.3 where the horizontal line, P_I, is the price (or average revenue) of investment goods, and where the average and marginal cost curves (derived from CC') are also shown. The equilibrium (profit maximizing) point is I_0, where marginal cost equals price.

This market investment logic[6] shows that the level of investment, I_0, as well as the price of investment goods, P_I, are functions of the price of industrial goods, p.[7] This framework is the only possible rational intrepretation of investment demand based upon profit maximizing behavior in a competitive market.

The short-run theory of investment demand is an integral part of the long-run growth mechanism. In the second period, for example, the capital stock is K_1 (i.e., $K_0 + I_0$), and the short-run analysis can be repeated to show determination of investment, I_1,

5. If w_n is the wage cost per unit of output, then, conceptually:

$$P_I I = \int_0^\infty (I/k)(p - w_n)e^{-rt}\, dt = I(p - w_n)/kr$$

6. This analysis is an adaptation of the Keynesian investment decision mechanism. We differ from the Keynesian method only in using a concept of "marginal efficiency of investment" in place of "marginal efficiency of capital."

7. From diagram 4.3, we see that P_I is the slope of the radial line, $P_I I$, and is causally determined by price, p, current costs, and the interest rate. The equilibrium level of investment, I_0, is a function of all of these, as well as capital construction cost. (See equation 4.3.)

and, similarly, for succeeding periods. This investment demand determination involving price, p, the interest rate, r, as well as current and capital costs, ultimately constitutes an essential and sensitive mechanism in the growth rules of a developing economy under a free market regime. This type of behavior is relevant to assessing the long-run growth prospects of a neocolonial system.

5

Typology of Transition Growth

The open dualistic economy inherits from its colonial background a particular structure, marked by coexistence between an export-oriented enclave and a large, stagnant, traditional agricultural sector. The operation of the enclave is dominated by the export of land-based primary products, in the production of which the non-agricultural sector plays a subordinate role. The traditional agricultural sector, isolated from the enclave, remains backward in technology and continues to emphasize subsistence production.

Modernization of the open dualistic economy requires the integration of the agricultural and industrial sectors, the growth and development of indigenous factors of production other than land (i.e., entrepreneurship, skilled labor, and capital), the expansion of manufacturing through industrialization, and the uplift of traditional agriculture. While all of these tasks must ultimately be accomplished to bring about the modern growth epoch, transition growth may, in the short run, take many different paths. A typological approach to transition growth gives recognition to this diversity and seeks to explain its causation.

I. DIVERSITY OF TRANSITION GROWTH

Economic nationalism and neocolonialism are the two major systems under which transition growth may be initiated. These systems differ in both economic and organizational content. Economic nationalism, which relies upon control measures to promote import substitution growth, leads to the rapid expansion of domestic industrial capacity to replace imports. Neocolonialism on the other hand, which employs a free market system to facilitate export promotion growth, results in expansion of primary product exports with modest industrial growth.

Of the two systems, neocolonialism represents a less abrupt break with both the economic and political aspects of colonialism. Economically, neocolonialism continues to rely upon primary product exports as the major growth force, while politically the services of aliens are retained as industrial entrepreneurs. In Southeast Asia, Malaysia and Thailand are examples of neocolonialism accompanied by export promotion growth, while the Philippines and Taiwan exemplify import substitution growth under economic nationalism.

1.1. Economic Differences

Under neocolonialism, continuous expansion of primary product exports is the key growth phenomenon. The nonagricultural sector plays a supporting role by accommodating and stimulating primary product exports. Domestic manufacturing is subject to competition from foreign products, and for this reason the development of import-substituting industries proceeds at a slow pace. In contrast, import substitution growth under economic nationalism employs the earnings from primary product exports primarily as a means to develop import-substituting industries at a rapid pace.

Because of neocolonialism's concentration upon expansion of primary product exports, there is less opportunity for integration between the enclave and traditional agriculture than in the case of economic nationalism. The slow pace of industrialization offers little opportunity for development of entrepreneurship, labor, and capital. The more rapid development of the industrial sector under import substitution growth offers opportunities for growth of an industrial labor force and entrepreneurship in the import-substituting industries.

1.2. Organizational Differences

The organization of economic nationalism is based on a strategy of government intervention designed to force industrialization through a wide variety of trade-related controls. These controls encourage indigenous industrial producers by protecting the domestic market, and they foster domestic investment by preventing capital flight. Profits are thereby transferred from agricultural export producers to industrial entrepreneurs, a strategy which discriminates against the agricultural export sector while favoring the industrial class.

The key organizational feature of neocolonialism is the maintenance of a free market system, both internationally and domestically. The allocation of export profits is guided by market forces which tolerate both import competition and capital flight. The government does not interfere in the market to discriminate against or favor any economic group. However, the government may support the development of agricultural infrastructure in order to encourage the growth of primary product exports.

1.3. Differences in Development Potential

In import substitution industrialization under economic nationalism, termination tendencies will eventually appear since the control system causes primary product exports to stagnate, or, at best, to grow slowly. Termination occurs when the domestic market for industrial consumer goods is completely supplied by domestic producers and producer goods are dominant in the import account. At this point the first transition phase of relatively easy industrial growth comes to an end, and entrepreneurs confront more difficult growth tasks.

The entrepreneurial response to these termination tendencies in import substitution growth may take either of two alternatives. In the first alternative, the entrepreneur shifts to producing labor-intensive exports for the foreign market and a phase of export substitution growth emerges. A second alternative occurs if entrepreneurs turn their attention internally to promote expansion of primary product exports. In this case, prolonged import substitution growth occurs.

Contrasts in transition growth experience between the Philippines and Taiwan are of this nature. Both countries shared an initial phase of about ten years of import substitution growth. Termination of this initial growth phase led to export substitution in Taiwan, while in the Philippines it led to prolongation of import substitution through the promotion of primary product exports. From our "generation" (i.e., 20 year) perspective of transition growth, therefore, the initial import substitution phase is short-lived, giving rise to a new transition growth phase.

Where the transition is initiated through export promotion growth under neocolonialism, different issues of development potential are raised. Export promotion growth offers longer viability as a transition system and may endure throughout the first generation. This was true in both Malaysia and Thailand, where export promotion growth has been the only growth phase occurring during the postwar generation.

Viability of export promotion growth during the first generation should not lead to the unwarranted conclusion that this system can endure indefinitely. Two factors threaten long-run viability. First, the supply of land resources for primary product exports may be eventually exhausted. Second, the slow pace of industrialization which characterizes this system may become politically intolerable. In both cases the likely outcome will be a shift toward import substitution growth.

1.4. Empirical Evidence

The typological characteristics of the four countries may now be supported by empirical evidence. Table 5.1 compares export promotion growth under neocolonialism in Malaysia and Thailand with import substitution growth under economic nationalism in the Philippines and Taiwan. Four indicators are used to show the essential characteristics of growth in these economies between 1950 and the mid-1960s.

Column 1 shows the export ratio (the ratio of exports to GNP) as a measure of the share of exports in the economy's income generation. The colonial heritage of all four countries is apparent from the fact that all show relatively high export ratios in the early 1950s. The high external orientation of Malaysia is particularly noteworthy. This feature of the colonial heritage is reinforced by the data in column 2 which shows primary product exports as a fraction of total exports. In all cases, primary product exports account for virtually all export earnings in the early 1950s.

The export promotion nature of transition growth in Malaysia is seen in column 1 from the maintenance of the unusually high export ratio; in the case of Thailand this may be seen from the significant increase in the ratio. Continued reliance upon primary product exports in these two neocolonial economies is further confirmed by the data in column 2 showing that primary product ex-

Table 5.1. Characteristics of Neocolonialism and Economic Nationalism

	(1) Export ratio		(2) Primary product exports/Total exports		(3) Share of manufacturing in value added		(4) Imported manufactured consumer goods/Total imports	
	Early 1950s	Mid 1960s	Early 1950s	Mid 1960s	Early 1950s	Mid 1960s	Early 1950s	Mid 1960s
Neocolonialism								
Malaysia	.46	.45	.97	.95	.09[a]	.11	.32[b]	.31
				(−2.1%)		(+22.0%)		(−3.1%)
Thailand	.16	.21	1.00	.98	.12	.13	.35	.31
				(−2.0%)		(+8.3%)		(−11.4%)
Economic nationalism								
Philippines	.20	.20	.97	.90	.09	.20	.39	.20
				(−7.2%)		(+122%)		(−48.7%)
Taiwan	.12	.24	.94	.59	.13	.20	.32	.13
				(−37.2%)		(+54%)		(−59.4%)

Sources:

Column 1: Douglas S. Paauw, "Economic Progress in Southeast Asia," *Journal of Asian Studies* 23, no. 1 (November 1963); and Douglas S. Paauw, "The Postwar Record of Open, Dualistic Economies," mimeographed (National Planning Association, May 1969).

Column 2: United Nations, *Yearbook of International Trade Statistics*, various issues.

Column 3: United Nations, *Yearbook of National Account Statistics*, various issues; Department of Statistics, Malaysia, *National Accounts;* and Directorate General of Budgets and Accounts and Statistics, Taiwan.

Column 4: United Nations, *Yearbook of International Trade Statistics*, various issues; Department of Customs, Thailand, *Annual Statement of Foreign Trade*, various issues; Statistical Appendix, below, tables 18 and 25.

[a] 1960.

[b] 1957.

ports continued to account for practically all exports in the mid–1960s.

In both countries where transition growth proceeded under economic nationalism (Philippines and Taiwan), the intertemporal comparisons given in column 1 obscure crucial characteristics. Since the import substitution phase in these countries lasted from 1950 to 1959, we need the following information for intertemporal comparison of export ratios:

Import Substitution Phase

	Early 1950s	Late 1950s	Mid-1960s
Philippines	.20	.16	.20
Taiwan	.12	.12	.24

In the Philippine's case, the import substitution phase is clearly seen to be a phase of internal orientation since the export ratio declines. In the case of Taiwan, the export ratio is maintained during the import substitution phase because agricultural exports expanded rather than remaining stagnant (see chap. 6, below).

In both countries the export ratios increased significantly when the first phase of import substitution growth ended. In the Philippines this growth of the export ratio was associated with the phenomenon of prolongation of import substitution, while in Taiwan it was associated with export substitution. This is substantiated by the data in column 2 which show that in spite of a modest decline (7.2 percent) in the Philippines, primary product exports still accounted for 90 percent of total exports in the mid 1960s. This contrasts sharply with Taiwan where the share of primary product exports fell by 37 percent under export substitution growth (between the late 1950s and the mid 1960s).

Column 3 shows the share of manufacturing in total value added. The colonial heritage of all four countries is apparent from the low share of manufacturing in the early 1950s. The moderate change in this ratio for the two neocolonial countries (Malaysia and Thailand) testifies to the slow pace of industrialization under export promotion growth. This contrasts sharply with the Philippines and Taiwan where economic nationalism was adopted. In both these countries there was a large jump in the share of manufacturing in value added testifying to rapid industrialization under import substitution growth.

Column 4 shows imported manufactured consumer goods as a fraction of total imports. A significant decrease in this fraction over a period of years is direct evidence of import substitution growth. In Malaysia and Thailand, only a slight decrease occurred, indicating the absence of rapid import substitution. In the Philippines and Taiwan, however, there was a marked reduction in imported manufactured consumer goods, demonstrating the existence of vigorous domestic import substitution.

These data show that there was, indeed, considerable diversity in patterns of transition growth during the first generation. They are sufficient to demonstrate the existence of export promotion under neocolonialism in Malaysia and Thailand in contrast to import substitution under economic nationalism in the Philippines and Taiwan. These cross-country comparisons will be supplemented in later chapters by more detailed time-series analysis of transition growth in the four countries.

2. Causes of Diversity

Although open dualistic economies all inherited a common structure from their colonial background (in particular, the coexistence of an export enclave and a stagnant traditional agricultural sector), the colonial heritage left important differences in the background factors among individual countries. These differences are both economic-geographic and political in nature. The emergence of economic nationalism or neocolonialism (and their variations during the course of transition growth) must ultimately be explained in terms of the inherited background factors of each country.

2.1. Economic-Geographic Background

The economic-geographic background inherited from colonialism includes two major dimensions: natural resource supply and indigenous entrepreneurship. In general, neocolonialism tends to emerge where the natural resource endowment is favorable and indigenous entrepreneurship is very scarce.

It is easy to understand why this is true. Export promotion growth under neocolonialism relies upon expansion of primary product exports, essentially comprising the export of land services. An adequate natural resource base enables the country to maintain a satisfactory rate of per capita income growth from primary product exports. In contrast, when the natural resource base is inadequate, a country must seek a new basis for growth through developing other primary factors (labor, entrepreneurship, and capital). Import substitution growth offers opportunities for this shift from land to other primary factors. Economic nationalism abruptly modifies the colonial pattern because the economy lacks the natural resources for the continuation of growth based on primary product exports.

For emergence of economic nationalism, indigenous entrepreneurs must be available to manage the newly created import-substituting industries. This contrasts with neocolonialism where there is no demand for new industrial entrepreneurs to participate in rapid import substitution, and where the entrepreneurial requirements are confined to the type of trade-related activities familiar in the colonial economy. Neocolonialism, thus, maintains continuity with colonialism because the country lacks the entrepreneurship for an abrupt break.

Neocolonialism emerged in Malaysia and Thailand because these countries had adequate natural resources to continue colonial-type growth while they did not possess the indigenous entrepreneurship for shifting to an industrial base for transition growth. Economic nationalism occurred in the Philippines and Taiwan because their natural resource bases were inadequate to continue the colonial growth system, and the entrepreneurial capabilities for a new departure were present.

2.2. Political Background Factors

The term "political background factors" refers to the distribution of political power among the important economic classes — in the case of the open dualistic economy, between agricultural and industrial interests. Under economic nationalism, development strategy emphasizes the transfer of agricultural export profits to industrialists for import substitution. A necessary condition for this strategy is domination of political power by industrial interests. In both the Philippines and Taiwan, the adoption of import substitution growth was a reflection of this political reality.

In the neocolonial countries of Malaysia and Thailand the political aspect is dominated by the ethnic composition of the population. In both, political power rests in the hands of the indigenous group representing agricultural interests, while alien minorities control industrial entrepreneurship but lack political power. In this situation a strategy favoring industrialists for import substitution growth is politically intolerable, and export promotion growth under a free market system is a natural response. This system represents a compromise in which the government leaves the (alien) industrial entrepreneur free to function subject to impartial competitive forces while the government focuses upon the uplift of the rural, indigenous population.

Summing up, the emergence of neocolonialism or economic nationalism at the outset of the transition is traced to coincidence of economic-geographic and political background factors. In Malaysia and Thailand neocolonialism emerged because the natural resource endowment was favorable to continuation of primary product export expansion while the supply of indigenous entrepreneurship and political conditions were inimical to import substitution growth under economic nationalism. In contrast, economic nationalism arose in the Philippines and Taiwan because entrepreneurial and political conditions were conducive to import substitution growth while the natural resource base was inadequate for continued reliance on primary product exports.

2.3. Diversity Within Growth Types

Scrutiny of open dualistic economies in transition forces us to recognize finer differences of growth experience within the two major transition types, economic nationalism and neocolonialism. Malaysia and Thailand have shown different growth characteristics although both belong to the neocolonial family. Similarly, there are variations in the experience of the Philippines and Taiwan although economic nationalism was adopted in both. These distinctions within the major growth types may also be explained by more subtle differences in the inherited economic-geographic background factors, i.e., natural resource endowments and entrepreneurship.

Assessment of a country's natural resource background includes two aspects, one involving conditions in the enclave and the other, conditions in the traditional agricultural sector. The enclave aspect refers to the abundance and diversity of natural resources for expansion and diversification of primary product exports. The second aspect refers to the relative size of the traditional agricultural sector, the degree of its backwardness, and its land-labor ratio.

Both Malaysia and Thailand have been characterized as having a natural resource base favorable to primary product exports. However, there is an important difference between the two. Malaysia's resource base is more diversified, and historically, has supported a large export enclave. Thailand, by contrast, has a favorable land-labor ratio in the traditional agricultural sector, which has been the major source of exports. For this reason, the postwar growth of Thailand's primary product exports has been based upon expansion and diversification of its traditional sector output (e.g., rice, maize, kenaf). Malaysia's export growth has continued to focus upon expansion of modern exports (palm oil, tin, rubber) in which modern technology and industrial processing play an important role.[1]

While neither the Philippines nor Taiwan inherited resource endowments conducive to the expansion of primary product exports, there was a significant difference between the two with respect to traditional agriculture. Preconditions favorable to the modernization of Taiwan's agricultural sector had been created during the Japanese period, while these preconditions were absent in the Philippines. This difference in background accounts for the emergence of export substitution at the termination of the import substitution phase in Taiwan. In the Philippines, it explains agricultural shortfall and the prolongation of import substitution.

Assessment of a country's entrepreneurial endowment must include attention to both public and private entrepreneurial capabilities. The Philippines and Taiwan shared a strong private entrepreneurial tradition, accounting for emergence of the first transition phase of import substitution growth. However, the Philippines differed from Taiwan in having a weaker tradition of public entre-

---

1. The difference between Thailand's indigenous exports and Malaysia's modern exports implies an important analytical difference evident in our construction of contrasting models of transition growth in chapters 8 and 9. In the case of modern exports, production is crucially dependent upon inputs (management, capital, intermediate goods) from outside the agricultural sector, a dependence causing pronounced intersectoral relationship. In the case of indigenous export products, this is much less true.

preneurship, particularly with regard to government participation in modernization of traditional agriculture. This deficiency in the Philippines helps to account for the agricultural shortfall which impeded the rise of export substitution when the import substitution phase neared termination.

Both Malaysia and Thailand confronted a shortage of indigenous private entrepreneurs. In the public sector, however, Malaysia inherited entrepreneurial competence from the British colonial regime. This advantage permitted the Malaysian government to undertake prompt and effective measures to disseminate modern technology in both export and traditional agriculture. The absence of an overt alien colonial government in Thailand left the public sector without a similar capability.

2.4. Empirical Evidence

Empirical evidence on background factors (political and economic-geographic) related to the diversity of transition growth is only partially quantifiable. While nonquantifiable aspects (e.g., diversity of natural endowments, the relative backwardness of agriculture, and the quality of entrepreneurship) will be discussed in later chapters, some quantifiable measures are presented in table 5.2.

Column 1 shows the ethnic composition of the population. Notice the large alien minorities in the two neocolonial countries, Malaysia and Thailand.[2] A difference between Malaysia and Thailand is that there is less integration between alien and minority groups in Malaysia. For this reason resistance to the import substitution strategy is likely to be even greater in Malaysia than in Thailand.

Column 2 shows the share of enclave enterprise controlled by the alien minority. Notice that for the two neocolonial countries alien control is clearly dominant, while this is not true for the Philippines and Taiwan. A high share of alien control obviously discourages the forced industrialization strategy which relies upon profit transfers to industrial entrepreneurs.

Two measures of the degree of population pressure on land are given in columns 3 and 4: arable land per capita (column 3) and

2. In the case of Thailand, the nonindigenous group is, in fact, considerably larger because the size of this group is obscured by intermarriage and social and cultural integration.

Table 5.2. Causes of Emergence of Neocolonialism

	(1)	(2) Percentage of enclave enterprise controlled by alien population	Population pressure on land	
	Aliens as percentage of total population		(3) Arable land per capita (in hectares)	(4) Population density (per square kilometer)
Neocolonialism				
Malaysia	50	99	1.04	22
Thailand	20	95	.38	64
Economic nationalism				
Philippines	1	9	.27	116
Taiwan	irrelevant[a]	irrelevant[a]	.10	365

Sources:
Column 1: For Malaysia, Frank H. Golay et al., Underdevelopment and Economic Nationalism in Southeast Asia (Ithaca: Cornell University Press, 1969), p. 324; for Thailand, ibid., pp. 289, 297; for the Philippines, ibid., p. 25.
Column 2: For Malaysia, Golay et al., p. 366; for Thailand, based on Robert J. Muscat, Development Strategy in Thailand (New York: Frederick A. Praeger, 1966), p. 189; for the Philippines, Golay et al., pp. 106–107.
Column 3: Norton Ginsburg, Atlas of Economic Development (Chicago: The University of Chicago Press, 1961), p. 46.
Column 4: United Nations, Demographic Yearbook (1967).
[a] In the case of Taiwan, a distinction might be made between the recent immigrants (Mainlanders) and the earlier immigrants (Taiwanese). This distinction is neglected in the analysis because the cultural differences are much less pronounced than those between aliens and indigenous groups in the other countries.

population density (column 4). These measures testify to the more favorable land endowment conditions in the two neocolonial countries. High population pressure on land in the Philippines and Taiwan made imperative a shift from land-based growth to import substitution.

In this chapter we have introduced a typological approach to transition growth by analyzing the effect of background factors on the transition growth process. A combination of background factors typically influences the course of transition growth and the sequence of phases which occur (e.g., export substitution naturally follows import substitution in a small labor-surplus economy). These causal relationships will be examined in the chapters which follow.

There is a legitimate question about the strength of this causal determinancy. The evidence that will be cited from the four case studies in this book must necessarily be regarded as a first step. More definitive causal relationships await the availability of more inductive evidence from application of the typological approach to many other countries.

Part 2

EMPIRICAL AND POLICY APPLICATION

6

Transition Growth in Taiwan

After World War II, Taiwan emerged from a half century of Japanese control with all the major features of a colonial economy. Growth experience in the intervening generation (1950–70) has been transitional in nature, terminating colonialism and moving toward the epoch of modern growth.

A unique feature of Taiwan's transition growth experience was the occurrence of two distinct phases. This gave Taiwan's growth an evolutionary character as its economy moved from an initial, import substitution phase (1950–59) to an export substitution phase (1959 to the present). During the first phase, growth focused upon the development of import substituting industries under control measures; in the second phase, growth emphasized the development of industries for the export of labor intensive goods under a liberalized market system.

This evolution represents successful transition growth in a labor-surplus, open economy. Within one short generation, Taiwan shifted from the land-based export system of colonialism to an export economy based upon labor efficiency and entrepreneurial ingenuity. This success was manifested not only through changes in the economy's structure but also in very rapid growth. Taiwan shares this successful contemporary transition experience with few other countries, among which South Korea and Israel may be mentioned.

This unique success may be attributed to unusually favorable background conditions. Taiwan inherited from Japanese colonialism a traditional agricultural sector well conditioned for further modernization. An adequate supply of industrial entrepreneurs was provided by an influx of immigrants from mainland China. The public sector was prepared for leadership in agricultural modernization

93

programs by its immediately preceding history. These favorable conditions more than compensated for the high population pressure on land resources.[1]

The empirical work in this chapter is focused on the verification of the two-phase feature of Taiwan's transition growth. This focus necessitates some attention to the reasons behind the economy's evolution from the first to the second phase.

1. THE IMPORT SUBSTITUTION PHASE

Taiwan began transition growth with an import substitution phase which lasted from 1950 to 1959. The economy's mode of operation during this phase was based upon a triangular pattern of resource utilization in which the foreign exchange earnings from primary product exports were used to finance capital goods imports to build up import-substituting industries. This mode of operation was analyzed in chapter 2. A brief recapitulation will serve our purpose here.

1.1. The Model of Import Substitution Growth

The model of import substitution growth is shown graphically in diagram 6.1. Total imports, M, are differentiated into two types, industrial consumer goods, M_y, and producer goods, M_p.[2] Producer goods imports, M_p, are employed to build up domestic industrial capital stock, K, thereby creating capacity for production of manufactured consumer goods, y. This output is supplied to the domestic market which now absorbs industrial consumer goods from two sources, imported (M_y) and domestic (y). The major phenomenon of import substitution growth is diversion of primary product export earnings, J, to importation of producer goods, M_p, in order to create domestic industrial capacity, K, enabling pro-

1. To these, the exogenous factor of large-scale foreign assistance might also be added. In this connection, however, it should be remembered that much of this assistance was related to an unusually large defense burden. Taiwan's success is also shown by the fact that public foreign assistance was terminated within the first generation of transition.

2. In practice, M_p contains two types of producer goods, raw materials, M_R, and capital goods, M_i. This distinction will be brought into the analysis at a later stage.

duction of consumer goods, y, to replace gradually imported goods, M_y, in the domestic market where purchasing power is generated by exports, J.

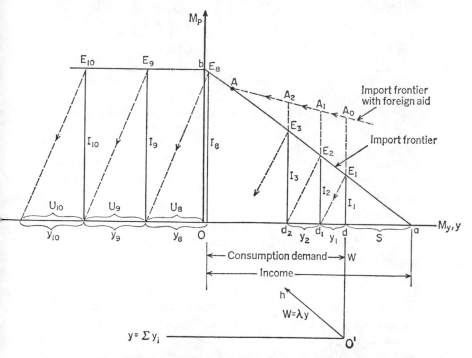

Diagram 6.1. The Import Substitution Growth Process

The dynamic process of import substitution growth may be briefly reviewed with the aid of diagram 6.1. The import frontier, ab, corresponds to a fixed volume of primary product exports. This frontier describes the alternative combinations of consumer and producer goods imports as well as the extent of the domestic market in terms of purchasing power, Oa, generated by exports. The dynamic growth path is described by the zigzag path $dE_1, d_1E_2, \ldots$ whereby producer goods imports in one period (e.g., I_1) lead to growth of domestic manufacturing capacity in the next period (e.g., y_1). The output created by this capacity replaces imports of consumer goods, thus releasing more foreign exchange for capital goods imports in the next period (e.g., I_2). With a fixed import frontier the process terminates after a finite period of time when the domestic market for manufactured consumer goods is completely supplied by domestic production.

1.2. Observable Properties

A number of observable properties may be readily deduced from the model of import substitution growth to facilitate statistical verification. They are enumerated, with a brief discussion of each, in the pages following.

P 1: *The import substitution phase (henceforth termed IS phase) both builds on the colonial heritage and modifies that heritage.* While retaining triangularism based on primary product exports, the IS phase departs from the colonial pattern by adopting an internal orientation for growth through the creation of a domestic industrial sector.

Empirically the colonial heritage may be shown by the fact that primary product exports dominate total exports at the outset of the transition. The shift toward an internal orientation (signifying an import substitution process) may be seen in the declining export ratio (E/GNP).

P 2: *The IS phase involves two basic substitution phenomena.* On the one hand, there is substitution in the foreign exchange allocation sense as producer goods imports, M_p, displace consumer goods imports, M_y. This may be seen from the movement of the equilibrium points, E_1, E_2, E_3, . . . upward along the frontier in diagram 6.1. On the other hand, there is substitution in the domestic market sense as domestic output, y, replaces imported consumer goods, M_y. These two phenomena can be empirically measured, and their simultaneous occurrence comprises the major empirical criterion for the identification of the IS phase.

P 3: *The IS phase represents an early transition growth phase inasmuch as the country lacks domestic productive capacity for producer goods, causing reliance upon importation.* For this reason the phase involves only consumer goods substitution. Two types of producer goods will be imported during the import substitution phase, i.e., capital goods and intermediate goods. (In diagram 6.1, M_p includes both types of producer goods.) Backward linkage import substitution is a concept referring to the replacement of these producer good imports by domestic production. Our theory hypothesizes that this type of import substitution is a more advanced transition phenomenon occurring only when entrepreneurs have become adept at technological adaptation. The sequence in which substitution occurs for intermediate and capital goods imports can only be determined by inductive evidence.

P 4: *Agricultural exports constitute the foundation for industrialization in two senses. First, they provide the means of expansion in terms of savings and foreign exchange resources. Second, they provide the market outlet and, hence, the incentive for industrial investment.* These characteristics occur because total exports are dominated by agricultural exports, while industrial exports are of minor significance.

P 5: *Import substitution is a cumulative and self-reinforcing growth mechanism.* Diagram 6.1 shows why an initially small amount of substitution leads to larger amounts in subsequent periods. Once started, capital and output can be sustained at the constant "high" rate of growth, even when primary product exports remain stagnant.[3] In this sense early import substitution growth is a deceptively easy growth process.

P 6: *There is a logical necessity for termination of the IS phase because of exhaustion of the domestic market.* This is associated with relative constancy (or slow growth) of exports. In diagram 6.1 this occurs after the substitution process has reached E_8, when all imports are producer goods or, equivalently, when the entire domestic market is supplied by domestic output. The inevitable termination of the IS phase is the basic cause of a multiple phase transition for countries beginning with an IS phase.

P 7: *As termination approaches, an observable symptom is the deceleration of the expansion rate of industrial output.* In diagram 6.1, after point E_8 when all foreign exchange, Ob, is devoted to capital goods imports, increments in industrial capacity will be constant, i.e., E_9, E_{10}, . . . implying deceleration in the rate of increase of industrial output.

P 8: *As the IS phase terminates, deceleration of growth is accom-*

3. This can be seen in diagram 2.2, chapter 2, where the time path of industrial capacity is shown.

panied by underutilization of productive capacity. This is shown
in diagram 6.1 by $U_8 + U_9 + U_{10}$. . . . Unutilized capacity appears because stagnant primary product exports lead to exhaustion
of the domestic market. Insufficiency of domestic demand may
cause capital flight unless the industrial sector finds a new outlet
for its output.[4]

Because of the appearance of these termination tendencies, the
import substitution phase is relatively brief (about one decade in
both Taiwan and the Philippines). This offers a brief period during which industrial entrepreneurs may gain efficiency through
learning by doing. When termination nears, entrepreneurs may or
may not be able to penetrate new markets. Property 8 refers to
the case where entrepreneurs fail in this regard and unutilized capacity and capital flight occur, as happened in the Philippines.
In contrast, the next property (P 9) is pertinent to Taiwan.

P 9: *Termination of the IS phase may lead to the launching of
a new growth phase, the export substitution phase, henceforth referred to as ES, in which expanding industrial capacity becomes
oriented toward the external market.* The term "export substitution" is used to emphasize the fact that for the first time in the
country's history industrial exports become significant, eventually
displacing and overshadowing exports of primary products.

P 10: *The shift from a primary product base to an industrial
export base in the ES phase produces two effects. The first effect
is a reversal from the domestic orientation of the IS phase to a
more externally oriented economy.* This reversal is reflected in a
rising ratio of trade to GNP.

P 11: *The second effect of the shift to an industrial export base
is rapid expansion of the country's own import capacity.* A realistic
model for postwar transition growth must recognize that a country's import capacity is determined partly by foreign aid as well as
by the country's export capacity. Our theory suggests that entry
into the export substitution phase enables the country to reduce
dependence on foreign capital inflow, particularly foreign assistance.

4. The paradox of appearance of unutilized capital capacity in a capital-
scarce country is often attributed to the lack of imported raw materials to
operate the capital stock during the IS phase. Our analysis shows this argument is subsidiary in nature.

The model structure of chapter 2 may be easily modified to incorporate foreign aid. Availability of foreign aid may be shown as an upward shift of the import frontier, *ab*, in diagram 6.1 by amounts equivalent to the magnitude of the additional import capacity provided by foreign aid through time. Suppose the dotted curve in diagram 6.1, shown as AA_0, represents such an import frontier including foreign aid; then dynamic equilibrium under IS growth will be represented by the sequence of points A_0, A_1, A_2, . . . moving toward point A where foreign aid terminates. Thus foreign aid, by adding to import capacity will increase the rate of the industrial sector's expansion and may affect the duration of the import substitution phase, but it does not affect the basic nature of the process.

The existence of an IS phase may be verified not only from the observable properties deduced from the economy's mode of operation (P 1–P 11) but also from the presence of the following organizational features:

P 12: *The IS phase is accompanied by foreign trade-oriented control policies emphasizing overvaluation of the exchange rate, quantitative import restrictions, and high tariff duties on consumer goods.*

P 13: *The termination of the IS phase and the emergence of the ES phase are accompanied by organizational changes that relax the foreign trade-oriented controls and emphasize an orientation toward free markets.*

2. EMPIRICAL VERIFICATION — THE IS PHASE

The primary purpose of empirical verification is to show the existence of an IS phase in Taiwan from 1952 to 1959, followed by an export substitution phase after 1959. This will be undertaken by using time series to verify the properties deduced from our theory.[5]

Our first task is to verify the existence of the two basic substitution phenomena described in P 2. Substitution in the foreign exchange allocation sense is shown in diagram 6.2. There are four components in total imports, *M:* industrial consumer goods, M_y,

5. Time series data behind diagrams used in the text are found in the Statistical Appendix (relevant tables for chapter 6 are tables 1 and 2).

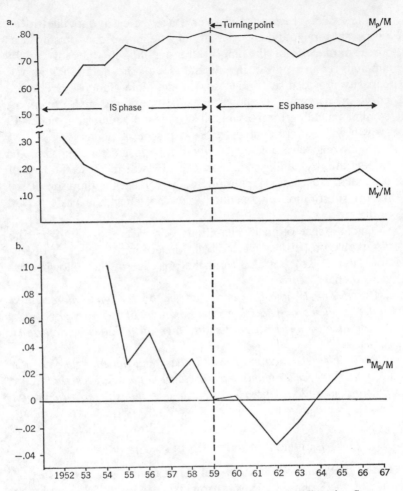

Diagram 6.2. Import Substitution, Foreign Exchange Allocation Sense
    a. Ratio of producer goods, M_p, and industrial consumer goods,
       M_y, to total imports, M
    b. Growth rate: ratio of producer goods imports to total imports

agricultural consumer goods, M_x; raw materials, M_R; and capital
goods, M_i (i.e., $M = M_y + M_x + M_R + M_i$). Imports on producer account, M_p, equal $M_R + M_i$. The time series, 1952–67, for
M_p/M and M_y/M are shown. The vertical dotted line at the year

1959 marks the end of the IS phase, referred to henceforth as the *turning point*.

As our theory predicted, M_p/M shows a consistent increase from about 57 percent to about 80 percent during the IS phase. This contrasts sharply with the ES phase, when the M_p/M ratio remains essentially constant. The same substitution phenomenon is seen from the behavior of the M_y/M curve. The rate of growth of M_p/M, i.e., $\eta_{M_p/M}$, is shown in diagram 6.2b.[6] During the IS phase $\eta_{M_p/M}$ is positive and decelerates to zero precisely at the turning point, leading to the ES phase. These time series all show a significant shift from consumer goods to producer goods imports throughout the IS phase.

Import substitution in the domestic market sense, as described in P 2, is shown in diagram 6.3. Imported and domestically produced industrial consumer goods are denoted by M_y and Y,[7] respectively, while imported and domestically produced agricultural goods are M_x and X. The time series in diagram 6.3a are the ratios M_y/Y, M_x/X and $(My + Mx)/(Y + X)$. Import substitution in the market sense is clearly shown from the U-shaped nature of the M_y/Y curve, reaching a minimum at the turning point. Notice that in the IS phase, import substitution is a phenomenon exhibited only by the industrial sector, as we have emphasized in our theory; the M_x/X ratio remains virtually unchanged during the IS phase. Throughout the IS phase, the growing self-sufficiency of industrial consumer goods, the essence of this phase, is clearly apparent, contrasting with agricultural goods.

As stated in P 3, during the IS growth phase the economy lacks domestic capability for producing producer goods, and backward linkage import substitution is reserved for a later phase. In diagram 6.4, let M_i and I represent imported and domestically produced capital goods and M_R and R imported and domestically produced raw materials. The delayed effect of backward linkage import substitution is clearly shown in diagram 6.4a by the inverse U shape of the M_p/P curve $(M_p = M_i + M_R;\ P = M_i + I + M_R + R)$, with a maximum occurring near the turning point. This signifies

6. $\eta_{M_p/M}$ is shown as three-year moving averages.

7. Y is total value added of the industrial sector, which is used as an approximation of domestic production of industrial consumer goods.

1. M_y/Y (Ratio of industrial consumer goods imports to industrial value added)
2. $(M_y + M_x)/(Y + X)$ (Ratio of consumer goods imports to total value added)
3. M_x/X (Ratio of agricultural consumer goods imports to agricultural value added)

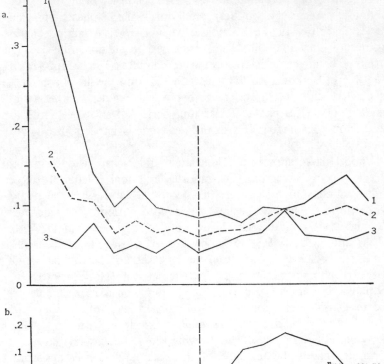

Diagram 6.3. Import Substitution, Domestic Market Sense
  a. Value added components
  b. Growth rate: import substitution in domestic con-
     sumer goods markets

an increasing share of imports in producer goods used by the economy during the IS phase, while backward linkage import substitution begins to occur during the ES phase as the country gains in
technological capacity.

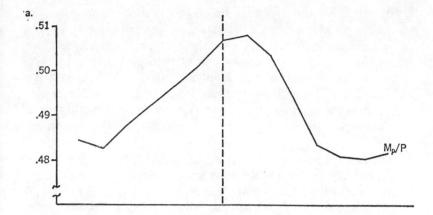

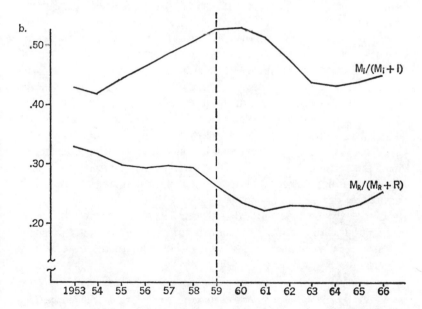

Diagram 6.4. Industrial Sector Producer Goods: Import Component
a. All producer goods
b. Capital goods, $M_i/(M_i + I)$ and intermediate goods, $M_R/(M_R + R)$

Inductive evidence suggests that import substitution begins to occur much earlier for raw materials than for capital goods. This is shown in diagram 6.4b where a continuously declining trend of the $M_R/(M_R + R)$ ratio occurs throughout both phases. The ratio of imported capital goods to total supply, $M_i/(M_i + I)$ shows delayed substitution of domestic production for imports. This evidence appears to suggest that domestic production of capital goods is more technologically demanding than is production of intermediate goods.

The dominance of exports by agricultural exports during the IS phase (property P 4) and the emergence of an ES phase (property P 9) are clearly shown in diagram 6.5. Let E_x and E_y denote agricultural and industrial exports, respectively. Notice that during the IS phase, total exports, $E(= E_x + E_y)$, are dominated by agricultural exports. This characteristic begins to be reversed at the turning point, with rapidly growing industrial exports eventually overwhelming agricultural exports as the dominant type of export in the ES phase.

Our theory has predicted that industrial sector expansion will proceed rapidly at the outset of the IS phase (P 5), eventually decelerating as termination approaches (P 7). In diagram 6.6a, let Y be the real (constant price) value added of the industrial sector.[8] The rate of growth of Y on a three-year moving average basis, i.e., η_Y, is shown in diagram 6.6b as a U-shaped curve, with a minimum near the turning point. Notice that during the IS phase, η_Y is sustained at a high value, i.e., between 7 and 10 percent, but there is a noticeable deceleration effect.

Our analysis has suggested that termination of IS growth is also associated with the near constancy of primary product exports (P 6). This phenomenon is shown in behavior of the E_x curve in diagram 6.5.[9]

---

8. The service and nonservice components of Y are shown; notice that there is no conspicuous difference between the behavior of these components.

9. The constancy of E_x was broken only after the economy had entered the ES phase. At this point, there was a bulge in agricultural exports (1962–67) reflecting the shift from land-based to labor-based agricultural exports (e.g., canned mushrooms and pineapple), a major shift emphasized in our theory below.

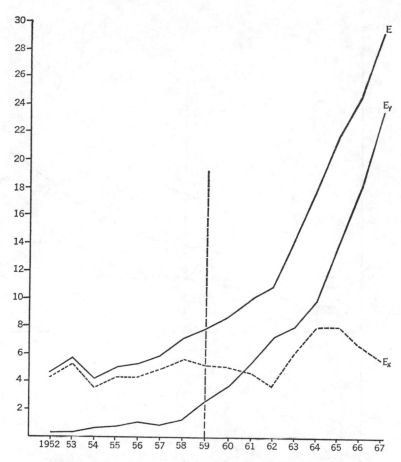

Diagram 6.5. Total Exports, *E*, Agricultural Exports, E_x, and
Nonagricultural Exports, E_y (Billion N.T. dollars, constant 1964
prices)

As the IS phase gives way to the ES phase, the economy's orientation shifts from internal to external (**P** 10). This may be verified
first by the generally U-shaped nature of all three curves in diagram
6.3a and is also shown by the $\eta_{(M_y + M_x)/(Y+X)}$ curve in diagram
6.3b, which crosses the horizontal axis at the turning point.

The orientation of the economy can also be measured by trade as

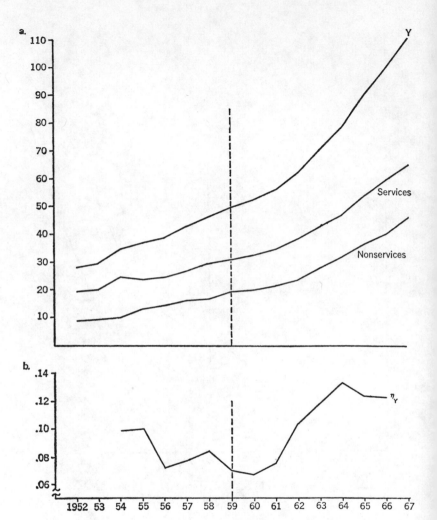

Diagram 6.6. Nonagricultural Sector Value Added (Billion N.T. dollars, constant 1964 prices)

    a. Total and components

    b. Growth rate of value added by nonagricultural sector

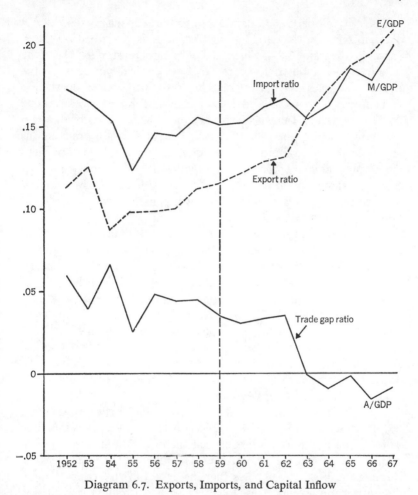

Diagram 6.7. Exports, Imports, and Capital Inflow

a fraction of GDP, shown in diagram 6.7. Let M, E and A ($= M - E$) be total imports, total exports, and import surplus, respectively. Their ratios to GDP (M/GDP, E/GDP, A/GDP) are given in diagram 6.7. Notice that during the IS phase both the import ratio and the export ratio are nearly constant, contrasting sharply with behavior during the ES phase when both the export ratio and the import ratio increase consistently, testifying to the growing external orientation of the economy.

To verify property P 11 concerning import capacity, we introduce diagram 6.8. Taiwan's total export capacity is described by the E curve in diagram 6.8a, which includes agricultural exports (the E_x curve) and industrial exports, E_y (the vertical gap between the E and E_x curves). Total imports are shown by the M curve, the vertical gap between M and E representing foreign capital inflow, A. The sources of Taiwan's import capacity as fractions of the total are shown in diagram 6.8b. The E_y/M curve shows a dramatic increase in the contribution from industrial exports beginning near the turning point. The declining significance of primary product exports is shown by the E_x/M curve. The A/M curve shows reduced reliance upon foreign capital inflow (foreign aid), which is phased out in 1963, four years after the turning point.

In order to verify the evolution of organizational features from the control policies of import substitution to the free market policies of export substitution (P 12 and P 13), we necessarily rely partly upon a chronology of events and partly upon statistical data. These major organizational changes near the turning point (1959) are well documented.[10] A multiple exchange rate system, employed throughout the IS phase, was converted into a unitary exchange rate in 1959. Foreign exchange rationing was gradually abandoned, and tariff protection for favored industries was progressively reduced.[11] Similarly, in domestic policy, inflation was brought under control and interest rates were liberalized.

Let b be the free market rate and r the official rate. In diagram 6.9, the time series for $(b - r)/b$ is shown. The fact that this time series is positive $(b > r)$ means that the official rate represents an overvaluation of domestic currency. The fact that the index declines through the IS phase signifies that the extent of this overvaluation diminishes through time, especially near the turning point. Finally, the fact that, after the turning point, the index approaches zero (and remains constant thereafter) signifies the institution of a free

10. See, for example, the accounts in Neil H. Jacoby, *U. S. Aid to Taiwan: A Study of Foreign Aid, Self-Help and Development* (New York: Frederick A. Praeger, 1966); and Ken C. Y. Lin, "Industrial Development and Changes in the Structure of Foreign Trade: The Experience of the Republic of China in Taiwan, 1946–66," *International Monetary Fund Staff Papers* 15 (July 1968): 290–321.

11. Jacoby, pp. 134–39.

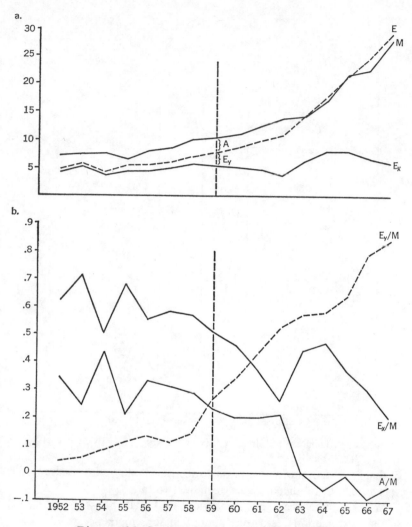

Diagram 6.8. Sources of Financing Import Capacity
a. Constant 1964 N.T. dollars (billions)
b. Fraction of total imports

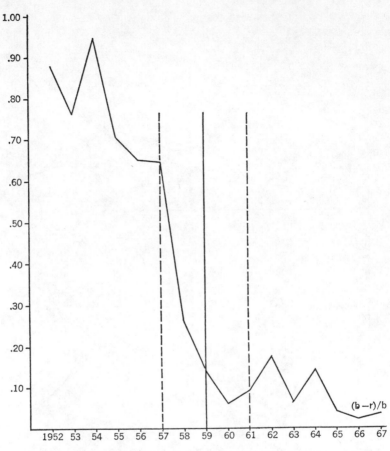

Diagram 6.9. Index of Exchange Rate Disparity

exchange system during the export substitution phase in which there was no significant disparity between the two rates.

Major growth accomplishments during the IS phase (discussed in the next section) laid the foundation for emergence of the ES phase which, in turn, constituted the basis for liberalization of economic controls. From diagram 6.9 we note that the full effect of liberalization occurred in 1965, lagging six years behind the turning point. While continuation of foreign aid in the early years of the ES phase (see diagram 6.8) eased the impact of the liberalization policies, these policies were the consequence of emergence of the ES phase rather than its cause. Hence, these major policy changes, while facilitating transition growth, were, in fact, the product of past growth accomplishments.

3. THE EXPORT SUBSTITUTION PHASE

3.1. The Significance of the Export Substitution Phase

While many less developed countries have begun the transition with an import substitution phase, the experience of Taiwan is unique in the subsequent emergence of export substitution during the first generation. The evolution of export substitution produced changes in the economy's mode of operation as well as in its organization. Organizationally, the phase of export substitution brought liberalization of the IS phase controls. These liberalization tendencies were essential for the external orientation of the industrial sector.

The mode of operation under export substitution growth, as described in chapter 2, may now be recapitulated with the aid of

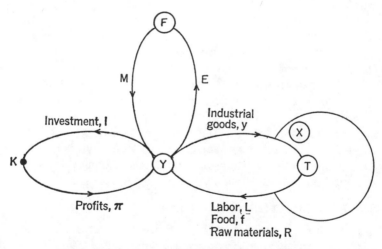

Diagram 6.10. Structure of the Economy: ES Phase

diagram 6.10, which shows the structural outline of the ES growth phase. The industrial sector, Y, now has an external orientation as output, *E*, is exported to the foreign market, F, in exchange for imports, M. Internal integration between the industrial sector and the traditional agricultural sector, T, is reflected in flows of labor, L, food, f, and raw materials, R, to the industrial sector in exchange for industrial products, y. As a result, industrial investment, I, to increase capital stock, K, is for the first time financed from industrial profits, π. This "three-leaf clover" structure of the ES phase (emphasizing external orientation, domestic integration, and self-finance in the industrial sector) is superimposed upon and gradually replaces the triangularism of the IS phase. The ES phase is thus a considerably more complex growth phase than its predecessors, colonialism and import substitution.

The mode of operation of the ES phase hinges upon the intersectoral allocation of labor through which the abundant supply of surplus labor in the traditional agricultural sector becomes utilized for exporting labor-intensive goods to the foreign market. Thus, the ES phase is a phenomenon unique to the labor-surplus type of open dualistic economy. The emergence of export substitution signifies that the economy has accomplished a shift from a land-based growth system to one based upon the export of labor services and entrepreneurial ingenuity.

The nature of profits, the major source of investment, changes as the economy moves from import substitution to export substitution. During the import substitution phase industrialists' profits are of a windfall nature, traced to profit transfers from the land-based surplus enforced through political controls. In the export substitution phase, industrial profits arise from entrepreneurial efficiency in using the abundant supply of labor to compete successfully in the international market. This accelerates the rate of growth of profits and savings, and in turn accounts for the more rapid rate of growth of capital accumulation and output in this phase.

3.2. Emergence of Export Substitution

Export substitution emerges from the natural termination of the import substitution phase and the fulfillment of two more positive preconditions which explain successful termination of that phase. The appearance of export substitution during the first generation of the transition is rare since these conditions are seldom fulfilled.

Taiwan's unusual success during the first generation of transition lies precisely in meeting these essential conditions for launching the new phase of ES growth.

The first condition is the development of market-oriented and efficient industrial entrepreneurship. Import substitution is a phase during which growth of entrepreneurship is forced through protection and profit transfer, offering opportunities for learning-by-doing. Success in this strategy initially depends upon a supply of potential entrepreneurial talent, capable of responding positively to the profit transfer stimuli. Given this condition, the strategy will be more successful where the protective measures are adopted in the spirit of the infant industry policy (i.e., to promote the development of entrepreneurial efficiency rather than to perpetuate inefficiency). In short, the qualities of entrepreneurship needed for export substitution (adoption of labor-intensive innovations, efficient management and penetration of new markets) must be cultivated during the import substitution phase by gradual relaxation of the protection and profit transfer measures.

These entrepreneurial conditions were present in Taiwan. An initial supply of capable entrepreneurs was readily forthcoming because of immigration from the Chinese Mainland. The government encouraged private entrepreneurial development by promoting the transfer of technology from advanced countries through a variety of foreign assistance programs. These positive measures were accompanied by gradual liberalization (e.g., devaluation) to accustom entrepreneurs to a more competitive market environment, paving the way for export substitution growth.

The second condition is modernization of agriculture. Growth of agricultural productivity is essential for the release of labor and food from the traditional agricultural sector, T. This enables the industrial sector to acquire labor at a low real cost, i.e., at favorable internal terms of trade. While the causation of agricultural modernization is complex,[12] we emphasize two forces which tend to appear

12. For an exhaustive listing of the many factors relevant to agricultural development, see M. Millikan and D. Hapgood, *No Easy Harvest: The Dilemma of Agriculture in Underdeveloped Countries* (Boston: Little, Brown and Company, 1967), chapter 2.

in the IS phase and to lead toward agricultural modernization: intersectoral integration and public sector participation. Labor reallocation from agriculture to industry begins during the IS phase as the industrial sector absorbs labor in import substituting industries.[13] This is accompanied by the exchange of food and industrial consumer goods between the two sectors. Thus, the intersectoral integration emphasized as an important phenomenon during the ES phase is actually the acceleration of a trend begun during the IS phase.

This interaction between industry and traditional agriculture is a basic factor contributing to modernization of traditional agriculture. This idea conforms to the emphasis of the "contact school" which stresses that contact between industry and agriculture is essential for transmission of modernizing forces to agriculture.[14] The agricultural sector benefits from growing contact with industry through acquisition of modern inputs and technology (e.g., fertilizer) and access to modern institutions (e.g., financial and research agencies). These forces stimulate the commercialization of agriculture. Taiwan inherited from Japanese colonialism adequate agricultural infrastructure to make traditional agriculture responsive to this stimulation.

Modernization of agriculture requires a combination of private initiative and government activities (e.g., land reform, agricultural cooperatives, extension services, and infrastructure investment). These government activities comprise a second modernizing tendency which must appear during the import substitution phase as a precondition for the emergence of the export substitution phase. In the case of Taiwan, the government had a long experience in such

    13. In diagram 6.1, let the horizontal axis $O'y$ (measuring leftward from O') be total industrial output (i.e., $y = y_1 + y_2 \ldots$) during the IS phase. Suppose the labor-output coefficient, λ, is constant; then during the IS phase, the amount of labor, W, absorbed by the industrial sector is given by the radial line $O'h$ (i.e., $W = \lambda y$)
    14. Douglas C. North, "Agriculture in Regional Economic Growth," in *Agriculture in Economic Development,* ed. Carl Eicher and Lawrence Witt (New York: McGraw-Hill Book Company, 1964); and Anthony Tang, *Economic Development in the Southern Piedmont, 1860–1950: Its Impact on Agriculture* (Chapel Hill, N. C.: The University of North Carolina Press, 1968).

agricultural development activities, and they became a major focus of government programs early in the import substitution phase.[15]

Modernization of agriculture brought about rapid gains in agricultural productivity, facilitating the release of labor from the agricultural sector. The presence of efficient industrial entrepreneurs enabled industry to use this labor supply in producing exports for the world market. These conditions gave rise to the export substitution phase, during which the economy's comparative advantage shifted from traditional land-based exports to labor-intensive exports. Taiwan shares with other countries currently in this phase (e.g., South Korea, Israel, Hong Kong and Singapore) a concentration upon the export of labor-intensive manufactures (e.g., textile products, plywood) directed mainly toward mass consumer goods markets in advanced countries.

Summing up, the successful termination of the import substitution phase and the emergence of export substitution result from a number of favorable factors exogenous to the process of import substitution itself. Taiwan began with an unusually favorable supply of industrial entrepreneurs and an agricultural sector well conditioned for modernization. This favorable background was fully exploited by effective government policy, aided by the infusion of large-scale foreign assistance. While one might be tempted to rank these factors according to their importance, our functional analysis of the operation of the economy as a whole empasizes that these favorable factors formed a complementary package which explains the rapid emergence of the export substitution phase in Taiwan.

3.3. Mode of Operation During Export Substitution Phase

The emergence of the ES phase signifies that the industrial entrepreneur, having achieved maturity, is able to utilize surplus labor released from the agricultural sector to exploit international trade

15. The Kuomintang government was amenable to institutional reform in agriculture because of its preceding history on the mainland. This orientation was reinforced by creation of the Joint Commission for Rural Reconstruction which provided American assistance for promoting both institutional conditions (particularly "land reform") and technology for rapid modernization of agriculture.

opportunities. Central to this process are the expansion of labor supply through population growth and the reallocation of labor from agriculture to the industrial sector. As explained in the familiar model of the closed labor-surplus economy, analysis of this process must emphasize labor absorption by the industrial sector and labor release by the agricultural sector.[16] The case of the open dualistic model may be analyzed by a slight modification of the closed model, which we briefly sketch.

For analysis of labor absorption by industry, the real wage in terms of industrial goods, w_i, is assumed to be relatively constant because of the labor-surplus condition ("unlimited supply of labor"). Rapidity of labor absorption then depends upon the rate of increase in the demand for labor, as caused by increase of capital stock which raises the marginal physical productivity of labor, MPP_L. Labor is absorbed rapidly when (1) labor-using innovation raises MPP_L, (2) the real wage, w_i, remains at a constant low level causing income distribution to favor industrial profits and leading to (3) a high rate of industrial capital accumulation (again raising MPP_L).

In the analysis of labor release from agriculture, expansion of agricultural productivity assures an increasing supply of labor as well as agricultural goods to the industrial sector. This, in turn, leads to internal terms of trade favorable to industry and, hence, to the relative "cheapness" of labor supply, i.e., a low real wage, w_i. Industrial profits are thus enhanced and capital accumulation is promoted. The traditional agricultural sector, T, now replaces the agricultural export sector, X, as the major source of intersectoral finance for industrial capital accumulation.

The opportunity of trade offers the open economy advantages not available to the closed economy. First, labor reallocation to the industrial sector can occur at a more rapid pace. This is true because the industrial sector in an open economy has the option of

16. See, for example, W. Arthur Lewis, "Economic Development with Unlimited Supplies of Labour," *The Manchester School* 22 (May 1954); 139–91; also, John C. H. Fei and Gustav Ranis, *Development of the Labor Surplus Economy* (Homewood, Illinois: Richard D. Irwin, Inc., 1964); and Dale W. Jorgenson, "The Development of a Dual Economy," *Economic Journal* 71 (June 1961): 309–34.

acquiring needed food and raw materials from abroad by concentrating on labor-intensive exports. Second, this permits a more rapid rate of capital accumulation than in the closed economy. The closed economy model implies a turning point thesis for the development of the labor-surplus economy. As population expands, continued expansion of industrial employment and labor reallocation will eventually lead to a turning point at which the economy's surplus labor is exhausted. At this point the real wage in the industrial sector will begin to rise sharply. The implication of this phenomenon for the open economy is that the economy will lose its cheap labor advantage after the turning point. This will necessitate that the industrial sector find a new comparative advantage in international trade (e.g., skilled labor, technology, or capital).[17]

As an economy moves from an import substitution phase to export substitution, the central growth phenomena change. Analysis must focus upon the labor reallocation process and the forces which determine the real wage. In the open economy the labor reallocation process is complicated by industry's external orientation as affected by both internal and external terms of trade. Long-run development prospects of export substitution growth are influenced by the gradual exhaustion of surplus labor and resultant pressure toward a rising real wage.

4. EMPIRICAL ANALYSIS OF THE EXPORT SUBSTITUTION PHASE

While a rigorous model for the export substitution phase is not difficult to construct, this will not be attempted here. Instead, in this section we cite empirical evidence from Taiwan to corroborate the central features of export substitution growth just discussed. These may be formulated as additional observable properties of Taiwan's transition growth.

P 14: *During the ES phase, the real wage of industrial labor, w_i, and the internal terms of trade between industry and agriculture,*

17. This implies that the export substitution phase is primarily based upon utilization of unskilled labor. Skilled labor becomes more relevant as the surplus of unskilled labor becomes exhausted.

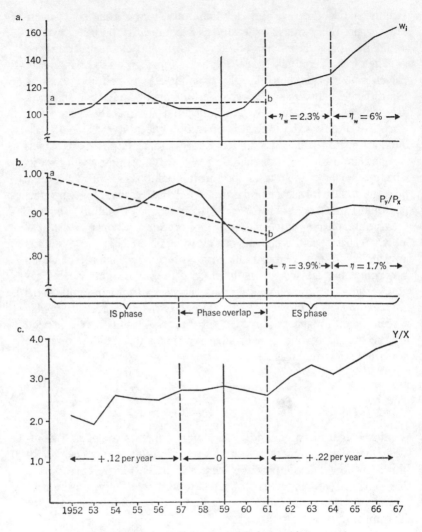

Diagram 6.11. Intersectoral Relationships
a. Nonagricultural sector real wage index
b. Internal terms of trade
c. Sector value added ratio

P_y/P_x, become growth relevant phenomena for the first time. Erratic behavior of these variables is replaced by more regular behavior.

The time series for w_i is given in diagram 6.11a and the time series for internal terms of trade, P_y/P_x, in diagram 6.11b. During the IS phase w_i is seen to show erratic fluctuations around a virtually constant trend line, i.e., the dotted line, *ab*; while during the ES phase (after 1961) w_i shows a sustained pattern of increase. Similarly, the internal terms of trade are seen to fluctuate around a decreasing trend line, the dotted line, *ab*, until 1961, after which they show a steady increase.

P 15: *During the IS phase internal terms of trade move in favor of agriculture, while the opposite is true during the ES phase.*

In diagram 6.11b the intersectoral terms of trade, P_y/P_x, are seen to move consistently in favor of the industrial sector during the ES phase (after 1960). This reverses the trend (the dotted line, *ab*) during the IS phase when the terms of trade tended to move consistently in favor of agriculture. Terms of trade favorable to agriculture during the IS phase promote the modernization of traditional agriculture, preparing it for its crucial role during the ES phase. The fact that the terms of trade shift in favor of the industrial sector during the ES phase signifies that the traditional agricultural sector becomes a major source of intersectoral finance.

P 16: *During the IS phase real wages, w_i, remain constant while they rise during the ES phase, reflecting gradual exhaustion of the economy's labor surplus.*

In diagram 6.11a the trend behavior of real wages, w_i, is clearly seen by comparing the dotted trend line, *ab*, for the IS phase with the rise in real wages during the ES phase. Thus, during the IS phase the condition of unlimited supply of labor prevails, while during the ES phase the surplus labor supply is gradually exhausted.

P 17: *During the ES phase, an initial period of modest and steady increase of the industrial real wage, w_i, will eventually give way to more rapid rises, signifying a gradual termination of the surplus labor condition. This eventual acceleration of the real wage is accompanied by movement of the terms of trade, P_y/P_x, against the industrial sector.*

In diagram 6.11, the year 1964 is identified as a bench-mark year in the ES phase. Diagram 6.11a shows that prior to 1964 the real wage grows at a rate of 2.3 percent, but it accelerates to 6 percent after 1964. In diagram 6.11b, the terms of trade, P_y/P_x, rise in favor of industry at the rate of 3.9 percent prior to 1964 while slowing down to a rate of 1.7 percent after 1964. In theory these effects are caused by retardation of growth of agricultural productivity.

P 18: *The economy's center of gravity will shift more rapidly toward the industrial sector in the ES phase than in the IS phase, measured by the relative value added contributions of industry (Y) and agriculture (X).*

In diagram 6.11c the time series for Y/X is plotted. During the entire transition period, 1952–67, the ratio of industrial to agricultural value added approximately doubled from 2.1 to 3.9. A third of this gain occurred during the IS phase, averaging .12 per year from 1952–57. In the interphase period, 1957–61, no gain occurred. In the ES phase years from 1961–67, two-thirds of the gain for the entire period occurred, averaging .22 per year.

P 19: *The ES phase is characterized by unusually rapid growth of per capita GDP.* This is the result of (1) higher gains in labor productivity in the industrial sector than in the agricultural sector (2) rapid reallocation of labor from agriculture to industry.

In diagram 6.12a the rate of growth of real per capita GDP is shown, revealing a marked acceleration of growth during the ES phase, beginning in 1961. In diagram 6.12b, the time series for labor productivity in the industrial and agricultural sectors, h and p, respectively, are shown. Their ratio, h/p, is exhibited in diagram 6.12c. The fact that labor productivity in industry is three to four times that in agriculture is a major cause of the increase in real GDP when labor reallocation occurs.

Accelerating reallocation of labor is shown by the increasing trend of the W/F curve in diagram 6.12d, where W is employment in the industrial sector and F, in agriculture. The increase of GDP is also explained by the gains in h and p. Although both increase consistently throughout the postwar transition, the growth of labor productivity in industry, h, is especially noticeable during the ES phase, reflected in the U-shaped h/p curve. This is the root cause of the conspicuous acceleration in the growth rate of GDP during the ES phase. Thus, it is the maturity of industrial entrepreneurship

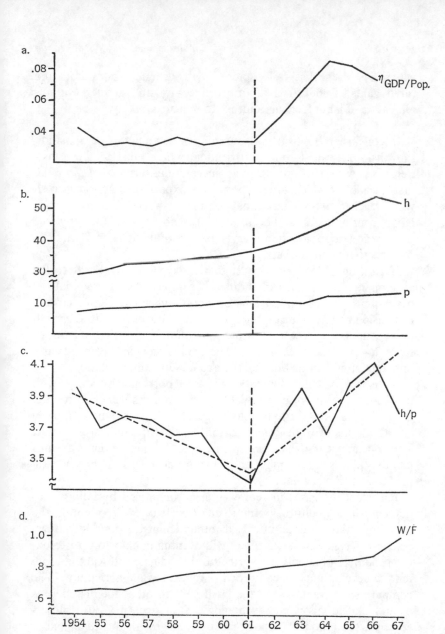

Diagram 6.12. Performance Variables
   a. Per capita GDP growth rate
   b. Labor productivity in nonagriculture, *h,* and agriculture, *p* (thousand
      N.T. dollars)
   c. Ratio of *h* to *p* (*h/p*)
   d. Ratio of nonagricultural to agricultural employment

which lies at the basis of rapid growth, accounting for both the rapid gains of industrial labor productivity and accelerating reallocation of labor from agriculture to industry.

In conclusion, let us briefly summarize our analysis of transition growth in Taiwan. Import substitution, which initiated the transition toward modern growth, was successfully terminated after the first decade, at which time a period of export substitution growth was launched. This phase was dominated by the reallocation of labor from agriculture. The industrial sector was enabled, by this reallocation, to rapidly increase its exports of labor-intensive manufactures to foreign markets.

Expansion of productivity in the traditional agricultural sector accompanied by growth of industrial capital stock is essential for development of a labor-surplus economy, whether open or closed. Expansion of agricultural productivity encourages industrial growth by maintaining a low real wage and offering favorable terms of trade to the industrial sector. These phenomena became clearly apparent after Taiwan entered the export substitution phase.

Statistical evidence suggests that as export substitution growth proceeded in Taiwan, new development problems were confronted. Beginning in about 1964, real wages began rising more rapidly and the terms of trade began to shift against the industrial sector. The appearance of these phenomena seems to indicate that Taiwan's labor surplus is approaching an end and that the gain in agricultural productivity is slackening.

Persistent increases in real wages, accompanied by falling productivity in agriculture, point to the necessity for reorienting the economy in two directions. Like other countries poor in natural resources (e.g., Japan), Taiwan will eventually have to turn to external sources of supply for agricultural products, and will therefore tend to develop unbalanced growth of industry and agriculture. The comparative advantage in labor will shift to other factors such as capital, skilled labor, and technology. Thus, seen in historical perspective, the phase of export substitution growth, based on labor intensive exports, may be rather short lived. Empirical analysis of these issues requires longer time series than are now available.

7

Prolonged Import Substitution Growth:
The Philippines

1. GENERAL FEATURES

1.1. Causes of Prolongation

In this chapter we investigate the particular type of transition growth in an open dualistic economy referred to as prolonged import substitution growth (prolonged IS growth). The postwar experience of the Philippines exemplifies transition growth of this type. The dominant features are that the transition is begun by import substitution (as discussed in chapter 5) and that this process fails to terminate during the first generation. Two initial questions may be raised: what is the specific meaning of failure, and why does failure occur.

For a labor-surplus economy, this growth type represents failure because the country fails to shift its source of income generation from the traditional land base to make effective use of its labor abundance.[1] We have seen in the previous chapter that some contemporary open dualistic economies (e.g., Taiwan, Korea) succeeded in accomplishing such a shift during their first generation of transition growth.

---

1. Specifically, failure in this case refers to the fact that export substitution does not emerge. This normative criteria is applicable to small, labor-surplus economies but may not be relevant for other types of less developed countries (e.g., large countries such as China and India and natural resource abundant countries, such as Malaysia, Thailand, and some Latin American countries). Selection of normative criteria is essentially an issue of the typology of transition growth, a subject which we discuss in chapter 10.

123

Failure through a prolonged import substitution phase occurs because background conditions inherited from colonialism are unfavorable. We may cite two economic background factors — both related to primary factor endowments — which lead to failure: (1) unfavorable conditions in the traditional agricultural sector; (2) weakness of indigenous entrepreneurship, public, private, or both. Although prolongation requires a supply of land resources for continuing primary product export, the supply is not adequate for an export promotion system under neocolonialism.

In the labor-surplus economy, at least two-thirds of the labor force is typically employed in the backward traditional agricultural sector. Hence, termination of the IS phase requires modernization of the agricultural sector to allow release of labor for more productive employment. Where conditions are unfavorable to agricultural modernization, import substitution growth can not terminate.

In the Philippines an unfavorable agricultural background is manifested in population pressure on natural resources. This population pressure is reflected in regional disparities between the densely populated islands of Luzon and the Visayan region, and the lower population density elsewhere. Such disparities indicate that the Philippines' traditional land surplus is nearing exhaustion. The densely populated areas reflect the labor-surplus characteristic, while the more sparsely populated areas provide the limited natural resource base for continuing primary product exports.

Successful termination of the IS phase also requires evolution of indigenous entrepreneurship in both private and public sectors. The development of private entrepreneurs is needed to provide alternative outlets for industrial output, and public entrepreneurship must provide infrastructure for agricultural modernization. The development of entrepreneurial capacities is the basic objective of the IS phase. Where the supply of potential indigenous entrepreneurs is unfavorable however, the country may be unable to terminate the IS phase successfully within the first generation.

In the Philippines, the background of an American educational system and extreme emulation of American institutions offered favorable conditions for a first wave of private entrepreneurs who were protected by powerful control measures adopted in the early postwar period.[2] However, the critical entrepreneurial deficiency was concentrated in the public sector: the government failed to provide the public infrastructure needed for modernization of traditional agriculture.

It is legitimate to ask why the public sector has failed to carry out national development functions during the post–World War II transition period. We have seen that these functions center on providing public infrastructure, particularly for initiating growth in the traditional agriculture sector.[3] In our judgment, the reasons for lagging performance of these functions lie in the political aspects of Filipino transition growth.

A fundamental factor in the Filipino society is the existence of a strong, private indigenous entrepreneurial group concentrated in a few large and powerful families. Their power is rooted in colonial history; their economic base grew out of a dominant position in colonial primary product exports, particularly in the sugar export industry. During the postwar transition period this group became the major source of private industrial entrepreneurship while also assuming positions of political and government leadership. The economic interests of this group came to be focused upon industrial processing of agricultural goods for export (e.g., sugar) and on import substituting industries. They showed only a very narrow interest in the agricultural sector (e.g., acquisition of sugar cane). This accounts for the failure of government to aggressively promote a broad-based program for the development of the traditional agricultural sector (e.g., rice and corn production) which employs about 80 percent of the rural population.

To summarize, import substitution tends to emerge after decolonization and to persist throughout the first generation (twenty–twenty-five years) of the transition where both natural resource and entrepreneurial conditions, inherited from colonialism, are relatively unfavorable.[4] These factors account for failure of termination of

2. See Frank H. Golay et al., *Underdevelopment and Economic Nationalism in Southeast Asia* (Ithaca: Cornell University Press, 1969), pp. 37–42.
3. In the previous chapter we have mentioned a wide range of public sector activities essential to modernization of agriculture.
4. See chapter 5 on these factors as the cause of emergence of IS.

the IS phase because they obstruct agricultural modernization and produce lagging entrepreneurial development.

1.2. Import Substitution and Backward Agriculture

We have just seen that prolonged import substitution growth occurs where the import substitution process is impeded by unfavorable background conditions, especially with regard to the backward traditional agricultural sector. Analysis of this transition growth system thus requires a model which emphasizes the interaction between the import substitution process and traditional agriculture.

The familiar triangularism of open dualism is pictured in diagram 7.1a. Primary product exports, J, provide foreign exchange for two types of imports, producer goods, M_p, to build up capital stock in the industrial sector, and consumer goods, M_y, to supply the domestic consumer goods market and supplement domestically produced consumer goods, y. In diagram 7.1b, this basic structure is modified by the addition of a new subsector, T, within agriculture, representing traditional (subsistence) agriculture. Thus, we explicitly postulate the condition of technological dualism within agriculture involving the coexistence of a backward traditional agricultural subsector, T, and a more modernized agricultural enclave X.

The development significance of the large and backward part of agriculture, T, stems from the fundamental condition of population pressure within this subsector. As a result of population pressure, reflected in low productivity, surplus population migrates to both the industrial, Y, and agricultural, X, components of the enclave, as shown by the two arrows designating labor flows. The fact that this migration is pushed by low productivity in the traditional subsector, T, rather than being pulled by enclave demand for labor, means that the migrant labor remains partially or fully unemployed.[5] Thus the surplus population transferred from traditional agriculture to the enclave represents a drag upon development rather than an asset available for productive employment.

---

5. W. Arthur Lewis cites many institutional arrangements which accommodate disguised unemployment of such migrants in the urban setting. See W. Arthur Lewis, "Economic Development with Unlimited Supplies of Labour," *The Manchester School* 22 (May 1954): 139–91.

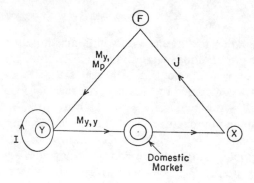

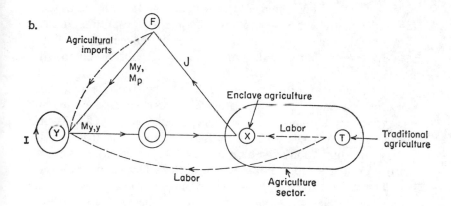

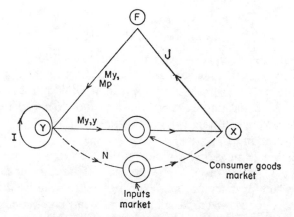

Diagram 7.1. Import Substitution: Intersectoral Aspects
  a. Import substitution
  b. Import substitution under agricultural shortfall
  c. Prolongation phenomena

The labor migration to the enclave would constitute a development asset if two preconditions were fulfilled. First, if the traditional agricultural sector were modernized, the release of labor to the enclave could be accompanied by adequate supplies of food for their maintenance and by raw materials with which to work. Second, if public and private entrepreneurship cooperated to encourage widespread introduction of labor-intensive technology, the transferred labor could be employed to produce goods for new market outlets. These conditions are precisely the ones which remain unfulfilled in prolonged import substitution, as we have just seen. Without accompanying food and raw material transfers, and given an inherent bias toward capital-intensive technology in import-substitution industries, the migrating labor constitutes a drag on the general development process and hampers the continued import substitution growth process.

Surplus labor exerts a depressing effect upon development because of political pressures to provide for its maintenance in the enclave sector, a phenomenon consistent with the nationalistic climate. When adequate food supply is not forthcoming from traditional agriculture, food must be imported. This leads to diversion of foreign exchange from import substitution. Given the political volatility of food supply, it is obvious that food imports will take priority over other types, giving them first claim upon foreign exchange use.

1.3. Phases of Prolonged Import Substitution Growth

The postwar generation of transition growth in the Philippines represents a case in which shortfalls in traditional agriculture increasingly impede the import substitution process. Three phases may be identified: (1) initial import substitution (1950–56); (2) retardation of import substitution (1956–59); and, (3) prolongation of import substitution (1959–   ).

In the initial IS phase, two major growth forces were apparent. On one hand, there was the phenomenon of import substitution proper in which primary product export earnings were used to import producer goods for the development of a consumer goods manufacturing industry. On the other hand, there was a gradual accumulation of growth-retarding forces stemming from stagnation in the agricultural sector. Stagnation in export agriculture restrained the basic growth-promoting force of primary products exports, while stagnation in traditional agriculture caused growing reliance upon imported food and agricultural raw materials. This interfered with the import substitution process, causing difficulties which came to the fore in the second phase. During this brief second phase (1956–59), the symptoms of retardation caused the society to seek correctives to bolster the economy's lagging growth.

During the third phase of prolongation of import substitution (1959–), the country sought to expand primary product exports. The duration of import substitution was lengthened by the growth of primary products exports, but the process was hampered by the continuing shortfall in traditional agriculture. Thus, since entrepreneurs turned to primary product export expansion rather than to labor-based manufactured exports, a new growth type did not emerge.

1.4. Organizational Aspects

Organization refers to the use of government policies to modify market mechanisms. As the economy moved through phases of prolonged IS growth, changes in mode of operation were accompanied by organizational changes. These reflected the underlying difficulties of an IS growth system impeded by agricultural shortfall.

In the initial IS phase the essential organizational feature is a control system whereby primary product export income is transferred to industrialists as artificial profits (see chap. 3). While this development strategy is instrumental in encouraging the growth of import substitution industries, it is deleterious to primary product export expansion. An even more serious shortcoming of this organizational system is its complete neglect of the backward traditional agricultural sector, T, which remains unimproved because of the government's failure to devote to it part of the agricultural export surplus. Thus, the basic weaknesses of the organizational system are that it discourages primary product export expansion in the export sector, X, and ignores modernization of the traditional sector, T.

These organizational features were manifested in economic difficulties at two levels. At the basic level, retardation of import substitution growth (1956–59) occurred. The retardation was reflected in both the deceleration of growth in agriculture and industry, and in the appearance of unutilized industrial capacity. At the level of governmental policy concern, balance of payments difficulties, inflationary tendencies, and budgetary problems become prominent in the second phase. It is at this latter level that political pressures appeared, inducing the government to undertake organizational change.

During the prolongation phase, reorientation should be aimed at correcting the basic organizational weaknesses, i.e., the discrimination against primary product exports and the neglect of traditional agriculture. However, given the inherited backwardness of the large traditional agricultural sector, T, the organizational reorientation in practice emphasizes short-run measures to promote primary export products through adjustments in foreign trade and foreign exchange policies. These policy changes may produce a favorable export response and give import substitution new momentum, but they fail to solve the longer-term problem of stagnation in traditional agriculture.

Prolonged IS represents a failure at transition growth inasmuch as a new growth base is not found to displace the inherited land-based growth system. A sequence of phases emerges from the cumulative difficulties caused by the lagging agricultural sector's interference with the IS process and by society's response to these difficulties. This involves interaction between the economic forces which arise from changes in the economy's mode of operation and the political forces expressed in the economy's organization.

2. IMPORT SUBSTITUTION AND AGRICULTURAL SHORTFALL

In the Philippines, transition growth was initiated by a phase of import substitution. However, the import substitution process developed against the background of the large, traditional agricultural sector, T, which remained stagnant. The dominant feature of this growth experience was the gradual interruption of the import substitution process by shortfall in the traditional agricultural sector. The purpose of the present section is to investigate this phenomenon analytically.

We begin with a brief review of the IS process. Agricultural shortfall encroaches upon this process by necessitating growing quantities of agricultural imports. Analysis of this phenomenon requires modification of the pure import substitution model. Static analysis is undertaken in section 2.1, followed by dynamic analysis in section 2.2. The economic significance of this growth process is assessed in section 2.3.

2.1. The Import Substitution Process

To begin our analysis, we reproduce in diagram 7.2 an import frontier, VO', determined by a given volume of primary product exports, J, from the agricultural export sector, X. This import capacity enables the country to import two types of goods, producer goods, M_p (measured on the vertical axis), and industrial consumer goods, M_y (measured on the horizontal axis). The fundamental meaning of import substitution is the gradual displacement in the domestic market of imported consumer goods, M_y, by domestically produced consumer goods, as domestic capacity is built up by importation of producer goods, M_p.

In diagram 7.2a, point O' is accepted as a second origin on the horizontal axis, measured leftward, to show domestic industrial sector capacity for producing consumer goods, A. Through time, this capacity can then be represented by points, such as A_0 and A'. These two points represent two contrasting situations.

On the one hand, an import gap exists if domestic capacity for industrial consumer goods (e.g., A_0) is less than export-generated purchasing power, OO'. This is shown in diagram 7.2a by point A_0 lying to the right of the first origin of the horizontal axis, O. The distance, Q, is referred to as the import gap since it represents the magnitude by which domestic output capacity falls short of the purchasing power, OO' ($=J/Py$), generated by export volume, J. This gap must be filled by imports of consumer goods, i.e., OA_0 units.

On the other hand, surplus domestic capacity exists if domestic capacity (e.g., at point A') lies to the left of O. The distance, U, represents a surplus of domestic output capacity over the domestic purchasing power. Export income fails to absorb domestic output, even when imports are zero.

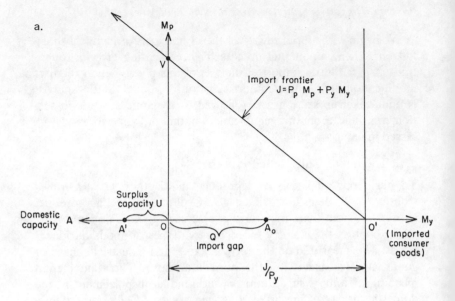

a.

Import frontier
$J = P_p\, M_p + P_y\, M_y$

M_p

V

Domestic capacity
A

Surplus capacity U

A'   O

Import gap
Q

A_o

J/P_y

O'

M_y
(Imported consumer goods)

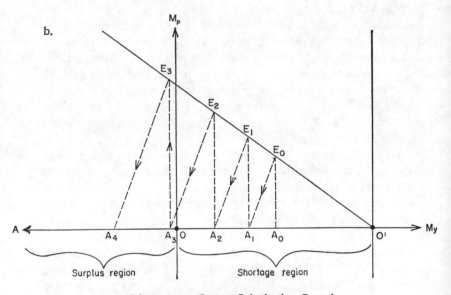

b.

M_p

E_3

E_2

E_1

E_0

A

A_4 A_3 O A_2 A_1 A_o

O' M_y

Surplus region

Shortage region

Diagram 7.2. Import Substitution Growth
a. Import frontier
b. Import substitution process

The import gap and surplus capacity are defined relative to domestic income generated by exports, which income determines the purchasing power in the consumer goods market. The implicit assumption is that activities related to primary product exports provide the main source from which such purchasing power is generated. Conceptually, such income includes not only income to original export producers but also income to all economic agents involved in the trade, processing, and transport of primary export products.

The distinction between import gap and surplus domestic capacity is crucial for the analysis of import substitution. As long as an import gap exists, there is a shortage of domestic capacity relative to purchasing power. This shortage can be transformed into effective demand, offering incentives for further expansion of domestic output, especially when protection is provided for domestic producers through the appropriate government policy for restricting imports. Thus, an import gap situation provides the economic precondition for bestowing favored treatment upon industrial entrepreneurs, and an output response that enables import substitution to proceed may be expected.

When the import gap is eventually replaced by surplus capacity, incentive for industrial expansion disappears. Even though all consumer goods imports have been eliminated, the surplus still exists and the government is powerless to encourage further expansion through protection. Redirection of output to a new market is necessary. If this redirection fails to emerge, as in the prolongation case, unutilized industrial capacity and unemployment will plague the country indefinitely.

The process of import substitution through time is shown by the dotted zigzag path in diagram 7.2b. Growing volumes of producer goods imports (shown as the vertical distances at E_0, E_1, E_2, . . .) lead to recurrent expansion of domestic industrial capacity (shown by A_0, A_1, A_2, . . .). Associated with this process is the gradual elimination of consumer goods imports (OA_0, OA_1, OA_2, . . .), as producer goods progressively displace consumer goods in the import account.

This process analysis of import substitution points to the inevitability of its termination. While a country begins the process from a point such as A_0 in the "shortage region," it eventually moves into the "surplus region" (e.g., A_3 and beyond). As the domestic market becomes satiated by domestically produced output, excess capacity emerges, weakening incentives to invest in further expansion of industrial capacity.

After this turning point (point A_3 in diagram 7.2b), the future course of growth in the economy depends not so much upon capital accumulation as upon the extent to which indigenous entrepreneurship, both public and private, has been prepared for the task of producing for new market outlets. This task is more difficult than import substitution because goods are manufactured for new foreign markets and production must therefore be based upon efficiency rather than protection.

When import substitution is interrupted by a backward agricultural sector, foreign exchange will be diverted from the IS process to importation of agricultural supplies. To analyze this phenomenon, let the import frontier, $O'V$, be reproduced in diagram 7.3. We now admit the possibility of importing food and agricultural raw materials, F, as well as industrial products. The magnitude of F is determined by the degree of population pressure in traditional agriculture, T, as well as by the quantity of surplus labor migrating to the enclave.

Let V and O' be the two corners of the import frontier in diagram 7.3. As before, we use point O' as an origin on the horizontal axis to measure domestic industrial capacity, A, for consumer goods. In addition to measuring imports of producer goods on the vertical axis (as before), we also measure agricultural imports (food and raw materials) on this axis. This is done by taking V as an origin to measure these imports, F. An import deficit of agricultural goods, $-F$, will now be represented by points below point V (e.g., F, F', F''), while surplus, $+F$, may be shown by points above V (e.g., F_1 and F_2). By measuring agricultural goods on the same axis as producer goods imports, we define the unit of measurement of F in terms of the value of producer goods. For example, if $F = -3$, three units of producer goods imports would have to be sacrificed to cover the agricultural deficit.

Suppose there exists an agricultural deficit of FV, and that this deficit is given highest import priority. The effect of this agricul-

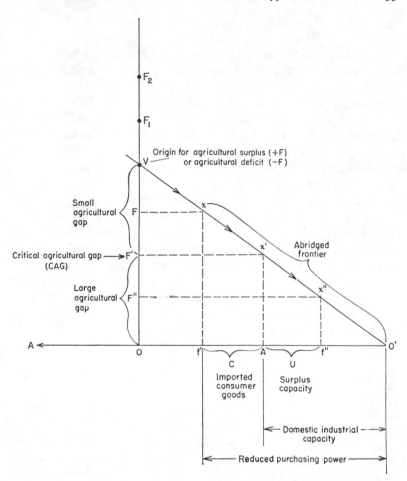

Diagram 7.3. Agricultural Shortfall and Import Frontier

tural deficit (at point F) is shown by the abridged import frontier, $O'x$, for the imports, M_p, M_y, relevant to import substitution. For example, the point x' on the abridged frontier indicates that the country will import C units of consumer goods (measured on the horizontal axis) and Ax' ($=OF'$) units of producer goods (measured on the vertical axis) in addition to the agricultural imports. Successive increases in the size of the agricultural deficit will result in progressive abridgement of the import frontier (e.g., from $O'x$ to $O'x''$).

Let us assume that domestic industrial capacity is given by $O'A$ in diagram 7.3. With the aid of point A, we may now locate point F' on the vertical axis. This point gives us the size of the *critical agricultural gap* (abbreviated as CAG) which we define as that magnitude of agricultural deficit which results in full utilization of domestic capacity without imports of industrial consumer goods. If the actual agricultural gap is less than the CAG, (e.g., at point F), the situation may be referred to as a "small gap." If the actual gap exceeds the CAG (e.g., at point F''), a "large gap" exists.

With the given initial domestic capacity at point A, the amount of consumer goods imports is OA when there is no agricultural gap. The occurrence of a gap may or may not cut into the country's ability to import producer goods. When the gap is small (e.g. at point F), the reduction of import capacity is matched by reduced demand for consumer goods imports (i.e., OA decreases to Af'), leaving producer goods imports unaffected (i.e., at Ax') and domestic productive capacity, $O'A$, fully utilized. Conversely, when the gap is large (e.g., at F''), the reduction of import capacity (with the import frontier abridged to $O'x''$) exceeds the reduction in the demand for consumer goods imports so that producer goods imports fall (from Ax' to $f''x''$) and surplus domestic capacity, U, appears.

An *increasing agricultural gap* through time is shown in diagram 7.3 by the downward movement of the points F, F', F'', ... In the first stage of the small gap, reduced consumption is accompanied by cutbacks in imported industrial consumer goods. Domestic industrial capacity. $O'A$, is fully utilized and the rate of industrial expansion is not affected. After the critical agricultural gap at F' is passed, however, reduced consumption causes unutilized domestic productive capacity and begins to have an adverse effect on the rate of industrial expansion.

2.2. Dynamic Analysis

We now investigate the dynamic process of import substitution as it is impeded by agricultural shortfall. The case of a constant agricultural gap may be distinguished from the more realistic case of an increasing agricultural gap.

Let us consider the simple case of a constant agricultural gap, G. The import frontier, VO', is reproduced in diagram 7.4, and the constant gap, G, is marked off on the vertical axis, producing

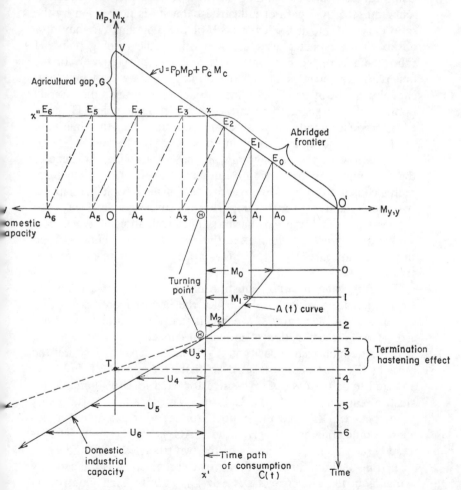

Diagram 7.4. Import Substitution Process under Agricultural Shortfall

the fixed abridged import frontier, $O'x$. Let the vertical line xx' and the horizontal line xx'' be constructed from point x. Suppose initial industrial capacity (for consumer goods) is A_0. The import substitution growth process is then described by the zigzag path, determining industrial capacity through time as $A_0, A_1, A_2, \ldots$ Using the vertical axis pointing downward from point O' to represent time, the time path of industrial capacity is now given by the solid curve, $A(t)$, in the lower deck of the diagram. We may now observe two distinct phases, marked off by the turning point, H (shown on both the horizontal axis and the $A(t)$ curve). In the first phase (prior to point H), the rapidity of growth of industrial capacity is not affected since the impact of the gap falls entirely upon consumer goods imports. After the turning point, H, however, producer goods imports become constant and the time path of $A(t)$ becomes linear, signifying a slower growth rate.

In the lower deck of diagram 7.4, the vertical line Hx' denotes the time path of consumption of industrial goods, $C(t)$, which remains constant through time. Before the turning point the gap between $C(t)$ and $A(t)$ shows imported consumer goods. Thus, even a constant agricultural gap hastens the termination of the import substitution process, while after the turning point, H, unutilized industrial capacity (U_3, U_4, U_5, U_6) appears and increases through time.

To investigate the import substitution process under the condition of an increasing agricultural gap, let the import frontier, $O'V$, be reproduced in diagram 7.5. We recall that the critical agricultural gap (CAG) is a function of industrial capacity, A. For example, if domestic industrial capacity is A_2, then the CAG is Vf_2. Let the straight line VM be constructed so that $OM = MO'$. This line is referred to as the *CAG Curve* since for each level of domestic industrial capacity, A_i, the CAG is now shown as the vertical distance between VM and the import frontier. For example, for domestic industrial capacity A_2, the CAG is $Tg_2(=Vf_2)$. This is readily seen from the similarity of the two triangles, Vf_2b and Tg_2b.

During the import substitution growth process, industrial capacity expands in the sequence $A_0, A_1, A_2, \ldots$ In each time period the actual agricultural gap can be shown as the vertical distances F_0, F_1, F_2. Suppose the actual gap curve intersects the CAG curve

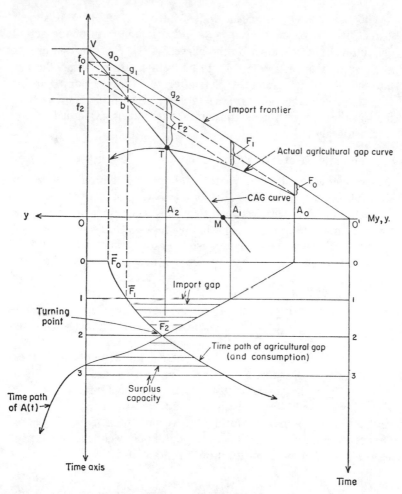

Diagram 7.5. Growing Agricultural Gap

at point T. Then to the right of point T, the actual gap is "small" since it is less than the CAG, while to the left of point T the gap is "large." Point T is a turning point similar to H in diagram 7.4. The rate of growth of industrial capacity is unaffected by the agricultural gap before T, but is depressed after T. Like H, this turning point denotes the appearance of unutilized capacity.

The time path of domestic industrial capacity, $A(t)$ is shown in the lower deck of diagram 7.5, and the time path of the actual agricultural gap is shown by the curve $\overline{F}_0$, $\overline{F}_1$, $\overline{F}_2$. The two curves intersect at a turning point, $\overline{F}_2$. Prior to this turning point, the import gap is rapidly reduced, and after the turning point surplus capacity accelerates. The greater rapidity of both phenomena here than in the case of a constant agricultural gap is explained by the increasing agricultural gap.

2.3. Growth Retardation Effects

We may now briefly summarize the impact of agricultural sector shortfall on the operation of the import substitution process. The effects of shortfall vary between two phases. During the first phase there is an adverse effect only on consumption through curtailment of imports. During the second phase the growth rate of capacity will be retarded for two reasons: reduction in capital goods imports, and impairment of investment incentives because of emergence of unutilized industrial capacity.

When an economy suffers a growing agricultural gap, the termination hastening effects are accentuated as more foreign exchange must be allocated to cover the agricultural shortfall. The priority given to agricultural imports causes balance of payments difficulties. Paradoxically, this coexists with tendencies toward capital flight resulting from the appearance of excess industrial capacity and the shrinking of domestic investment opportunities. This sequence of difficulties was apparent during the second phase (1956–59) of Philippine transition experience and led to policy changes conducive to prolonging import substitution (1959–   ).

3. IMPORT SUBSTITUTION AND PRIMARY PRODUCT
EXPORT EXPANSION

We have seen that there is an inherent tendency in import substitution toward termination and that this tendency may be hastened by agricultural shortfall. The fundamental cause of termination is stagnation of primary product exports which restricts demand for industrial consumer goods in the domestic market. When retardation of industrial growth sets in, a natural social response is expansion of primary product exports through which the IS process can be prolonged. The third phase of postwar transition experience in the Philippines (1959–   ) can be interpreted as such a process of prolonging IS growth. It is the purpose of this section to analyze this prolongation phenomenon.

There are positive and negative reasons for the occurrence of prolongation. Import substitution does not culminate in export substitution during the first generation (as in Taiwan) because traditional agriculture remains backward and deficiencies of public and/or private entrepreneurship continue. Hence, the economy is unable to develop an external industrial orientation based upon efficient utilization of its surplus labor. On the positive side, there are natural resource endowments (e.g., lumber, minerals) which offer conspicuous comparative advantages so that with modest promotion on the part of government and cooperation of alien entrepreneurs, indigenous entrepreneurs are capable of producing and selling new primary products in the world market.

During the initial phase of import substitution, as we have seen, the basic strategy was transfer of export profits to industrial producers through a controlled system involving an overvalued exchange rate, import controls, and protective tariffs. During prolongation this strategy is eased by partial dismantling of controls to encourage growth of primary product exports. Hence, policy becomes hybrid in nature, as it must accommodate both continued import substitution and the expansion of primary product exports.

3.1. Structural Outline of the Economy

The structural outline of the economy under prolonged IS growth is shown in diagram 7.1c. The only modification is that, in addition to consumer goods, y, a part of industrial output, N, now constitutes intermediate inputs for agriculture (e.g., fertilizer, processing, implements, transport) to raise the productivity of and to diversify primary product exports. While the country still exports primary products, J, it continues to import consumer goods, M_y, and producer goods, M_p, at international prices, P_y and P_p, respectively.

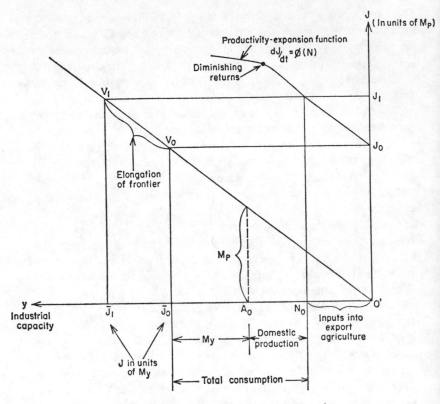

Diagram 7.6. Elongation of Import Frontier

In diagram 7.6 let primary product exports, J, be shown on the vertical axis with its origin at O' and measured in terms of prices of imported producer goods, M_p, as a numeraire. Assuming import prices, P_p and P_y are given and that J_0 represents the initial value of J, we can determine the import frontier, V_0O', resulting from this level of exports. If, in the next period, primary product exports are increased to J_1, the import frontier will be elongated to V_1O', i.e., extended by V_0V_1.

The horizontal axis with its origin at O' is used, as before, to measure domestic industrial capacity, A. Suppose the initial capacity is located A_0. Under our present assumption, this capacity will be used for two types of output, consumer goods (e.g., A_0N_0), and

N, intermediate inputs for export agriculture (e.g., $O'N_0$). Domestic income, $\bar{J}_0O'$, generated by the import frontier $O'V_0$, will be used to purchase $O'N_0$ units of intermediate inputs and $\bar{J}_0N_0$ units of industrial consumer goods, of which M_y will be imported and the remainder (A_0N_0), domestically produced. In addition to M_y, foreign exchange earnings will be used to import producer goods in the amount of M_p, which, as before, are directly related to expansion of domestic industrial capacity, A.

3.2. Prolongation of Import Substitution

Our structural outline of the economy suggests two key analytical issues in prolongation, the magnitude of N and the productivity-raising effect of N. The second aspect may be described as a productivity-expansion function:

(7.1) $dJ/dt = \phi(N)$ (Productivity expansion function)

It states that the amount of increase of J through time is causally determined by the magnitude of N. In diagram 7.6 this function is represented by the rising curve beginning from point J_0. Given the magnitude of N, e.g., $O'N_c$, we can determine the amount of increase of J (i.e., J_0J_1) and hence primary product exports, J_1, as well as the elongated import frontier, $O'V_1$, in the next period.

The magnitude of N is functionally related to J in the following equation:

(7.2) $N = N(J)$ (Propensity to expand)

It specifies that income recipients devote a part of export-generated income, J, to the purchase of producer inputs, N. Thus, the magnitude of N is based upon the propensity of exporters to acquire productive inputs rather than consumer goods.

Prolongation of IS involves the interaction of two dynamic mechanisms: the basic import substitution process and the process of primary product export expansion. In the top deck of diagram 7.7, the familiar zigzag process of import substitution growth is shown as $A_0, A_1, A_2, \ldots$. In the time series diagram in the lower deck, the time path of industrial capacity, $A(t)$, is shown by the curve labeled I. The process of primary product export expansion through time, $\bar{J}_0, \bar{J}_1, \bar{J}_2, \ldots$ is summarized by the time

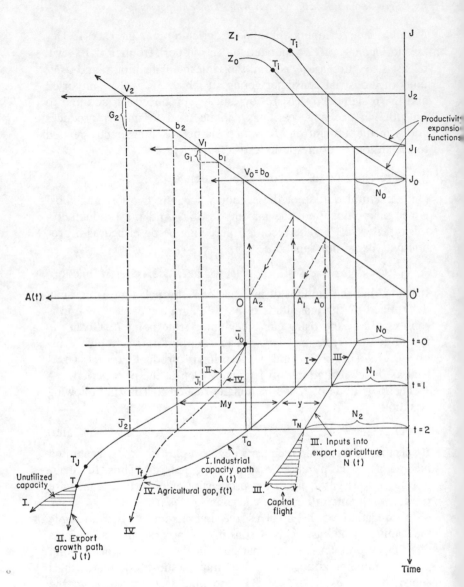

Diagram 7.7. Export Expansion and Growing Agricultural Gap

path, $\bar{J}(t)$, labeled II. Determination of these two basic paths through time involves simultaneous interaction between the two.

Given the original value of primary product exports, J, in diagram 7.7, we have the initial import frontier, V_0O'. This determines the income to export producers, OO' on the horizontal axis of the top deck and, with the aid of the "propensity to expand" (equation 7.2), the initial value of N, i.e., N_0 is determined. With the aid of the productivity-expansion function in the top deck (the Z_0 curve), we can determine the amount of increase of primary product exports, J_0J_1, and hence, the new import frontier, V_1O', in the next period. In this way the process is dynamically determined.

From the time paths of $\bar{J}(t)$ (i.e., the curve labeled II) and $A(t)$ (i.e., the curve labeled I), we see that industrial capacity, $A(t)$, appears to be pursuing the expanding volume of primary products exports, $\bar{J}(t)$. (The horizontal gap between the two curves, I and II, is imported industrial consumer goods, M_y.) At point T, the $A(t)$ curve overtakes the $\bar{J}(t)$ curve, and this point is construed as a turning point. At this turning point, T, imports of industrial consumer goods are eliminated, and unutilized capacity appears (shown as the horizontal distance between $A(t)$ and $\bar{J}(t)$ after point T). Thus, even with export expansion, we find the two-phase phenomenon in import substitution growth, with unutilized capacity appearing in the second phase. Retardation and termination are also inherent in this prolongation case.

3.3. Economic Significance of Prolongation

Expansion of primary product exports extends the means and markets for industrialization. Prolongation thus lengthens the duration of the import substitution process. The crucial issues involved are the duration of the process and the inevitability of its termination.

The duration of the process depends basically upon the availability of land resources for primary product exports. In practice, extractive products (e.g., lumber, minerals) are most likely to serve as major prolongation exports since they do not directly compete with scarce agricultural land needed for food and raw materials.

These resources are clearly exhaustible. Thus, in diagram 7.7, the productivity-expansion functions Z_0 and Z_1 are shown as eventually turning down, i.e., at T_i. When this occurs, the prolongation effect begins to weaken because of natural resource depletion, a tendency reflected in the retardation of the $\overline{J}(t)$ path after point T_J in the lower deck. This hastens the arrival of the turning point, T, since $A(t)$ continues to expand at a sustained high rate. In short, a turning point is inevitable if the natural resource base is exhaustible.

Exhaustion of the natural resource base will cause returns to investment from primary product export promotion to deteriorate (indicated by the bending downward of the productivity-expansion functions). Retardation of export growth will, in turn, depress investment incentives for investment in import substitution industries. Underutilization of industrial capacity will cause capital flight unless a new orientation is found for industrial sector growth.[6]

When these symptoms occur in a labor-surplus economy, a new orientation for industrial sector growth must be found in foreign market outlets. A new phase of export substitution growth will then be initiated. We now clearly perceive prolongation as merely postponing the inevitable termination of the import substitution growth process. This postponement effect, however, may assume growth significance by allowing more time for meeting the preconditions for export substitution, i.e., versatile public and private entrepreneurship and agricultural modernization.

3.4. Impact of Agricultural Shortfall

A realistic analysis of prolonged import substitution growth under agricultural shortfall must encompass the operation of three dynamic mechanisms: (1) the basic import substitution process, (2) elongation of the import frontier through primary product export

---

6. This dissipation of the economy's savings may affect both inputs into export agricture, $N(t)$, and investment in the industrial sector. In diagram 7.7, the first type of capital flight may be shown by referring to the $N(t)$ curve, labeled III. After point T_N, the dotted curve shows the effect of declining export-promotion opportunities, and the distance between this curve and the solid $N(t)$ curve represents capital flight. Similarly, in the industrial sector the appearance of unutilized capacity after point T on the $A(t)$ curve will tend to lead to flight of industrial sector savings.

expansion, and (3) truncation of the import frontier by a growing food and raw material deficiency.

We may employ a slight modification of diagram 7.7 to analyze the combined effects of these three forces. The points V_0, V_1, V_2, . . . are the upper ends of the elongated import frontier as the system moves through time. Assuming the agricultural gap at V_0 is zero, let G_1, G_2, . . . represent increasing agricultural gaps through time. Truncation of the import frontier is now shown by the length of the frontier falling back toward point O', e.g., from $O'V_1$ to $O'b_1$, from $O'V_2$ to $O'b_2$, etc. This phenomenon can be transposed to the bottom deck of diagram 7.7, where the dotted time path, labeled IV, forms an increasing agricultural gap, $f(t)$, through time, and where the magnitude of the gap is now measured as the horizontal distance between curve II and the agricultural gap curve, $f(t)$. This distance represents the export-generated income which must be diverted to expenditure on imported agricultural goods.

Since the horizontal distance between the export curve, II, and the time axis pointing downward from O' represents domestic income generated by exports, diversion of this income for agricultural imports leaves less purchasing power available for purchasing the growing output from domestic industrial capacity, $A(t)$. This is the basic cause of an earlier termination (i.e., appearance of excess industrial capacity) under the growing agricultural gap condition. This may be seen from the fact that the dotted time path of $f(t)$, shown by curve IV, lies below the time path of $\bar{J}(t)$, the distance between them now construed as representing the extent of import frontier truncation. Since curve IV intersects the $A(t)$ curve (at turning point T_f) earlier than the $\bar{J}(t)$ curve (at turning point T), we know that both unutilized industrial capacity and termination occur earlier. This represents the termination-hastening effect of a growing agricultural gap during prolongation.

In summary, import substitution is a type of transition growth system that tends to arise naturally in open dualistic economies with an unfavorable set of background factors, i.e., a large and stagnant traditional agricultural sector, population pressure on land resources, and entrepreneurial deficiencies. The dominant growth missions of import substitution are to create a class of industrial entrepreneurs and to modernize agriculture to pave the way for emergence of export substitution.

The duration of import substitution is determined by two sets of conditions in the agricultural sector. The traditional agricultural sector constitutes a threat to the viability and duration of import substitution growth. Where population pressure is severe, short-falls in traditional agriculture impose a food and raw material import burden on the earnings from primary product exports. This burden both reduces the means (import capacity) for growth and also diverts the domestic purchasing power (generated by exports) from demand for industrial goods to agricultural imports. These effects will shorten the IS process.

The export enclave within agriculture may contribute to pro-longing the phase by providing continued growth of primary export products. This, however, requires access to new natural resources for export, relaxation of controls, and participation of the evolving entrepreneurs in export expansion activities. Successful export expansion postpones the inevitable termination implicit in eventual exhaustion of land resources, offering more time for entrepreneurial development and agricultural modernization.

4. STATISTICAL VERIFICATION

4.1. Phases of Transition

We have just analyzed prolonged import substitution as a transition growth type. In this section we will verify this thesis statistically by using Philippine time series data. The purpose of statistical verification is to show that the first generation of transition growth experience in the Philippines can, indeed, be characterized as prolonged import substitution. This will be done by demonstrating that the statistical data of the Philippines show the observable characteristics predicted by the thesis expounded in this chapter.

We have noted (in section 1.3) that three phases may be identified during Philippine postwar transition growth:

1. Initial import substitution   (1950–56)
2. Retardation of import substitution   (1956–59)
3. Prolongation of import substitution   (1959–   )

The emergence of the three phases of import substitution in the given sequential order portray the central thesis of transition failure in a labor-surplus economy. Heuristically, one may think of the first phase (1950–56) as the phase of IS growth proper and the last phase (1959–   ) as prolongation of IS growth through promotion of primary product exports. The brief second phase of retardation (1956–59) reflects the accumulation of economic difficulties associated with tendencies toward termination of IS growth. These difficulties induced the government to modify some of the policy measures employed during the initial IS growth phase, leading to prolonged IS growth in the third phase.

To verify this phase aspect of Philippine transition growth, we first concentrate on characteristics of the transition period (1950–70) as a whole (section 4.2). The three phases will then be examined in turn (sections 4.3, 4.4 and 4.5).

4.2. A Synoptic View of the Generation

Viewing the first generation (1950–70) of Philippine transition growth as a whole, the dominant growth characteristic is the economy's failure to evolve from a land-based primary product export economy to a labor-based economy.

At the time of decolonization the Philippines inherited from colonialism an economy based upon primary product exports. Throughout the first generation of transition growth this basic property was maintained. In diagram 7.8 time is shown on the horizontal axis, covering the period 1950–65.[7] The two vertical lines at the years 1956 and 1959 mark off the three phases in the postwar transition. Diagram 7.8a presents the time series for total exports, E, disaggregated into three components, agricultural exports, E_x, extractive exports, E_m, and industrial exports, E_i. Primary product exports are defined as $E_x + E_m$. The persistence of primary product exports as the dominant component is clearly shown by the close proximity of the $E_x + E_m$ curve to the E curve throughout the period.

The continued dominance of primary product exports signifies that the economy remained land-based in nature. Scrutinizing the

7. Data behind all diagrams introduced in this section are presented in the Statistical Appendix, tables 3–10 for chapter 7.

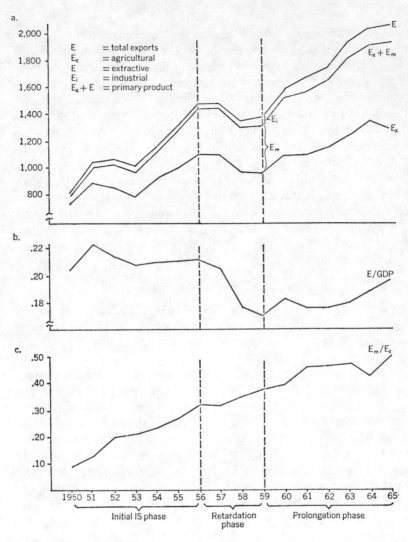

Diagram 7.8. Export Series
  a. Total exports and components (in million constant 1955 pesos)
  b. Export ratio, E/GDP
  c. Ratio of extractive exports to primary product exports, E_m/E_x

two components of primary product exports more closely, we may hypothesize that extractive exports, E_m, are more land-intensive than agricultural exports, E_x. In diagram 7.8c the time series for E_m/E_x is shown. We see that the relative importance of extractive exports to agricultural exports increased consistently from less than .10 to about .50.

This relative expansion of extractive exports at the expense of traditional agricultural exports may be explained by two factors. First, from the viewpoint of resource endowments, arable land had become increasingly scarce while land for extractive exports (e.g., lumber, minerals) was still available. Second, production of these extractive exports was appropriate as a new outlet for the evolving Filipino entrepreneurship, frequently in cooperation with foreign capital, management, and technology.

We have pointed out in our theoretical analysis that prolonged IS growth emerges where land resources are available for export and where modernization of the traditional agricultural sector does not take place. The fact that Philippine transition growth was impeded by agricultural shortfall may be verified by investigating the trend of labor productivity in the agricultural sector. The agricultural labor productivity index (1952 = 1.0) for the Philippines is shown by the dotted curve in diagram 7.9a. Failure in agriculture is reflected in the declining trend of labor productivity, which became pronounced in the retardation phase (around 1958).

The significance of this failure may be brought out more clearly by comparison with the successful transition case of Taiwan. The basic difference between the first generation of transition experience in Taiwan and the Philippines is that export substitution emerged in Taiwan while failing to appear in the Philippines. This is shown clearly in diagram 7.9b where exports of industrial goods, E_i, as a fraction of total exports, E, are given. The dramatic rise of the external orientation of the industrial sector in Taiwan after 1959 did not occur in the Philippine case. It is a central thesis of this study that this failure in the Philippine case to shift to labor-based export growth is in large part traceable to agricultural stagnation. For purposes of comparison, the solid curve in diagram 7.9a shows agricultural labor productivity in Taiwan (using the same base year as for the Philippines). In sharp contrast to the

a.

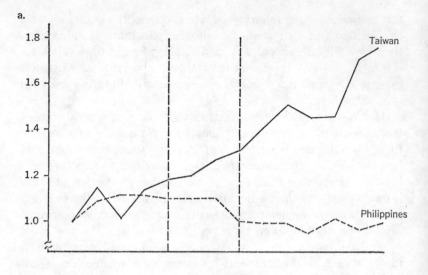

b.

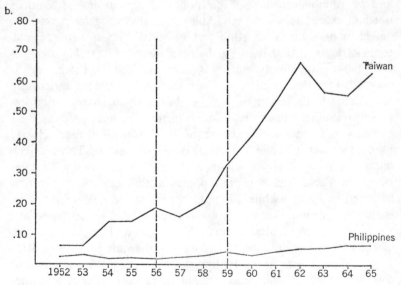

Diagram 7.9. Comparison: Philippines and Taiwan
a. Labor productivity in agriculture (1952 = 1.0)
b. Ratio of industrial exports, E_i, to total exports, E

Philippines, the emergence of export substitution growth in Taiwan about 1960 was accompanied by acceleration of agricultural labor productivity growth.

In the context of an open dualistic economy in transition, reallocation of labor from agriculture to the industrial sector is a complex phenomenon. In the success case (i.e., Taiwan), two conditions were satisfied. First, entrepreneurship was adequate to employ effectively reallocated labor in labor-intensive manufacturing for export. Second, the expansion of agricultural productivity permitted the transfer of food and raw materials to industry so that foreign exchange was not dissipated in acquiring these agricultural goods through imports. Hence, Taiwan's success is explained by satisfactory entrepreneurship and the availability of internal real finance based upon an agricultural surplus.

It is quite possible that reallocated labor may be used to build up labor-intensive export industries even where agricultural productivity is stagnant and internal finance fails to occur. This is possible under fortuitous circumstances as in Hong Kong and South Korea. In the case of Hong Kong, the development of export manufacturing industries drew upon labor from mainland China, obviously unaccompanied by an agricultural surplus. Hong Kong was able to control the inflow of labor migrants and entrepreneurs were efficient enough to purchase agricultural requirements from export earnings. South Korea's success is explained by liberal injections of foreign aid throughout the transition period which provided needed agricultural imports, enabling industrial entrepreneurs to expand rapidly labor-intensive manufactured exports.

In the Philippine case, substantial labor migration to the industrial sector occurred because of agricultural stagnation. However, labor-intensive manufacturing industries devoted to export failed to develop so that labor migration merely caused growing unemployment. Filipino entrepreneurship continued to emphasize land-based exports (e.g., lumber, minerals) for which the country enjoyed a conspicuous comparative advantage. Even with more favorable entrepreneurial conditions, however, the agricultural shortfall would have impeded industrialization because of the need to import agricultural requirements.

Thus, the postwar transition in the Philippines was dominated by failure to modernize traditional agriculture and by continued reliance upon primary product exports. It is precisely for this type of country that our theory predicts prolonged IS growth. Central to verification of this growth type, therefore, is evidence that import substitution remained as a central growth phenomenon throughout the first generation. This feature of the Philippines transition is borne out by our statistical analysis of the three phases in the next sections.

4.3 Initial IS Phase (1950–56)

Transition growth in the Philippines was launched by import substitution. This can be verified by the presence of the two basic import substitution phenomena, i.e., import substitution in the foreign exchange allocation sense and substitution in the domestic market sense.

Import substitution in the domestic market sense is shown in diagram 7.10. Imported industrial consumer goods, M_y, as a fraction of total domestic production, y, is shown by the M_y/y curve in diagram 7.10a. The persistence of import substitution over the entire period is seen from the gradually declining trend of the curve as a whole. Notice that substitution in the market sense proceeded rapidly early in the first phase as our theory predicted. Over a seven year period (1949–56) consumer goods imports declined from an initial value of 140 percent of domestic production to about 50 percent. Much slower decline, from 50 to 30 percent, occurred in the following 9 years.

Import substitution in the foreign exchange allocation sense is shown in diagram 7.11. Diagram 7.11a presents time series for the ratio of producer goods imports to total imports, M_p/M, for the ratio of industrial consumer goods imports to total imports, M_yM, and for the ratio of finished agricultural consumer goods imports to total imports, M_x/M. The major import substitution phenomena are shown by the consistent increase of the M_p/M curve and the consistent decline of the M_y/M curve.

Our theory of import substitution growth predicted (1) an initial high and sustained rate of industrial growth because of the cumu-

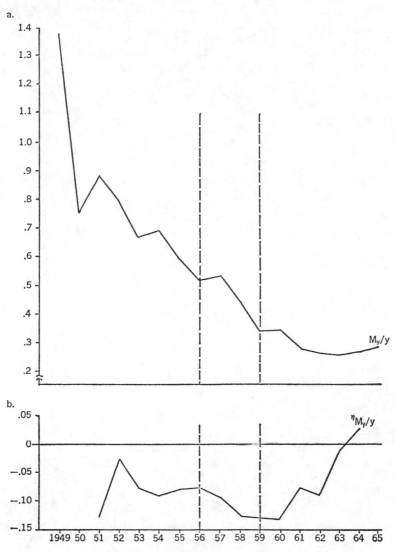

a.

b.

Diagram 7.10. Import Substitution, Domestic Market Sense
   a. Ratio of imported industrial consumer goods, M_y, to domestic pro-
      duction, y
   b. Growth rate: ratio of imports to domestic production (industrial con-
      sumer goods)

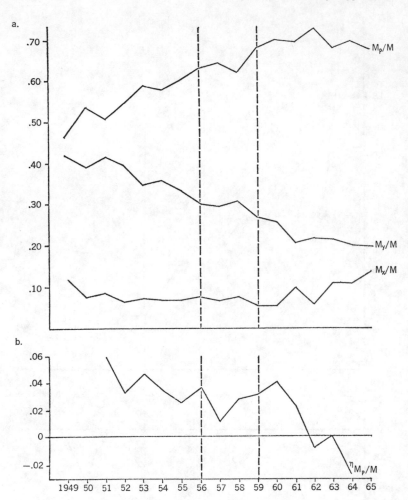

Diagram 7.11. Import Substitution, Foreign Exchange Allocation Sense
  a. Ratios of imported producer goods, M_p, industrial consumer goods,
     M_y, and agricultural goods, M_x, to total imports, M
  b. Growth rate: ratio of producer goods imports to total imports

lative tendencies inherent in the import substitution process and
(2) tendencies toward termination, as the rate of industrial expansion becomes retarded. Diagram 7.12 shows the rate of growth of
value added in the manufacturing sector. During the initial phase

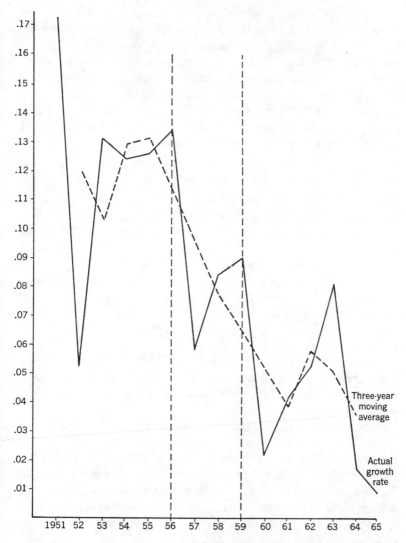

Diagram 7.12. Manufacturing Value Added: Annual Growth Rates
(1955 constant prices)

(1950–56) this rate of growth was sustained at a high value of about 12 percent. Just after the end of the initial phase, however, the termination tendencies produced a sharp decline in the growth rate (from 12 to 6 percent), and a declining trend was maintained during the retardation phase (1956–59). During the prolongation phase, a slight recovery occurred, but manufacturing value added grew at a much lower rate (under 4 percent) than during the initial phase. The dotted curve is a three-year moving average of the growth rate over the entire period.

4.4. The Retardation Phase (1956–59)

The period of sharp retardation was a phase in which the economy confronted difficulties associated with the termination of import substitution growth forces. Our statistical interest in this phase centers upon the economic difficulties that emerged as well on the policy reversals that were evoked by these difficulties.

The two substitution phenomena and eventual deceleration of the manufacturing sector's growth rate are the basic symptoms of import substitution growth. These symptoms were observed during Taiwan's IS phase as well as in the Philippines'. The failure of export substitution to evolve in the Philippine case, however, led to a new phenomenon not shared by Taiwan, i.e., a period of prolonged retardation of industrial sector growth. The uniqueness of Philippine experience lies in difficulties of this latter type, to which we now turn.

At the economic level, the basic difficulties can be measured in terms of output and productivity trends in both the agriculture and the industrial sector. We have seen, from diagram 7.12, that the rate of expansion of the manufacturing sector fell drastically during the retardation phase. From diagram 7.9a we also see that a significant decline in agricultural labor productivity appeared during this phase, a decline which aggravated the difficulties traced to the termination of the import substitution process.

Our theory predicts that, as the import substitution process terminates and as the economy fails to find a new orientation for its industrial output, unutilized industrial capacity, industrial unemployment, and capital flight will appear even if primary product exports are maintained.[8] In the Philippine case, however, the volume of exports fell during the retardation phase, the only such period of declining exports occurring during the Philippine transition experience—as may be seen from diagram 7.8a. The clear implication is that without reviving export performance, there was no further possibility for import substitution growth.

The decline of primary product exports during the retardation phase was a direct consequence of development strategy during the initial IS phase (1950–56). This strategy, as we have seen, was based upon exploitation of primary product exports to transfer profits to the industrial sector. Profit transfer was accomplished by the use of an overvalued exchange rate and high tariffs on consumer goods imports, policies which imposed a dual burden on the export sector. Thus a natural escape from the difficulties attending retardation was a reversal of these policies to revive the growth of primary product exports.

Pressures for political action to overcome these difficulties stem from practical problems in the balance of payments. Diagram 7.13 shows the value of imports, M, exports, E, and the import surplus, A, all in constant 1955 prices. From the A curve we see that the import surplus problem gradually worsened during the initial IS phase, reaching a maximum for the entire period precisely during the retardation phase.

Pursuit of economic recovery through policy naturally centered upon devaluation of the exchange rate to encourage primary product exports. In diagram 7.14, the free market exchange rate is denoted by b, and the official exchange rate to exporters by r. While the continuously rising b curve reflects the chronic difficulties traced to agricultural shortfall and export sluggishness, the r curve reflects the use of government policy. Notice in particular the gradual reversal from an overvalued official export rate to one approximating the free market rate (by 1962), a reversal aimed at reviving primary product export growth.

8. Consistent time series to document these phenomena are lacking so we must rely only upon chronological records of events for their verification. For such a record of difficulties appearing during the retardation phase, see Frank H. Golay, *The Philippines: Public Policy and National Economic Development* (Ithaca: Cornell University Press, 1961), pp. 89–99.

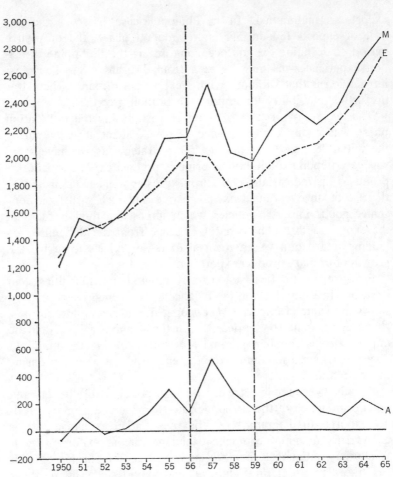

Diagram 7.13. Exports, *E*, Imports, *M*, and Import Surplus, *A*
(Constant prices, million 1955 pesos)

The stimulation of primary product exports through devaluation
leads directly into prolongation of IS in the next phase. As that
phase emerges, policy, which becomes more selective in nature, is
aimed at encouraging specific exports and domestic industries—
as we emphasized in the theoretical section. This was accomplished

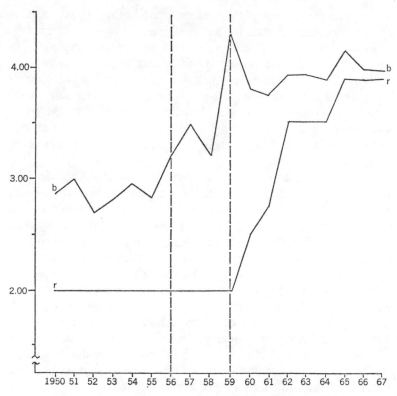

Diagram 7.14. Exchange Rates: Free Market, *b*, and Official
Export, *r* (Pesos per U.S. $1.00)

by use of a more diversified tariff rate structure and judicious use
of public subsidies.[9]

4.5. Prolongation of IS (1959–　)

During the prolongation phase there was a noticeable entrepreneurial response to the policy changes just described. This may be
seen from diagram 7.8a, which shows the revival of primary prod-

9. See John H. Power, "The Structure of Protection in the Philippines,"
University of the Philippines, School of Economics, Discussion Paper no.
69-68 (April 1968).

uct exports at the turning point after a period of retrogression. This revival provided the basis for a new phase of prolonged IS growth. Prolonged IS growth differs from IS proper as experienced in the initial phase. Our theory specifies that under IS proper the economy exhibits an internal orientation. Under prolongation, however, where a conscious export promotion policy exists, the economy assumes an external orientation. In diagram 7.8b, the curve shows exports as a fraction of GDP. A decreasing trend in this ratio occurs until the 1959 turning point, after which an increasing trend is apparent.

The revival of exports induced expansion of manufacturing activity, as seen in diagram 7.12. This expansion was short-lived, however, as a brief three year period of acceleration was followed by deceleration, beginning in 1963. After that year a marked weakening of import substitution forces in both the foreign exchange allocation and domestic market senses became apparent. In diagram 7.11b, the curve shows the rate of growth of M_p/M (share of imported producer goods in total imports) becoming negative in 1962 for the first time in the entire transition period. In diagram 7.10b, the curve shows the rate of growth of M_y/M (imported industrial consumer goods to domestic production) becoming positive in 1964 for the first time. Thus the two basic forces of import substitution showed marked retrogression a few years after the prolonged IS phase was begun.

The agricultural shortfall, i.e., the failure of traditional agriculture to supply adequate food and raw materials to the industrial sector was the major impediment to the IS process during the prolongation phase. From the dotted curve in diagram 7.9a we see that labor productivity in agriculture was virtually stagnant after 1960. Diagram 7.11a shows that imports of finished agricultural consumer goods, M_x, as a fraction of total imports, began to increase during the prolongation phase. To elaborate this point on agricultural shortfall, we show in diagram 7.15 the time series for imported agricultural raw materials, M_x', and M_x, as shares of total imports. Their sum, $F(=M_x' + M_x)$ as a fraction of total imports is given by the F/M curve. The sharp increase of this curve after 1962 shows the impact of agricultural shortfall upon the economy's import capacity. In three years (1962–65) foreign ex-

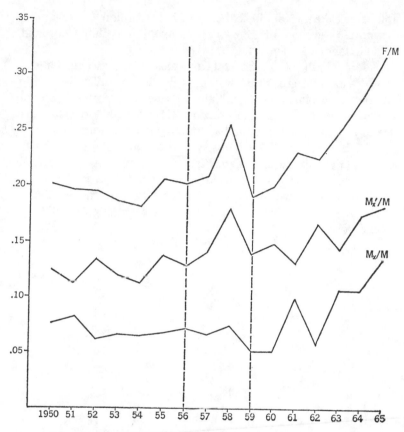

Diagram 7.15. Agricultural Shortfall, *F*, and Components (As fractions of total imports)

change allocated to import of *F* goods rose from 23 to 32 percent. This was the basic cause of the arrested IS process just noted.

In summary of our discussion of the Philippines, we find that the postwar generation of transition growth in that country represents a case of prolonged IS growth in which the society sought to achieve modernization by reliance upon primary product exports for import substitution industrialization. This case may be construed as a failure of transition growth, both in the sense of the gradual weakening of the basic growth promotion forces and in the more basic sense of the economy's inability to shift from land-based to labor-based growth.

In looking ahead, we find that the most likely avenue for successful transition growth in the future is efficient utilization of the economy's surplus labor to initiate a phase of export substitution growth. The most essential precondition for this development strategy is modernization of the traditional agricultural sector to assure labor reallocation to industry, and expansion of the domestic market. Given the relatively abundant supply of indigenous private entrepreneurship, the prime need is for government leadership to provide the infrastructure for agricultural modernization. Events since 1966 suggest that the government is beginning to fulfill this crucial role.

8

Export Promotion Growth under Neocolonialism: Thailand

In this and the next chapter we investigate postwar transition growth in Thailand and Malaysia as examples of export promotion growth under neocolonialism. In contrast to Taiwan and the Philippines, Thailand and Malaysia did not emphasize development of import substitution industries. Instead, the emphasis was upon continuation of expanding primary product exports, as under colonialism. Industrial activity was oriented toward servicing this export sector.

Neocolonialism arises from favorable resource endowments, i.e., from an abundant supply of land and a diversified natural resource base, assets which permit continued reliance upon land-based exports. The major organizational feature of neocolonialism is a free market system which, in the context of an open economy, regulates the interaction between primary product expansion and domestic capital accumulation. In this free, open economy system, domestic industrialization is subject to import competition. Capital flows are unregulated and capital outflows tolerated. In Thailand and Malaysia, this system arose from a political compromise between colonialists, minority groups, and indigenous interests (see chapter 5).

Two major growth-relevant issues dominate the analysis of export promotion growth. The first issue concerns the rapidity of growth, i.e., whether or not reliance upon primary product exports will offer a satisfactory rate of per capita real income growth. The second issue concerns the likelihood of structural change, which may be defined in terms of balance of growth between (1) primary product exports, J, and (2) accumulation of industrial capital stock, *K*. Heuristically, we may let $j = J/K$ represent the *index of relative agricultural orientation*.[1] A decreasing trend for *j* signifies that the industrial sector is gaining ground relative to the agricultural sector as the country becomes industrialized. An increasing trend for *j* signifies that the industrial sector is lagging as the economy fails to escape from colonial enclavism. From a long-run perspective, export promotion growth under neocolonialism offers continued viability only if growth is relatively rapid and if the structure of the economy shifts toward industry.

When exogenous factors, such as world market demand are given, the expansion rate of primary product exports is primarily determined by the real costs or inputs involved in export production. Four categories of real costs may be distinguished: (1) labor and natural resources internal to the agricultural sector; (2) commercial services (e.g., transport, handling, wholesale, and retail distribution); (3) processing services (e.g., packing, grading, and simple transformation); and (4) modern inputs of intermediate goods. Of these four, only the first is supplied from within the sector; the others are purchased from the nonagricultural sector.

In neocolonialism, real costs of categories (1) and (2) are indispensable. The presence of categories (3) and (4) depends upon the nature of the export commodity. If the exported good is an indigenous agricultural product (e.g., rice in Thailand), modern inputs (category 4) can be neglected since production of these indigenous crops involves traditional production techniques. Conversely where the exported good is a product introduced from abroad (e.g., rubber in Malaysia), modern inputs become crucial, and a substantial amount of industrial processing (category 3) is likely to be present.

On the basis of these real cost distinctions, two variants of neocolonial export-led growth may be identified. The first case will be referred to as growth led by indigenous export products. The dominant characteristic of this type is that primary product export expansion is determined by momentum within the agricultural export sector. The second variant will be referred to as growth led by

1. This concept assumes that technology remains constant so that the capital-output ratio also remains constant. Hence, *j* can be construed as measuring the ratio of agricultural to industrial output.

modern export products. The dominant characteristic of this variant is that primary product export expansion is determined by forces of modernization transmitted from the industrial sector through delivery of modern inputs. The remainder of this chapter will be devoted to analysis of the indigenous export product case and its application to Thailand. The modern export case will be analyzed in the next chapter, where its relevance to Malaysia will also be discussed.

I. Indigenous Export-Led Growth

1.1. The Model Structure

The essential characteristic of transition growth led by the export of indigenous agricultural products is that the expansion of primary product exports, J, is determined by growth momentum within the agricultural sector—a momentum ultimately traced to population growth and to the supply of land and other natural resources. The following static assumptions (equations 8.1a, b, c), and dynamic assumptions (equations 8.1d, e) may be postulated.[2]

(8.1a) $y = hJp^{-\alpha}$ (Demand function; $\alpha > 1$ is price elasticity of demand; $h \geqq 0$ is agriculture-pull coefficient)

(8.1b) $y = K/k$ (Production of y; k is capital-output ratio)

(8.1c) $I = a'p^{\beta}$ (Investment demand function; $\beta \geqq 0$ is price elasticity; $a' \geqq 0$ is coefficient of demand level)

(8.1d) $dK/dt = I$

(8.1e) $\eta_J = i$, or $J = J_0 e^{it}$

Let y denote industrial goods purchased by the agricultural sector, including consumer goods as well as trading, commercial, and processing services. Equation 8.1a is a demand function for y, based on income generated by primary product exports. This demand equation takes into consideration both the price effect (through α, the price elasticity of demand) and the income effect

2. See chapter 4 for a diagrammatic presentation of this system.

(through h, the agricultural-pull coefficient). Notice that in an open economy, in which the industrial sector is subject to import competition, the price elasticity of demand is bound to be elastic (hence $\alpha > 1$).[3] The supply of y is given by the production function in equation 8.1b in which K is industrial capital stock and k is a constant capital-output ratio.[4] Capital stock, K, is mainly of the liquid, commercial type, supplemented by fixed capital for production of consumer goods.

Equation 8.1c is the investment demand function, showing investment in the industrial sector, I, to be a function of price of industrial goods, p, where β is the price elasticity of demand and a' denotes the strength of the investment demand. Equation 8.1d states that industrial capital stock, K, is augmented through time by investment, I. Equation 8.1e states that primary product exports, J, grow at the constant rate, $\eta_J = i$, a key assumption of the present model.[5] There are thus six parameters (h, α, k, a', β, i) and five variables (y, J, p, K, and I) to be determined by the five equations.

Heuristically, industrial capital stock, K, which plays only a passive role, facilitates primary product exportation. The key analytical issue of structural change is whether the growth of K will tend to lag behind J, which grows by its own internal momentum.

Since investment, I, is a price-sensitive phenomenon, more favorable (higher) prices of y will lead to more rapid capital accumulation (equation 8.1c). The magnitude of price, p, is in turn determined by conditions of supply and demand. A higher i and more rapid expansion of primary product exports will increase demand for y (through the income effect in equation 8.1a) and thereby contribute to higher price and more rapid capital accumu-

3. For example, when the price of industrial goods is determined completely by import prices, the demand curve is horizontal and α approaches infinity. An upward shift of the demand curve (see diagram 4.2 of chapter 4) will be represented by a higher value of h.
4. In diagram 4.2 of chapter 4, the production function is represented by a radial line, reflecting this assumption of the constancy of the capital-output ratio, k.
5. In contrast, the major assumption of the next chapter (growth led by modern export products) is that the rate of expansion of J is affected by modern inputs.

lation. More rapid investment *I*, and capital accumulation, *K*, however, will increase the supply of industrial goods, *y*, and thereby depress their price (equation 8.1b).

Thus, more rapid expansion of primary product exports (higher *i*), while contributing to a more rapid pace of capital accumulation, *K*, in the short run, tends, in the longer-run, to discourage investment because of the initial output expansion and its price-depressing effect. Owing to the balancing of these forces, a dynamic equilibrium is achieved through time. The key question which we seek to answer is whether this dynamic equilibrium will produce balanced growth or whether the economy will show a tendency to revert to enclavism, with an agricultural orientation and a lagging, service-oriented industrial sector.

1.2. Reversion to Enclavism

To investigate the economy's long-run growth orientation, let us express *p* (price of industrial goods) and *py* (expenditure on industrial goods) in terms of $j = J/K$, the index of relative agricultural strength:

(8.2a) $p = k'j^{1/\alpha}$ where $k' = (hk)^{1/\alpha}$
Proof: $p^\alpha = hJk/K = hjk$ (by 8.1a, b)

(8.2b) $I = aj^{\alpha/\beta}$ where $a = a'(hk)^{\beta/\alpha}$
Proof: $I = a'(k'^\beta j^{\beta/\alpha})$ (by 8.1c and 8.2a)

(8.2c) $py = hJp^{1-\alpha}$ (by 8.1a)

We can then also deduce the rate of growth of industrial capital, η_K, in terms of *j* and *J*:

(8.3a) $dK/dt = aj^{\beta/\alpha}$ (by 8.1d and 8.2b)

(8.3b) $\eta_K = aj^u/J$ where $u = 1 + \beta/\alpha$ (by 8.3a)
Proof: $\eta_K = aj^{\beta/\alpha}j/J = aj^{1+\beta/\alpha}/J$

The definition of $\eta_j = \eta_{J/K}$ leads to the following differential equation in *j* (equation 8.4b):

(8.4a) $\eta_j = \eta_J - \eta_K$

(8.4b) $\eta_j = i - aj^u/J_0e^{it}$ (by 8.4a, 8.1e and 8.3b)

We can readily see from equation 8.4b that the value of j cannot be bounded from above.[6] To see this more precisely, let us compute from equation 8.4b the rate of acceleration of j:

(8.5a) $\quad d\eta_j/dt = (i - \eta_j)(i - u\eta_j)$ $\qquad$ (Rate of acceleration)

(8.5b) $\quad \bar{\eta}_j = i/u = i/(1 + \beta/\alpha)$ $\qquad$ (Stationary value of η_j)

(8.5c) $\quad j \to \infty$ as $t \to \infty$ $\qquad$ (j approaches infinity)

$$\text{Proof: } d\eta_j/dt = -\frac{a}{J_0}\frac{e^{it}uj^{u-1}dj/dt - j^u i e^{it}}{e^{2it}}$$

$$= (aj^u/J_0 e^{it})(i - u\eta_j)$$

$$= (i - \eta_j)(i - u\eta_j) \quad \text{(by 8.4b)}$$

Let η_j be measured on the horizontal axis in diagram 8.1a. Let the values of i and i/u be marked off on the horizontal axis through which points the two dotted straight lines are drawn to represent the two factors on the right-hand side of equation 8.5a.[7] The acceleration, $d\eta_j/dt$, is now seen to be represented by the parabola shown in the diagram. There are two long-run stationary values for η_j (i.e., i/u and i), of which the former i/u (equation 8.5b) is stable equilibrium. The direction of change of η_j through time is indicated by the arrows on the parabola. As long as the initial value of η_j is less than i, η_j will always converge toward i/u in the long run.[8] If the initial value of η_j is greater than i, then η_j will increase without bound. Thus in all cases, j will increase indefinitely in the long run.

This analysis allows us to predict the behavior of the index of agricultural orientation, j, through time. If η_0 (the initial rate of growth of j) is negative (e.g., $j_0 = \bar{\eta}$ in diagram 8.1a), the growth rate of j will always accelerate to a positive value. The time path

---

6. For, suppose that $B \geqq j$ is an upper bound for j. Then equation 8.4b implies: $\eta_j \geqq i - aB^u/J_0 e^{it}$ which approaches i as t approaches infinity. This is a contradiction, as a value of η_j close to i is inconsistent with a bounded value for j. Hence, j must increase without bound in the long run.

7. From equation 8.3b we see that $u > 1$ so that $i/u > 1$.

8. There are two types of transient behavior of η_j as it returns to the stable equilibrium of i/u, either monotonically decreasing (if the value of η_j is less than i/u or monotonically increasing (if the initial value of η_j is greater than i/u) — as shown in diagram 8.1a.

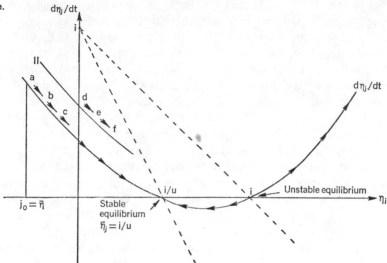

a.

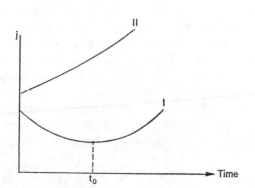

b.

Diagram 8.1. Time Behavior of Agricultural Orientation, *j*
  a. Rate of acceleration
  b. Time path of *j*

of j in this case is described by the U-shaped curve labeled I in diagram 8.1b. This implies that an initially declining trend of j will give way to an increasing trend at a turning point, t_0. Conversely if $\eta_0 > 0$, the value of j will increase monotonically, as shown by the curve labeled II in diagram 8.1b. For a country which begins transition growth with a slow start at export promotion, the U-shaped curve is the more realistic description of the behavior of j. For such a country, the predicted tendency toward reversion to enclavism (i.e., increasing values for j) is observable only after an initial period of transition growth.

Despite the short-run behavior, our conclusion shows that, in the case of indigenous export-led growth, there is always a tendency toward reversion to enclavism in the long run. Notice that this conclusion is inevitable, regardless of the rapidity of primary product export expansion (i.e., regardless of the value of i). This tendency is caused by the fact that the industrial sector merely plays a passive role of serving the agricultural export sector.[9]

In the indigenous export economy, industry is geared to export growth. Expansion of primary product exports will, indeed, cause an increase in industrial prices, p, through the income effect, and this will serve to stimulate investment. However, this stimulation is only temporary since the resulting increase in capital and output will prevent prices from increasing excessively, thus dampening investment incentives. In spite of price increases, therefore, industrial capital stock, K, and output, y, will tend to lag behind export growth. We conclude that the failure of industrialization in an indigenous export economy is attributable to weak investment incentives. This is all the more true in an open economy where investment incentives are further dampened by import competition.

9. This interpretation is supported by investigating the long-run stationary value of $\eta_j = i/(1 + \beta/\alpha)$. A more rapid rate of primary product export expansion, i, reinforces the tendency toward an agricultural orientation. Similarly, a large value of price elasticity of demand, α, has the same effect by inducing a large reduction in demand for domestic industrial output when the price increases. Conversely, a large value of β, the price elasticity of investment, will contribute to greater balance between agricultural and industrial growth. Regardless of the values of the coefficients, i, α and β, however, the underlying tendency toward reversion to enclavism cannot be avoided.

1.3. Import Competition

In the indigenous export product economy under colonialism, continuous expansion of exports and domestic income generated growing demand for industrial goods (consumer goods and intermediate good inputs). While some of these were necessarily supplied domestically (e.g., commercial services), other industrial goods (e.g., consumer goods) were traditionally imported. Domestic manufacturing of these latter goods failed to appear because import competition was permitted by the free market system. This was tantamount to regulation of domestic prices by international price levels, a situation which reflected the comparative advantage of industrially advanced countries in producing industrial goods. Under these conditions, colonies remained specialized in producing primary products for export, with industry providing only accommodating commercial and processing services.

As we have seen, the strategy of import substitution (through protection and an overvalued exchange rate) is designed to alter this free market mechanism to favor the growth of infant consumer goods industries. Industrial sector growth under neocolonialism continues to lag precisely because an import substitution strategy is avoided as a part of the political compromise by which the system is created at the outset of the transition.

We can incorporate the effect of import competition under neocolonialism by a slight modification of our basic model of the last section. Notice from equation 8.2a that there is a tendency for price, p, to increase as j increases; but we have seen that this increase is an inadequate stimulant for industrial investment. Let us now impose an upper ceiling, p_M, for the price level $p(t)$. Although continuous export expansion occurs, the domestic price level will now not exceed the price, P_M, determined in the international market. Once $p(t)$ approaches P_M, price will remain pinned at P_M because of import competition. When this occurs, domestic investment incentives will be further weakened. The net result is that industrial capital accumulation and output, y, will be discouraged even more, causing industrial sector growth to lag further behind primary product exports and accentuating reversion to colonial enclavism.

In inheriting this free market mechanism from colonialism, neo-colonialism also retains colonialism's mode of operation with regard to capital movements. Under this system, export profits tend to be partly reinvested in export-servicing industries when export prospects are favorable as indicated by export prices. When export prices are unfavorable, however, capital flight is likely to occur as export profits seek external outlets.

Certain observable properties, which can be verified by statistical data, may be deduced. The argument in the last two sections is summarized by the time series in diagram 8.2. The uppermost curve, J, shows agricultural exports expanding at the constant rate, i. This leads to a U-shaped time path for j (the index of agricultural orientation), which eventually increases at a constant rate $i/(1 + \beta/\alpha)$ until the turning value of j_t is reached. At the turning point, the force of rising prices, p, for industrial goods is replaced by the constant price p_m as import competition comes into play. After the turning point, the dotted curve for j is replaced by the solid j curve, which shows a higher growth rate and signifies that industrial expansion lags further behind export growth. Now, the growth of capital, K, output, y, and investment, I, slows down, as compared to their behavior before the turning point.[10] In the long run, not only will the economy tend to revert to colonial enclavism, but also its growth will become retarded as industry fails to become a more dominant component in the economy. Income deceleration is likely to occur even in the first generation of transition growth because of failure to shift to a more rapid industrialization process.

2. EMPIRICAL VERIFICATION

We now turn to the empirical verification of export promotion growth under neocolonialism as it appeared in Thailand in the form of indigenous export-led growth. We verify the existence of this growth type by considering two aspects, (1) its organizational

---

10. After the turning point, investment is constant since $p(t) = p_m$ is fixed. Thus, K and y will grow linearly instead of growing at a constant rate as in the previous stage.

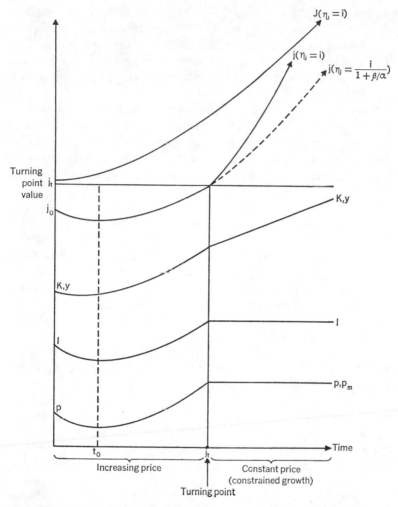

Diagram 8.2. Indigenous Export Economy, Long-run Potential

features, and (2) the performance of the economy as reflected in statistical data.

2.1. Organization for Export Promotion Growth

During most of the period since 1950 Thailand has exhibited all the organizational requirements for export promotion growth under neocolonialism. As we have seen in chapter 5, the political condition for the emergence of this system consists of a compromise between indigenous and alien interests. In the case of Thailand, this has been reflected in the rapid spread of compromise arrangements between Chinese entrepreneurs and the indigenous bureaucracy.[11]

This political compromise was manifested in three aspects of government economic policy: (1) the maintenance of a free market system permitting unrestricted participation of alien entrepreneurs; (2) an emphasis upon an agricultural orientation in public development expenditures; and, (3) a moderate industrial promotion policy.

Free market system. In an open economy the primary test of a free market system is absence of government control over foreign trade and investment flows. A tendency toward freeing these flows from government control in Thailand began with the abolition of the previous multiple exchange rate system in 1955. This step was followed by adoption of other liberalization measures. These changes terminated Thailand's earlier controls and established a free market system for export promotion growth.

Since 1955, the monetary exchange rate has been maintained near the free market value by an Exchange Equalization Fund. Profit and capital transfers have been liberally treated as a facet of the official policy of private foreign investment promotion.[12] Tariffs have not been raised to levels where they have a serious effect on restricting imports, and the impact of a limited number of continuing quantitative import restrictions has been minor.[13] Moreover, domestic price policies have been deliberately anti-infla-

11. See, for example, Hans-Dieter Evans, "The Formation of a Social Class Structure: Urbanization, Bureaucratization and Social Mobility in Thailand," Yale University, Southeast Asia Studies, Reprint no. 36 (1969); and G. William Skinner, *Leadership and Power in the Chinese Community in Thailand* (Ithaca: Cornell University Press, 1958).

12. National Economic Development Board, *Evaluation of the First Six-Year Plan, 1961–1966* (Bangkok: Government of Thailand, June 1967), pp. 62–63.

13. T. H. Silcock, ed., *Thailand: Social & Economic Studies in Development* (Durham: Duke University Press, 1967), pp. 163–64.

tionary.[14] As a result of the 1955 exchange rate reform and subsequent policies representing more active export promotion, the economy moved from a passive to an active phase of primary product export-led growth.

The noninterventionist feature of this free market system has been reinforced by other aspects of government policy. The government, by divesting itself of the industrial holdings acquired during the earlier bureaucratic industrialization era, opened entrepreneurial opportunities to all contenders, alien as well as indigenous. Profits from industrial and commercial undertakings could be freely disposed of, either reinvested domestically or transferred abroad. In short, the policy changes after 1955 established a neocolonial organizational system consisting of the maintenance of a free market and unrestricted participation of alien entrepreneurs.

Agricultural orientation in public investment. As a primary product export economy, Thailand relied upon a fiscal structure dependent on taxation of the agricultural surplus, particularly rice exports. This was manifested in the "rice premium" (in fact, a tax on rice exports), in effect since the exchange rate reform of 1955. The significant factor for export promotion growth was the government's employment of this revenue for export promotion through infrastructure investment (e.g., irrigation, transportation, and communications).[15]

This orientation of public policy is clearly stated in Thailand's current development plan:

> The agricultural sector is the foundation upon which the country's economic development must be based. About 80% of the country's population is engaged in agricultural employment; agricultural exports earn the foreign exchange required for capital imports to modernize the economy; and the agricultural sector is the primary market for industrial production. The government will encourage increased agricultural production and higher

14. National Economic Development Board, *The Second National Economic and Social Development Plan, 1967–1971* (Bangkok: Government of Thailand, n.d.), p. 25; and Silcock, pp. 174–78.
15. T. H. Silcock, p. 151.

quality, as well as further diversification of products which command high prices in the world market. . . .[16]

The public development program has been consistent with this emphasis on agricultural development. The government has participated heavily in investment in sectors related to agriculture and promotion of primary product exports. This is documented in table 8.1, which shows, for selected years, the share of public investment

Table 8.1. Share of Public Investment as Percentage of
Total Fixed Capital Formation, by Key Sectors,
Selected Years: Thailand

Sector	1952	1956	1960	1965
Agriculture	35	35	24	33
Transportation and communication	52	63	35	43
Manufacturing	4	4	2	8
Commerce	30	15	12	17
Total	33	32	25	29

Source: National Economic Development Board, *National Income of Thailand*, 1964 and 1965 editions.

in total fixed capital formation by major sectors. The government's investment orientation toward agriculture and toward infrastructure supporting exports (transportation and communication) is demonstrated by the large share of public investment in these sectors.

Moderate industrial promotion.   After the demise of the bureaucratic industrialization strategy in 1955, industrial promotion became moderate and indirect, relying essentially upon investment incentives provided by prices in a free market system. Two noteworthy features of government policy in this regard are its nondiscriminatory nature and its avoidance of profit transfer mechanisms as under import substitution.

The nondiscriminatory nature of Thai industrial promotion

16. National Economic Development Board, *The Second National Economic and Social Development Plan, 1967–1971* (Bangkok: Government of Thailand, n.d.), pp. 5, 23, 24.

policies may be seen, for example, from the ethnic composition of firms to which industrial promotion certificates (the major promotional device) were awarded. Since this program's inception, 55 percent of promotion certificates were issued to joint ventures between Thais and foreigners, 31 percent to wholly Thai-owned firms, and the remaining 14 percent to totally foreign-owned firms.[17]

Industrial promotion certificates entitle investors to receive benefits in the form of tax exemptions and reduced import duties on capital goods and raw materials (the maximum reduction being 33 percent). These benefits are modest indeed, compared to the advantages conveyed by the profit transfer and protection features of an import substitution strategy. It is significant to note that 57 percent of the promoted industries were export-oriented industries (agricultural processing and minerals).[18]

While we do not have access to a study of the effective rate of tariff protection in Thailand, indications are that protection is moderate, with tariffs largely employed for revenue purposes.[19] In Thailand's official statement on industrial development policy, a very moderate position is enunciated in regard to use of tariffs for protection, with emphasis on reducing duties on intermediate goods rather than placing tariffs on final products for protection.[20] Hence, the policy intent in regard to tariffs is very different from that expressed in countries where tariffs are aggressively used to foster import substitution industries.

To summarize, the organizational features of the Thai economy since 1955 have closely resembled the system we described in chapter 4 as "organization under neocolonialism." The dominant characteristics apparent in Thailand were: (1) a free market system which, with little government intervention and an absence of protection to entrepreneurs for industrialization, leaves investment incen-

17. National Economic Development Board, *Evaluation of the First Six-Year Plan, 1961–1966* (Bangkok: Government of Thailand, June 1967) p. 64.

18. Ibid.

19. Robert J. Muscat, *Development Strategy in Thailand* (New York: Frederick A. Praeger, 1966), pp. 232–35; and T. H. Silcock, ed., pp. 163–65. The latter contains an account of Thailand's tariff policies as a whole.

20. Ministry of Industry, *Industrial Development & Investment in Thailand* (Bangkok, 1966), pp. 74–75.

tives to be determined by free market price, p, subject to import competition, p_m, as specified in our model; and, (2) concentration of government infrastructure expenditure upon the promotion of primary product exports, a policy which is basic to growth momentum (summarized in our model by the parameter i).

2.2. Growth Performance

The purpose of statistical verification is to demonstrate that Thailand's postwar transition growth has followed the neocolonial pattern based on indigenous primary product exports. The uniqueness of this experience in Thailand can be best brought out by contrast with Taiwan and the Philippines where a more nationalistic course was pursued by developing import substitution industries. The viability of neocolonialism as a transition growth system depends upon whether or not reliance upon primary product exports can sustain adequate expansion of labor productivity and per capita income. This aspect of growth rapidity will also be considered.

In diagram 8.3, the time series for total exports, E, and primary product exports, J, are shown with the vertical gap between the two representing manufactured exports.[21] The striking feature is that exports are completely dominated by primary products throughout the entire period. The contrast between Thailand and Taiwan in this regard is dramatically shown in diagram 8.4 which shows the time series for primary product exports as a fraction of total exports, J/E, for four countries. In Taiwan the initial dominance of primary product exports is completely reversed, while in Thailand the ratio J/E remained constant signifying that the economy continued to be based upon primary product exports. In the third country, the Philippines, the behavior of J/E resembled that of Thailand, as the industrial sector also failed to develop an external orientation (see chapter 7).[22]

Returning to diagram 8.3, the year 1962 (marked off by a vertical line) appears to be a significant year. The rate of expansion of primary product exports, J, was much faster in the second than in

21. Data behind all diagrams introduced in this section are presented in the Statistical Appendix, tables 11–17 for chapter 8.

22. The experience of Malaysia, the fourth country, will be discussed in the next chapter.

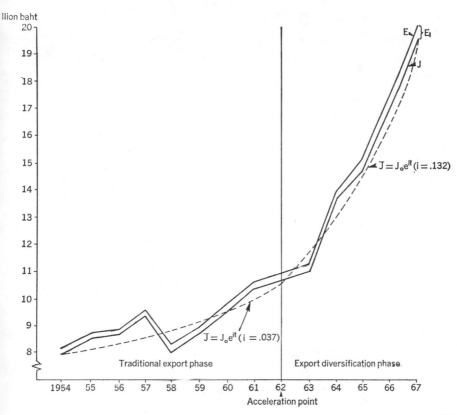

Diagram 8.3. Thailand: Composition of Exports by Type

the first phase. The dotted curves represent the constant rate growth paths, fitted separately for the two phases. While in the first phase J grew at the modest annual rate of .037, this growth rate accelerated in the second phase to .132. This acceleration reflects the eventual success of the post-1955 policy reorientation whose purpose was to foster the primary product export economy. The economy responded by rapid diversification of indigenous agricultural export products.

The constant rates of expansion of primary product exports in the two phases corroborates the basic assumption postulated in equation 8.1e about the major growth force in this type of econ-

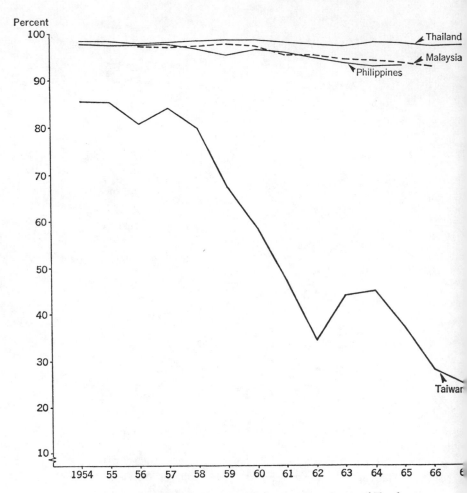

Diagram 8.4. Primary Product Exports as Percentage of Total
Exports, J/E: Malaysia, Philippines, Taiwan, Thailand, 1954–67

omy, namely, that the steady expansion of primary product exports
at a constant rate, i, constitutes the economy's major growth promotion force. In the application of our model to Thailand, the data
must be interpreted in this context. A regime of a higher growth
rate of primary product exports replaced an earlier regime with a
lower rate of expansion. This change is explained by the exogenous

force of government policy, resulting in an acceleration point in 1962. In the first phase, Thailand's traditional primary product exports continued to dominate, but in the second phase growth was led by rapid diversification of indigenous agricultural exports (e.g., maize, kenaf, tapioca).

We have asserted in section 1 that primary product export expansion in Thailand was dominated by indigenous export products,

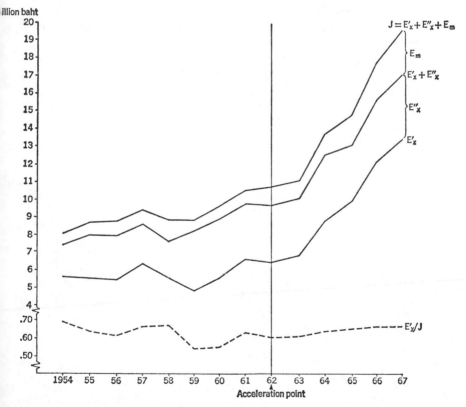

Diagram 8.5. Components of Primary Product Exports, *J*: Thailand

rather than modern export products. In diagram 8.5, total primary product exports, *J*, are disaggregated into three components: unprocessed indigenous products, E_x', processed agricultural products,

E_x'', and mineral products, E_m. The dotted curve in the lower part of the diagram shows the share of unprocessed agricultural goods in total primary product exports, E_x'/J. From the behavior of this curve we see that unprocessed (indigenous) export products were the dominant component of primary product exports, normally accounting for 60 to 70 percent of primary product exports, J. Thus throughout the period Thailand relied primarily upon indigenous, unprocessed primary product exports.

For an economy based on indigenous primary product exports, our theory predicts that reversion to enclavism is inevitable in the long run. This may be measured by the long-run increasing trend of the index of agricultural orientation, $j = J/K = J/yk$, or, as a proxy, $j = J/y$ (primary product exports divided by industrial output). In diagram 8.6, the time path of $j = J/y$ is shown. The dotted

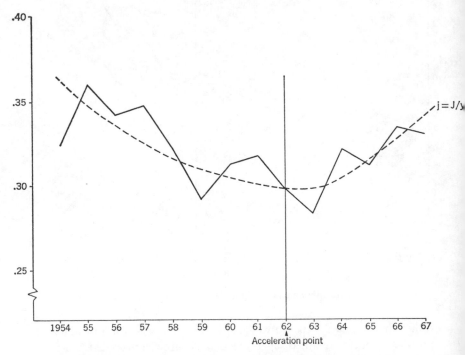

Diagram 8.6. Index of Agricultural Orientation, $j = J/y$: Thailand

curve is fitted to this time series by free hand. Notice that this curve is U-shaped with a turning point occurring at 1962 and coinciding with the acceleration point in diagram 8.3. This corroborates our theoretical prediction for a country with a slow start at export promotion (see curve I in diagram 8.1).

Our theory can predict such a turning point even when J is expanding at a constant rate, i. In the case of Thailand, we have observed (diagram 8.3) that J in fact accelerated from a slow growth rate to a more rapid one around the same turning point (i.e., the year 1962). Thus, the observed turning point phenomenon for j is due to the compounding of the endogenous force (i.e., based on the constancy of i) and an exogenous force (i.e., based on the acceleration of i).[23] Thus, from 1962 on, the economy, led by indigenous primary product expansion, exhibited an unmistakable tendency toward reverting to enclavism as industrial sector growth lagged behind primary product exports.

The major difference between Thailand and the two other countries (Taiwan and the Philippines) is that import substitution phenomena did not occur in Thailand. Import substitution can be measured either in the domestic market sense or the foreign exchange allocation sense (see chapter 6). Import substitution in the domestic market sense is measured here by the ratio of domestic manufactured goods output, y, to total availability of manufactured goods (i.e., the sum of domestic output, y, and imports, M_y). The time series for this ratio in the four countries are shown in diagram 8.7. Notice that in both the Philippines and Taiwan the ratio increased significantly until about 1959, signifying that in these countries the transition was begun by import substitution.[24] In Thailand, however, the ratio remained essentially constant in the first phase,[25]

23. In diagram 8.1, the exogenous force is represented by an upward shift of the parabola to the position labeled II, showing a higher value for i. The development path is now shown as $a, b, c, d, e, f, \ldots$ hastening the arrival of the turning point when j increases.

24. In Taiwan import substitution gave way to export substitution when industry developed an external orientation — as we have seen in chapter 6. In the Philippines, import substitution was prolonged after 1959 after the resumption of primary product export promotion (see chapter 7).

25. Notice that in Thailand there was a trend toward import substitution between 1950 and 1955. We have noted above that this attempt was abandoned in 1955.

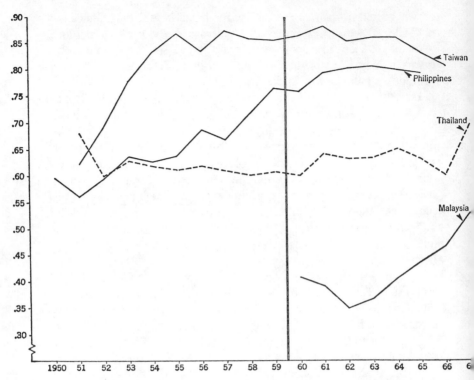

Diagram 8.7. Import Substitution, Domestic Market Sense,
$y/(y + M_y)$: Malaysia, Philippines, Taiwan, Thailand

signifying that import substitution was not operative. During the second phase, there is some indication of a slight tendency toward import substitution. Over the period as a whole, however, there is no significant increase in the domestic share of manufactured goods.

This conclusion is substantiated by a comparison of the four countries with regard to import substitution in the foreign exchange allocation sense. In diagram 8.8 the ratio of industrial consumer goods imports to total imports, M_y/M, is shown for the four countries. We observe a rapid and consistent decline in this ratio (until 1961) for both Taiwan and the Philippines, while for Thailand the ratio remains essentially constant until 1960, after which it behaves erratically. Thus, this import substitution measure also

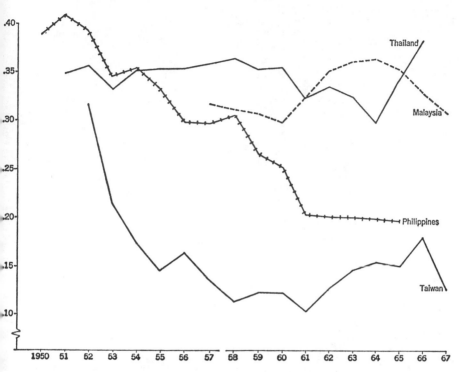

Diagram 8.8. Import Substitution, Foreign Exchange Allocation
Sense, M_y/M: Philippines, Taiwan, Thailand, Malaysia

demonstrates that import substitution failed to take hold in Thailand during the first generation of the transition.

In export promotion growth under neocolonialism, our theory envisages the maintenance of an external orientation, which may be empirically measured by the economy's export ratio (E/GDP). In diagram 8.9, this ratio is shown for the three countries. The U-shaped curve for this ratio for Thailand and the Philippines was rather similar, but was attributable to different causes in the two countries. In Thailand, the U-shaped time path of the export ratio (with a turning point near 1962) resembles (and thus corroborates) the U-shaped behavior of j in diagram 8.6.[26] In the first phase,

26. As a proxy for the export ratio measure of export orientation, we may use $J/(J + y) = 1/(1 + 1/j)$, which is an increasing function of j.

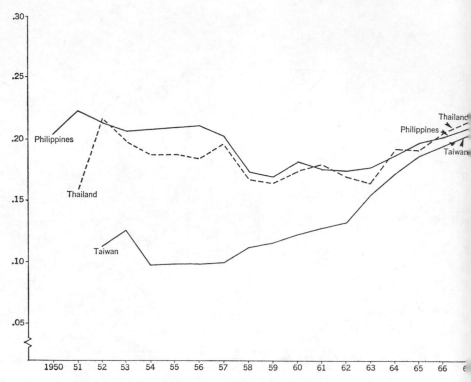

Diagram 8.9. Export Ratios, E/GDP: Philippines, Taiwan, Thailand

before 1962, the declining j was associated with an internal orientation, as reflected in the falling export ratio. This was reversed after 1962 signifying reversion to colonial enclavism, as the agricultural sector became increasingly tied up with the outside world through trade, and development of the industrial sector lagged. In the Philippines, a declining export orientation accompanied import substitution during the 1950s, and this trend was reversed only with efforts to prolong import substitution by promoting exports through the relaxation of controls (see chapter 7). In Taiwan, the relatively constant value of the economy's export ratio during the 1950s was replaced by a rapid rise in the 1960s, reflecting the export orientation associated with the phase of export substitution after 1959 (see chapter 6).

During the first generation of the transition, foreign capital flows played an important role in all less developed countries. This role, however, varied, depending on the nature of transition growth. In diagram 8.10, three year moving averages are shown for capital

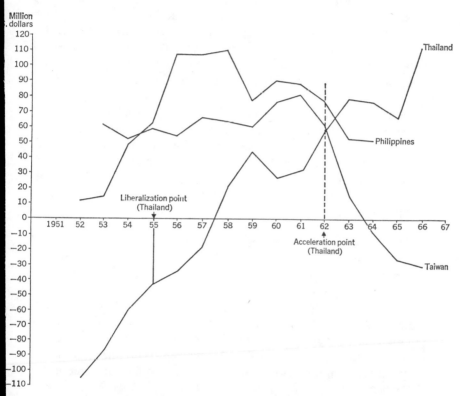

Diagram 8.10. Capital Inflow, *A*, 3-Year Moving Average: Philippines, Taiwan, Thailand (Million U.S. dollars)

flows for Thailand, the Philippines, and Taiwan. Taking the year 1962 as a reference year, we see that import substitution growth in the Philippines and Taiwan was accompanied by consistent use of foreign capital inflows which accommodated the import substitution process. The development of export substitution in Taiwan in the 1960s led not only to a termination of capital inflows but also to capital outflows after 1963. In the Philippines, the failure of export manufacturing industries to appear resulted in continued reliance on foreign capital inflows during prolongation of import substitution.

The record of capital flows in Thailand is very different and reflects the experience under export promotion growth. Following the colonial pattern, capital outflow occurred during the passive phase when primary product growth was slow, and capital inflow occurred during the active phase of rapid export expansion. We see verification of this thesis in a comparison of diagrams 8.3 and 8.10. During the 1950 decade, before the acceleration point, primary product exports expanded at a slow rate and capital outflow occurred. During the 1960s capital inflows grew rapidly in response to growing primary product exports and to the initiation of modest import substitution efforts. This capital movement experience suggests that capital inflows were a response to the liberalization policies adopted in 1955 and later, anticipating, or perhaps even precipitating, the acceleration which occurred after 1962.

Thailand's postwar economic experience confirms our typological characterization of the Thai economy as a neocolonial transition system. Once the strategy of primary product export promotion became firmly entrenched, growth was led by diversification of indigenous agricultural products. The acceleration of primary product exports and the economy's j index (index of agricultural orientation) after 1962 verify our theoretical conclusion that, under such a regime, rapid agricultural export growth will lead toward an agricultural orientation, at the expense of industrialization for the home market.

This signifies that Thailand retained the colonial characteristic of land-based growth during the first generation of postwar transition growth. It is true that the growth of indigenous product exports provided additional employment opportunities for the labor force. However, this expansion of employment was dependent upon the simultaneous opening of new arable land. This process of expanding labor employment is very different from that which occurs in export substitution growth where labor-intensive exports are based upon utilization of labor jointly with capital. In the long run, export substitution leads to more advanced transition growth phases, while Thailand's economy remains land-based.

This neocolonial growth system afforded Thailand modest increases in real per capita income, but the inherent threats to continued viability of the system are now becoming apparent. The tendency toward reversion to colonial enclavism and a growing agricultural orientation are producing a perceptible income deceleration effect, as predicted by our theory (see diagram 8.2). These symptoms are causing political pressures toward the adoption of a more aggressive industrialization strategy, involving greater import substitution. Assessment of growth rapidity and consideration of the typological issues raised can best be undertaken by comparison with the other countries in our study. This will be done in the concluding chapter where we adopt a typological approach to growth performance and development strategy issues.

9

Export Promotion Growth under
Neocolonialism: Malaysia

In this chapter we investigate another case of export promotion growth under neocolonialism as it occurred in Malaysia. In many basic respects, Malaysia's transition experience is similar to that of Thailand. Development continued to be based upon primary product export expansion, with little emphasis upon import substitution. Organizationally, a free market system prevailed to facilitate this export orientation and to accommodate the compromise between alien and indigenous participation in the economy. These organizational features and the accompanying mode of the economy's operation differ sharply from growth under economic nationalism as in the Philippines and Taiwan.

In certain important respects, however, transition experience in Malaysia and Thailand has differed. These differences are largely traced to the nature of primary product exports. While indigenous products dominated Thailand's exports, Malaysia concentrated upon modern export products. The operational difference between the two is described by the nature of inputs into the production process. In both cases export production must be accommodated by commercial and processing activities supplied to agriculture by the industrial sector. In the case of Malaysia, however, these services are supplemented by a significant flow of modern inputs from industry to export agriculture.[1] While the industrial sector provides

1. In the year 1965, for example, gross output of manufacturing was Malaysian $4,286 million, which was allocated as follows: export industries, $2,368; consumption, $1,014; and other, $904. This shows the dominant orientation of manufacturing to serve exports. Data from Malaysia, Department of Statistics, *Interindustry Accounts* (1960, 1965).

a passive servicing function in Thailand, industry actively stimulates primary product export expansion in Malaysia.[2]

The contrasting experience of the two countries is primarily a consequence of this basic distinction between indigenous and modern export products. The utilization of natural resources in Malaysia is based upon transmission of modern technology from abroad as, for example, in the production of rubber, tin, and palm oil. In contrast, native traditional technology is used in the production of indigenous product exports (e.g., rice) in Thailand. Hence, in Malaysia there is a sharper contrast between the modern export sector and traditional subsistence agriculture. This difference accentuates ethnic specialization. The modern export sector requires the presence of alien entrepreneurs (Chinese, British) while subsistence agriculture is the domain of indigenous Malays. This economic reality renders a political compromise between aliens and indigenous agents particularly crucial.

There is also a difference in respect to utilization of the primary products. In the case of indigenous products in Thailand, exports are a surplus accumulated after domestic consumption demand for food and other agricultural goods is satisfied. Hence the import of basic food requirements is not a crucial development issue. In Malaysia, however, the modern export products are not goods consumed domestically, and export earnings must be partly devoted to importation of food. Hence, the Malaysian economy is more open than Thailand's, and this is reflected in a larger foreign trade share (both exports and imports) in the economy. It also follows that import substitution for food constitutes a significant development issue in Malaysia while this is not true in Thailand.

These characteristics of the economy, which Malaysia inherited from colonialism, produced a sharp dichotomy between the modern enclave and the traditional agricultural sector, T, as depicted in diagram 9.1. The mode of operation in the inherited enclave continues to resemble that of colonialism, showing a triangular pattern

2. This distinction is based upon our familiarity with these countries. Statistical verification requires analysis of inputs into the primary product producing sector in an input-output framework. The necessary data is not yet available for Thailand. Malaysian data bear out our observation as the previous footnote indicates.

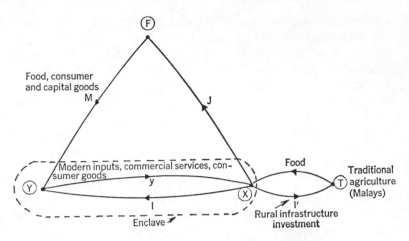

Diagram 9.1. Structure of the Malaysian Economy

of resource utilization. Primary product export earnings from the modern export sector, X, provide imports of both food and industrial goods to sustain the industrial sector, Y, which, in turn, delivers industrial goods and services, y, (including modern intermediate goods as well as commercial and processing services) to X in order to stimulate primary product expansion. The agricultural surplus generated by this triangular pattern is used mainly to augment productive capacity in the enclave through reinvestment, I.

The structural dichotomy between the enclave and traditional agriculture, T, coincides with ethnic specialization: minority groups dominate enclave functions and indigenous Malays are largely confined to T. During the colonial era, traditional agriculture remained isolated from the triangular growth dynamics in the enclave. As the transition got underway, however, the newly independent government sought to develop the traditional agricultural sector by diverting a part of the agricultural surplus to rural infrastructure investment, I', (e.g., roads, land clearing, irrigation). Though the enclave continues to dominate growth, the emphasis of rural development creates a second growth phenomenon, the gradual substitution of domestically produced food for food imports. This causes the country to gradually move toward food self-sufficiency.

Malaysia's enclave-dominated economy, with its concentration upon modern primary product exports, shows an excessive degree of openness to foreign trade. The result of this unique condition is that endogenous growth forces are complicated by exogenous influences transmitted from abroad. Fluctuations in world demand for Malaysia's primary product exports, reflected in changes in external terms of trade, produce sharp repercussions on the domestic economy, more so than in the other countries with lower foreign trade ratios. Hence, an understanding of Malaysia's postwar transition experience requires analysis of the impact of these exogenous influences upon the underlying endogenous growth process.

To summarize, Malaysia's transition experience closely resembles the typical colonial system of a highly export-oriented economy, with a modification involving efforts to develop traditional agriculture. In Malaysia's modern export economy, foreign entrepreneurship, capital, and technology continue as the essential ingredients that are transmitted from industry to agriculture to stimulate primary product export expansion. This process of expansion is highly sensitive to world market conditions. External stimulation and export expansion are vigorous only when world prices for primary products are favorable.

In such a highly export-oriented neocolonial economy, unfavorable world market conditions produce both short and long-run effects which dominate development policy. In the short run, declining prices for existing export products will induce efforts to diversify exports through exploitation of new land-based resources. In the long run, the country will confront the issue of shifting away from the colonial economy with its high degree of export specialization and its sensitivity to world market conditions. This will lead to the consideration of an import substitution strategy adapted to the necessity for political compromise between alien and indigenous interests.

1. Growth Led by Modern Export Products

Postwar transition growth in Malaysia has been characterized by the continued dominance of growth phenomena in the colonial enclave, although the traditional sector has played a secondary role.

The formal part of our analysis emphasizes the modern enclave. We also briefly touch upon the informal aspects of traditional sector growth.

1.1. The Model Structure

The growth model for analysis of the modern export case is based on a slight modification of the model presented in the previous chapter. In contrast to the indigenous export products, modern export products rely heavily upon modern inputs (e.g., fertilizer, insecticides, farm implements, and modern technology) delivered to the agricultural export sector by the industrial sector. Thus, in addition to consumer goods, processing, and commercial services (discussed in the last section), industrial goods, y, purchased by the agricultural sector, include such modern productive inputs. The source of productivity gains in the export sector in the present case lies in the injection of these modern inputs and the improved technology they embody. The model used for the modern export case is given by the following equations:

(9.1a) $y = hJp^{-\alpha}$

(9.1b) $y = K/k$

(9.1c) $I = a'p^{\beta}$

(9.1d) $dK/dt = I$

(9.1e) $dJ/dt = u(qy/J)^{\gamma}$ $u > 0$; $\gamma > 0$

Compared with the model in the last chapter, the only modification is that the last equation (8.1e) is now replaced by 9.1e. We now define qy as that part of industrial sector output, y, which constitutes modern productive inputs into agriculture and qy/J as modern inputs per unit of exports. The key behavioral assumption (equation 9.1e) may be referred to as the *agricultural stimulation function*, which states that the higher the value of modern inputs per unit of exports (qy/J), the larger will be the gain in output per unit of time (dJ/dt), with an elasticity $\gamma \geqq 0$ (and a coefficient, u).

Postulation of the agricultural stimulation function is based on the fact that modernization of agriculture originates from contact with the industrial sector, and that productivity gains are associated with the transmission of technology and resources embodied in modern inputs. This assumption is consistent with a learning-by-doing thesis, according to which greater application of modern inputs will not only affect the existing level of output but also will continue to engender productivity gain in the future.

The difference between this model and that of the last chapter signifies that the cause of primary product export growth is here governed by a different set of rules. Instead of assigning the momentum entirely to the agricultural sector, we now postulate that export growth derives from modernization resulting from the introduction of modern inputs to the agricultural sector from a source external to it. While the rate of expansion of primary product exports is given exogenously in the model of the previous chapter, it is determined endogenously in the modern export model of this chapter.

When transition growth is led by expansion of modern primary product exports, the industrial sector does not merely respond to export growth in a passive way, as in the previous case. Rather, it plays a positive role in stimulating primary product export growth. Unlike the indigenous product case, mutual growth stimulation occurs between the two sectors (agriculture and industry) of the dualistic economy. On the one hand, expansion of primary products exports, J, stimulates industrial investment, I, and capital accumulation, K, through income and price effects similar to the previous case. On the other hand, expansion of industrial output, y, and capital capacity, K, in turn stimulate primary product exports through the agricultural stimulation function. Thus, dynamic equilibrium in the present model is traced to the interaction of these mutually stimulating forces.

As in the indigenous export case, there are two key issues of development potential in this growth type, the balance and rapidity of growth. The first issue concerns the economy's orientation, as measured by the index, $j = J/K$. The heart of this issue is whether j will increase or decrease through time. Intuitively, when $j = J/K$ is large, a dominant agricultural sector will offer much stimulation to the relatively small industrial sector, while the reverse stimulation (i.e., industrial sector stimulation of agriculture) will be weak.

For a small value of j the opposite is true. Hence, if balanced growth is to eventuate, the value of j must be reasonably moderate, neither too large nor too small.

The second development issue is the rapidity of primary product export expansion, which is determined endogenously. However, as emphasized in the opening section of this chapter, this endogenous growth rate is strongly influenced by exogenous forces emanating from the world market. Anticipation of favorable primary product prices will stimulate investment activity. In the context of our model, such stimulation is reflected in higher values for the parameters a' and β, in the investment function of equation 9.1c.

1.2. Potential for Balanced Growth

To investigate the long-run development potential of this growth type, we express dJ/dt in terms of j (in equation 9.2a) and, through an expression for the rate of growth of J (equation 9.2b), we obtain the equation in 9.2c:

(9.2a) $dJ/dt = bj^{-\gamma}$ where $b = u(q/k)^{\gamma}$
      Proof: $dJ/dt = uq^{\gamma}(K/kJ)^{\gamma} = u(q/k)^{\gamma}j^{-\gamma}$ (by 9.1d, e)

(9.2b) $\eta_J = bj^{-1-\gamma}/K$
      Proof: $\eta_J = bj^{-\gamma}/J = bj^{-\gamma}/jK = bj^{-1-\gamma}/K$ (by 9.2a)

(9.2c) $K\eta_j = bj^{-1-\gamma} - aj^{\beta/\alpha}$ (by 8.3a, 8.4a and 9.2b)

To investigate behavior of the system, let j be measured on the horizontal axis and let the two terms on the right-hand side of equation 9.2c be represented by the two curves in the upper deck of diagram 9.2. The increasing curve represents stimulation of industrial investment (see equation 9.1c) while the decreasing curve represents stimulation of agricultural productivity. Notice that as relative strength shifts to agriculture (i.e., increasing j), stimulation of agricultural productivity is diminished because of the lagging industrial sector while stimulation of industrial investment increases. The two curves necessarily intersect at a point, E, determining a long-run stationary value for j, marked on the horizontal axis as j_e, the value of which is:

(9.3a) $j_e = (b/a)^v$ where

(9.3b) $v = \alpha/(\alpha + \beta + \gamma\alpha)$

(9.3c) $b = u(q/k)^\gamma$ and
$$a = a'(hk)^{\beta/\alpha}$$

If $K = 1$, we see from equation 9.2c that the vertical gap between the two curves in the upper deck is η_j, which may be represented by a negatively sloped curve, as in the lower deck of diagram 9.2. For a sequence of increasing values of K, e.g., K', K'', K''', . . . the corresponding values of η_j may be shown as a family of such curves,

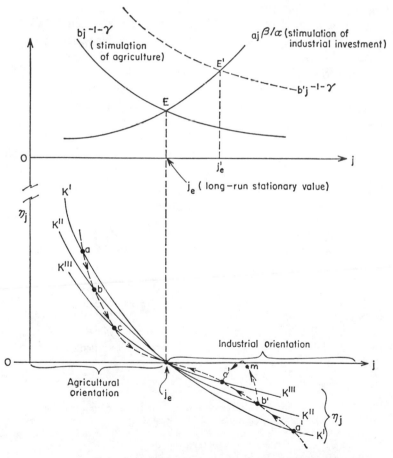

Diagram 9.2. Modern Export Economy: Long-run Potential

each indexed by a fixed value of K. Note that flatter curves are indexed by larger values of K.

Beginning with a point, a, lying between the origin and j_e, we observe that η_j is positive and the value of j moves increasingly toward the long-run stationary value, j_e. Simultaneously, an increase in the value of K causes a shift to a lower η_j curve. Thus, the typical growth path is shown by the dotted curve a, b, c, . . . toward j_e. Conversely, beginning from a point, a', beyond j_e, produces a growth path a', b', c', . . . representing decreasing values of j. Thus, j_e is the long-run stationary value of j.[3]

In diagram 9.3, with time measured on the horizontal axis, the behavior of j is represented by the two j curves which converge toward the long-run stationary value, j_e. The value of j increases monotonically to j_e if its initial value is less than j_e; otherwise, j decreases monotonically. There are two types of transient behavior toward the long-run equilibrium value, j_e, for j: an agricultural orientation (j increases) or an industrial orientation (j decreases). The latter will occur when the initial value for j is large (i.e., $j_e < j_0$). This is the case when a country does not initially have the industrial capacity to fully exploit the long-run balanced growth potential as shown by j_e. For less developed countries, this is obviously the normal case.

Thus, as a result of intersectoral interaction, growth led by modern export products will eventually lead to balanced growth. The agricultural and industrial sectors will grow in a proportional way characterized by a tendency toward constancy of price of industrial goods, p, and investment, I.

The long-run viability of this type of neocolonialism depends not only on the balanced growth phenomenon, but also on the rapidity of growth. Because of the long-run constancy of investment, I, in this model, capital stock, K, primary product exports, J, and industrial output, y, all grow linearly in the long-run as described by the pattern shown in diagram 9.3. Hence, the growth rate of all

3. When equations 9.3b and c are substituted into equation 9.3a, we can investigate the direction of changes in j_e resulting from changes in any of the parameters, u, α, k, γ, β, and q. It can be shown that j_e is an increasing function of u, q, and α, and a decreasing function of k, γ, and β — with obvious economic interpretations.

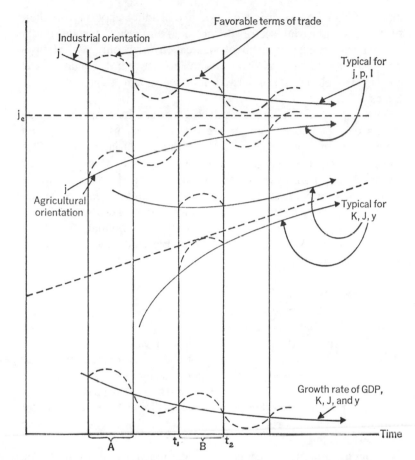

Diagram 9.3. Dynamic Equilibrium: Balanced Growth and
Retardation

these variables, as well as GDP, will approach zero, as indicated in the bottom curve. Thus we see that long-run balanced growth is accompanied by slow growth.

Colonial history offers abundant evidence on the inevitability of long-run stagnation. In spite of an initial flurry of investment activity associated with the introduction of modern export products in a colonial economy, the rate of growth eventually slackened and modest balanced expansion of primary product exports and their supporting industrial sector occurred. This result ensued under colonialism because investment was called forth only by anticipation of future profits based on favorable price trends for industrial goods. Neocolonialism inherited these long-run stagnation tendencies.

In summary, the inherent tendencies toward long-run stagnation in this type of neocolonialism are traced to exclusive reliance on the free market system for guiding entrepreneurial activity. This contrasts sharply with import substitution growth where economic nationalism is manifested in the forced transfer of profits to industrialists, who are favored by political measures to engage in nationalistic growth. In the absence of such encouragement in Malaysia, industrial investment, as guided by forces emanating from international markets, involves an inevitable tendency toward long-run stagnation.

1.3. Open Economy Complications

The model just presented is relevant to the closed economy. Since Malaysia is a highly open economy, the model structure must be extended and modified to take account of this fact. A dominant characteristic of an open economy of the neocolonial type is that the volume of primary product exports is highly sensitive to their prices, as determined in the world market. Favorable terms of trade (i.e., export prices/import prices) will cause an expansion of primary product exports, while unfavorable terms of trade will have the opposite effect.

To incorporate this open economy complication into our model, we reinterpret equation 9.1e in which the three parameters, u, q, and γ, are all affected by terms of trade, T (a higher value of T will cause a higher value for all three parameters). Referring to equation 9.3c, we see that the parameter b will also be positively related to favorable terms of trade. This can be summarized by:

(9.4) $b = f(T)$ with $db/dT > 0$

The impact of more favorable terms of trade on the economy can be analyzed in terms of both their long- and short-run effects. Referring back to diagram 9.2, more favorable terms of trade (higher T) will raise the curve labeled $bj^{-1-\gamma}$ (stimulation of agriculture curve) to a higher level, as shown by the dotted curve. The new long-run equilibrium point, E', leads to a long-run stationary value for j at j_e' which is greater than j_e. This confirms our intuition that more favorable terms of trade for a primary product export economy will lead to a higher degree of agricultural orientation in the long run.

It is well known that a primary product export economy is highly sensitive to short-run fluctuations in the international terms of trade. Such short-run fluctuations are superimposed on the long-run trends in the economy, analyzed in the last section. In diagram 9.2, let us suppose that a country is moving through a transition process shown by the sequence of points a', b', c', in the lower deck, signifying a steadily decreasing value for j. If between b' and c' there is a temporary improvement in the terms of trade, T, (i.e., the $bj^{-1-\gamma}$ curve in the upper deck is temporarily raised to the dotted position and then shifts back to the original position), the value of η_j will exhibit a temporary spurt upward, as shown by the curve b', m, c'. The rate of decrease of j is temporarily slackened. The value of j may even increase for a brief period if the favorable terms of trade effect is sufficiently strong.

In an unusually open economy, such as Malaysia, the long-run growth process is highly sensitive to these short-run fluctuations emanating from price changes in the world market. A short boom in world primary product prices may temporarily lead toward an agricultural orientation (i.e., increasing j). The long-run tendency toward a declining growth rate will also be briefly interrupted. Moreover, the transient export acceleration will normally be accompanied by increased capital inflow or reduced capital outflow, as foreign and domestic capital is attracted to export industries. An unusually open economy is characterized by a high export ratio (exports/GDP), and temporary export acceleration may be expected to cause a rapid increase in this ratio (and vice versa).

The imposition of short spurts of favorable international terms of trade upon the long-run paths may be pictured by a slight modification of diagram 9.3. Suppose during the phases marked A and B

on the horizontal axis there are brief rises in the terms of trade. These will cause temporary upward bulges in all of the growth curves shown, resulting in wavelike movements along the trendal paths. Each peak will reflect the most favorable terms of trade and each trough, the least favorable. The performance of the highly open primary product export economy will thus reflect a combination of the endogenous growth forces and the exogenous influences transmitted from abroad through terms of trade movements.

1.4. Development of Traditional Agriculture

While Malaysian transition growth has been dominated by this set of growth dynamics in the enclave, it has been supplemented by the beginning of development in the traditional agricultural sector. In order to incorporate traditional sector growth, the model of the previous section may be slightly modified. Earnings from primary product exports may be divided as follows:

$$(9.5) \quad J = y + I + I'$$

where y is purchases of industrial goods on current account, and the remainder $(I + I')$ constitutes the agricultural surplus or savings. This surplus is now divided into two parts: I is that part of the surplus under private control, either reinvested in the enclave or transferred abroad, while I' is that part which is channeled to the government through taxation of the export sector.

The previous section has been devoted exclusively to the disposition of private sector investment, I. The development significance of the public sector surplus, I', is that it is devoted to long-gestation rural infrastructure investment. This investment emphasizes the development of the economy's land-based resources, thereby benefitting both export and traditional agriculture. In traditional agriculture, the impact is mainly in terms of raising domestic productive capacity for food. This produces a tendency toward food import substitution, as domestic food production replaces imports. Throughout the transition, this phenomenon of the traditional agricultural sector is superimposed upon the dynamics of the enclave's growth as analyzed in the previous section.

2. EMPIRICAL VERIFICATION

We now turn to empirical verification of this modern, export-led transition system in Malaysia. Verification will emphasize the typological characteristics of this system as well as its operational aspects. The distinctive typological feature is the dominance of the export enclave in growth, with efforts to develop the traditional agricultural sector playing a supplementary role. The operational aspects include the economy's organization under the free market system and growth performance as measured by statistical data.

2.1. Typological Characteristics

The uninterrupted sway of the neocolonial system of export promotion growth in Malaysia deserves emphasis for its rarity. A peaceful transfer of sovereignty from the British to the newly independent government offered a climate for an effective compromise among several contending power groups, i.e., the former British colonial masters, the Chinese and Indian minorities who dominated the economic roles in the enclave, and the indigenous Malays to whom political power was transferred but whose economic base lay in the traditional agricultural sector. Neocolonialism emerged as an attempt to harmonize relationships among these interest groups with specialized economic functions. The result was a system which preserved the inherited colonial enclave, supplemented by efforts to integrate the backward Malayan traditional agricultural sector into the national economy.

Malaysia's system of export promotion growth did not require a period of decontrol and liberalization for its launching; it was rather a natural continuation of the colonial system, with some modifications associated with independence. The spirit of compromise was instrumental in preventing experimentation with a nationalistic control system, which marked decolonization in many newly independent countries. This difference is helpful in explaining the typological characteristics of Malaysian growth as distinguished from the import substitution growth in the Philippines and Taiwan.

Neocolonialism, as it emerged from this background in Malaysia, exhibited four typological characteristics: (1) abundance of land-based resources; (2) dominance of an export-oriented enclave; (3) ethnic specialization in economic functions; and (4) a rural development focus in public investment. We shall briefly discuss each of these characteristics.

Land abundance. Land abundance is a prerequisite for neocolonial growth based upon diversification of primary product exports and modern intermediate goods inputs. In Malaysia, primary product export expansion has been accompanied by expansion of the traditional sector to improve the economic status of the indigenous Malay component of the population. The supply of land available to Malaysia has been consistent with this land-based growth system. While West Malaysia itself possessed a land surplus at the time of independence (1957), this favorable land endowment was further enhanced by the merger with East Malaysia (Sabah and Sarawak) in 1963.[4] While population density per square kilometer was 65 in West Malaysia in 1967, it was only 8 in Sabah and 7 in Sarawak. The average population density for Malaysia as a whole is thus 22. This compares with a population density of 64 for Thailand, 116 for the Philippines, and 365 for Taiwan.[5]

Data verifying postwar expansion of land use are available only for West Malaysia. Table 9.1 shows cultivated area under agricultural crops for the period 1951–66. During this period, land under cultivation increased by one-fourth. Land devoted to export crops increased by 24 percent while that for domestic crops grew by 28 percent. After independence in 1957, land devoted to export crops grew slightly more rapidly than land under domestic crops.[6]

Economic geographers foresee the possibility of further expansion of cultivable land as well as access to unexploited mineral

4. Contemporary Malaysia contains West Malaysia (previously known as the Federation of Malaya) and East Malaysia (Sabah and Sarawak). West Malaysia accounted for 85 percent of Malaysia's estimated 1967 population of 10 million, but only 39 percent of its land area.
5. Data from United Nations, *Demographic Yearbook, 1967* (New York: United Nations, 1968).
6. In the East Malaysia area of Sabah, cultivated land devoted to export crops grew by 81 percent in the brief six-year period, 1960–66 (Malaysia, Department of Statistics, *Annual Bulletin of Statistics: Sabah, 1964–66*).

Table 9.1. West Malaysia: Cultivated Area
under Agricultural Crops

	Thousands of acres			Percentage increase		
Crop	1951	1957	1966	1951-57	1957-66	1951-66
Chiefly export						
Rubber	3557	3721	4342	5	17	22
Oil palm	97	116	304	20	162	213
Coconut	486	518	506	7	−2	4
Subtotal	4140	4355	5152	5	18	24
Chiefly domestic						
Rice	726	748	898	3	20	24
Fruits	161	214	239	33	12	48
Other food crops	67	107	124	60	16	85
Miscellaneous	116	124	108	7	−13	−7
Subtotal	1070	1193	1369	11	15	28
Total	5210	5548	6521	6	18	25

Source: Malaysia Department of Statistics, *Monthly Statistical Bulletin of West Malaysia* (August, 1968).

resources. According to one, "there is as yet no absolute shortage of land for settlement in the Federation, and indeed, provided that the market for Malayan export produce remained unsated, vast areas in the eastern two-thirds of the country could be planted with rubber, and many others might well be found to contain mineral deposits no less intrinsically valuable than those of the West." [7] Thus, despite the rapid increase in utilization of the society's natural resources during the postwar period, West Malaysia's land surplus does not appear to be nearing exhaustion. Moreover, land frontiers in East Malaysia have hardly begun to be exploited.

Dominance of the export-oriented enclave. Against this background of "unlimited supply of land," Malaysia entered the postwar transition with a predominantly export enclave economy. The dominance of enclave activities in the economy may be seen from table 9.2. At the time of Malaysian independence (1957), 78 percent of land under cultivation was devoted exclusively to export crops and 67 percent to the economy's major export, rubber. These

7. Charles A. Fisher, *Southeast Asia: A Social, Economic and Political Geography* (London: Methuen & Co., Ltd., 1964), p. 628.

Table 9.2. Allocation of Labor Force and Land, Malaysia, 1957
(Percentage of total)

Activity	Labor force	Land
Enclave		
Export agriculture	32	78
Rubber	29	67
Other	03	11
Mining	3	
Commercial services	32	
Manufacturing	6	
Total enclave	73	
Traditional agriculture		
Rice	19	13
Other	8	9
Total traditional agriculture	27	22

Sources: Table 9.1, and 1957 Census of Malaya.

percentages have remained unchanged after the first decade of independence. In addition, tin and other extractive exports (e.g., tim-
ber, iron ore) from the natural resource base grew rapidly during
this period.

The domination of the enclave in Malaysian economic activity
is further confirmed by the high degree of urbanization and its
rapid increase during the postwar period. The percentage of the
population living in urban areas was 35 percent in 1947 and 51
percent in 1957.[8] This high degree of urbanization is attributed by
Caldwell to the preeminence of the enclave sector in the economy.
The most fundamental indicator of the relative sizes of the export
enclave and the traditional agricultural sector is the share of the
total labor force absorbed by each, shown in table 9.2. In 1957
rice growing, the major traditional sector occupation, accounted for
only 19 percent of the employed labor force, compared to 29 percent engaged in rubber cultivation. In the same year, traditional
agriculture, as a whole, absorbed 27 percent of the labor force
while 73 percent were employed in the enclave, with export agri-

8. J. C. Caldwell, "The Demographic Background," in *The Political Economy of Independent Malaya*, ed. T. H. Silcock and E. K. Fisk (Berkeley:
University of California Press, 1963), p. 83.

culture alone absorbing 32 percent. Services, commerce, transport, storage, communication, building, and construction together absorbed 32 percent; mining 3 percent; and manufacturing 6 percent.

Ethnic specialization and income disparities. Malaysia's enclave-dominated economy, as inherited from colonialism, left a relatively high per capita income — in the neighborhood of U.S. $200 — at the time of independence in 1957. However, income was unequally distributed between the Malays and the Chinese and Indian minorities. While Chinese annual per capita income was approximately U.S. $280, and Indian, U.S. $225, Malay annual per capita income was only U.S. $120.[9] These discrepancies principally reflected the concentration of a large part of the Malay population in the low-income traditional agricultural sector and their relatively low level of attainment in the modern enclave sector. There is a historical basis for this income disparity. During the colonial period, indigenous Malays failed to assume entrepreneurial and managerial roles in the enclave as these roles continued to be dominated by aliens. The one exception was British tutelage of Malays for positions in the government bureaucracy.[10]

This pattern of ethnic specialization and income disparity was a basic factor affecting the society's choice of neocolonialism and its avoidance of nationalistic import substitution policies. As Golay points out:

> Inasmuch as the Malays are precluded by their economic backwardness from substituting for existing alien entrepreneurial and managerial resources and capital, policies of indigenism would benefit primarily citizens of Chinese and Indian descent. The absence of pressure on alien enterprise, therefore, is a manifestation of Malayism, rather than a denial of Malayan indigenism.[11]

Rural development focus in public investment. The enclave-dominated growth dynamics of Malaysia's economy have been supple-

9. Silcock and Fisk, appendix A, p. 279.
10. See Robert O. Tilman, "Education and Political Development in Malaysia," Yale University, Southeast Asia Studies, Reprint Series no. 27 (1968), especially section II.
11. Golay et al., *Underdevelopment and Economic Nationalism in Southeast Asia* (Ithaca: Cornell University Press, 1969), pp. 346–47.

mented by a public rural investment program which is entirely consistent with export promotion growth under neocolonial organization, as was also true in Thailand. (See previous chapter.) Two aspects of this program deserve emphasis. On the one hand, its agricultural orientation has strengthened the primary product export base of the growth system. On the other hand, the focus upon improving productivity in the traditional sector is a natural response to independence. The compromise solution which provided the political basis for neocolonialism endorsed the principle of elevating the depressed sector, populated by Malays, by application of resources made available from the primary product export surplus. Given the large size of the export-oriented enclave, the economy had historically been able to support a persistent food deficit without difficulty. The emphasis on modernizing traditional agriculture has stemmed not so much from the existence of this food deficit as from the political necessity to improve the welfare of the Malay component in the population, who are predominantly involved in subsistence food-crop agriculture. The impact of these programs, however, has reduced the economy's food deficiency, thus bolstering export promotion growth.

The rural focus of Malaysia's public development programs is apparent from both public pronouncements[12] and the actual public expenditure programs. The Ministry responsible for supervising and expediting the execution of national development plans, in fact, was known as the Ministry of Rural Development until 1964, when its name was changed to the Ministry of National and Rural Development. In the First and Second Malayan Five-Year Plans (1956–60 and 1961–65), expenditures for agriculture and Malay-oriented social services absorbed almost half of total expenditures, the remainder concentrated in infrastructure development. Such expenditure as was made for industrial development (2 percent of the total) was largely intended as assistance to Malay nationals. Expenditures for agricultural development emphasized both exports and the traditional sector, with rubber replanting alone rep-

12. This focus has been reiterated in each of the national plans (the First and Second Malayan Five-Year Plans and the First Malaysian Five-Year Plan).

resenting 16 percent of total development expenditures during the 1956–60 period.[13]

The concentration of social services upon efforts to modernize the Malay community have gone hand in hand with the rural infrastructure program. These efforts, according to Golay, "are concentrated presently in blanketing the countryside with agricultural extension, education, and public health services. At the same time a disproportionate share of public investment is allocated to feeder roads and other communication facilities, land settlement, and rural water supply and electrification works." [14]

The magnitude of the government's efforts to promote agricultural development and the improvement of the economic status of Malays in the traditional sector is indeed remarkable. One estimate places these expenditures during the 1963–65 period at 59 percent of total government expenditures, equivalent to at least one-eighth of the economy's real product.[15] Public expenditures were clearly financed from taxation of export enclave activities, since the country's tax structure was almost entirely oriented toward foreign trade and export production.[16] Thus, the massive program to raise the Malay-dominated traditional sector into modernization was fed by resources made available by the economy's export-oriented sector.

2.2. The Organizational System[17]

The organizational system adopted by the Malaysian government, and steadfastly adhered to since independence in 1957, reflects the force of the typological conditions just discussed. The compromise political arrangement which accompanied independence and which allowed Western residents, minority group, and indigenous Malays

13. Data in this paragraph are taken from First Malaysia Plan, 1966–70. For emphasis on rural development programs in the 1961–65 plan, see Clair Wilcox, *The Planning and Execution of Economic Development in Southeast Asia,* Harvard University, Center for International Affairs, Occasional Papers in International Affairs, no. 10 (January, 1965), pp. 23–24.

14. Golay et al., p. 344.

15. Ibid., p. 389.

16. Ibid., p. 353.

17. Only those aspects of Malaysia's free market system most relevant to our analysis are emphasized here. For a fuller description of the system as a whole, see Golay et al., chapter 6; and Silcock and Fisk, chapter 11.

212   *Empirical and Policy Application*

equal access to the export sector and domestic industrialization, required the continuation of the colonial laissez-faire system. Emphasis upon efficiency and competitiveness in export industries has precluded the use of control devices involving serious bias against exports. Nevertheless, the objective of advancing the economic position of the Malay segment of the population has been vigorously pursued, but without imposing serious limitations upon the free market system.

Because it is a highly open economy, as reflected in a ratio of exports to GNP near 50 percent, the test of Malaysia's maintenance of a free market system lies in the foreign trade arena. In this area, Malaysia stands out among less developed countries for the degree of restraint exercised in abstaining from the imposition of controls after independence was achieved. Flows of both factors and goods have remained relatively uncontrolled.[18] Capital movements have been subjected only to the restrictions applicable to the general sterling area. No quantitative restrictions have been imposed on foreign trade, and, in general, tariff policy has been employed for revenue, rather than for protection purposes.

Freedom of capital flows has been accompanied by freedom of entry for all nationalities, Western, Asian, and Malay, into domestic industries. The Malaysian government states, in its First Five-Year Plan, that "foreign entrepreneurs will be accorded the same incentives as local industrialists and, in addition, will continue to be given guarantees regarding the security of foreign investment."[19] The Pioneer Industries Ordinance, which seeks to promote industrial development by tax holidays, has been carried out with no serious distinctions between foreign and domestic investment.[20] Similarly, government assumes no direct role in industrial development and leaves industrialization to the dictates of the market. Assistance provided to Malay entrepreneurs takes the form of credit, training, and advisory services on a modest level. As we

18. An exception to the freedom of factor flows is the presence of politically induced barriers to immigration imposed to avoid the increase of minority group (Chinese and Indian) representation in the total population above the present politically volatile level of nearly 50 percent.
19. *First Malaysia Five-Year Plan* (Kuala Lumpur, 1965), p. 131.
20. Golay et al., pp. 376–79.

noted above, the government's major effort for Malay uplift has been concentrated in rural development programs.

Modest consumer goods industrialization has occurred in the absence of import controls and tariff protection. According to John Power, who has studied protection systems in several less developed countries, industrial development has been prompted by free market forces:

> Contrary to the experience of some less developed countries, the initial impetus to industrialization did not come from a sudden and drastic attempt to control imports . . . natural comparative advantage factors plus growth of the market played a larger role in initiating industrial growth in Malaysia than in many other countries more dependent on protection.[21]

There is a clear efficiency emphasis in official Malaysian government statements on the use of tariff policy for infant industry protection, a concern which has appeared in Malaysia only within recent years. While the government's principal role is defined as maintaining stability and providing proper incentives, infrastructure, and education,[22] attention has recently been given to protective tariffs, to be employed with a proper infant industry orientation, as is clear from the following official pronouncement on tariff policy:

> In recognition of the problems of infant industries and those which arise from the limited industrial experience of the country, major attention will be given to the imposition of protective tariffs and the establishment of common tariff arrangements for the whole of Malaysia . . . The government, however, is intent on ensuring that no more protection than is necessary will be accorded, for the cost of industrialization to the domestic consumer must be minimized . . . The growth of the industrial sector in the long run will demand that eventually production

21. John H. Power, "The Structure of Protection in West Malaysia," University of the Philippines, School of Economics, Discussion Paper no. 69-11 (July 8, 1969), p. 7.
22. See, for example, the statement in the *First Malaysian Five-Year Plan,* pp. 130–31.

be extended to supply not only the domestic market but also markets overseas. This makes it essential that domestic enterprise be constantly prodded to increase efficiency so that there will be progressive reductions in production costs.[23]

The system of tariff protection envisaged is very different from the indiscriminate use of tariff policy to foster rapid import substitution regardless of efficiency — the pattern which evolved in the Philippines (described in chapter 7). In implementing this moderate tariff policy in the 1960s, protection afforded to domestic manufacturing industries remained low as may be seen from table 9.3.

Table 9.3. Average Rates of Protection by Major Sectors, 1965
(In percentages)

	Value added	Whole product
Forestry	−17	−14
Mining	−17	−14
Rubber planting	0	0
Fishing	1	2
Agriculture and livestock	2	6
without tobacco	−1	4
Manufacturing	−5	2
without exports	14	8

Source: John H. Power, *The Structure of Protection in West Malaysia*, University of the Philippines, School of Economics, Discussion Paper no. 69-11 (8 July 1969), table 12, p. 3–12.

The average rates of protection offered are clearly modest when compared to other less developed countries. For all manufactures, for example, value added protection was slightly negative (−5 percent), compared to 52 percent in the Philippines. However, there was considerable variation of protection within the manufacturing sector, with some consumption goods industries receiving high levels of protection.[24] Nevertheless, these exceptions, which were introduced during the 1960s, represent isolated attempts to implement the infant industry principle in the case of a few indus-

23. Ibid., pp. 132–33.
24. Power, pp. 3–11.

tries rather than a broad policy of profit transfer and forced import substitution.

There is evidence, however, that a decade of neocolonial growth under relatively free markets may be producing stresses and strains that are pushing Malaysia toward more aggressive import substitution policies. Serious fluctuations in primary product export earnings and a persistent tendency toward rising capital flight have caused concern about the future of Malaysia's high degree of primary product export orientation under free markets. Moreover, the slow pace of industrialization (as predicted by our model) appears to be creating a revaluation of the political viability of the neocolonial system.

2.3. Growth Performance

We now turn to an examination of the Malaysian economy's growth performance during the postwar period, as reflected in statistical time series. We begin by comparing the experience of Malaysia with that of other countries in our study from a typological viewpoint. In certain respects, Malaysia's growth resembles that of Thailand since both countries, as examples of neocolonialism, contrast sharply with economic nationalism in Taiwan and the Philippines. There are also, however, unique characteristics of growth that distinguish Malaysia from Thailand.

A chief difference lies in the fact that Malaysia's exports are dominated by modern export products, while Thailand has concentrated upon indigenous export products. This difference produces a larger and more sharply defined enclave sector in Malaysia, reflected in a much higher export ratio. This particular colonial heritage means that Malaysia's long-run growth trends are more sensitive to short-run interruptions caused by fluctuations in the international terms of trade. This aspect of Malaysia's postwar growth was analyzed in our theory, and the theoretical conclusions will be verified in this section.

Typological comparisons. In diagram 9.4, the time series for total exports, E, and primary product exports, J, are shown, the vertical gap (labeled E_i) between the two representing manufactured exports. The striking feature is that exports are dominated by pri-

mary products throughout the entire period. This feature emphasizes similarity with Thailand, as can be seen by comparing this
diagram with the same series for Thailand in diagram 8.3.[25] The

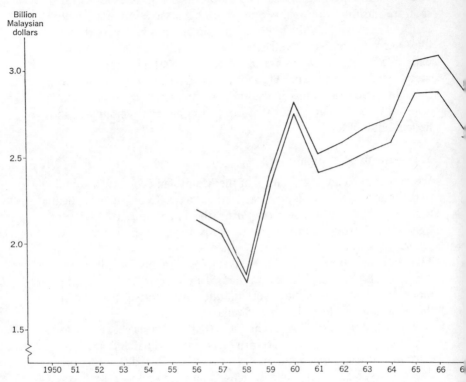

Diagram 9.4. Primary Product Exports, *J*, Industrial Exports, *E*ₜ,
and Total Exports, *E*

contrast of this feature of neocolonial growth with the export substitution experience of Taiwan is clearly apparent from diagram
8.4 in the previous chapter. While primary product exports as a
fraction of total exports declined drastically in the case of Taiwan,
there was little change in this ratio for either Malaysia or Thailand.

25. Data behind all diagrams in this section are presented in the Statistical
Appendix, tables 18–21 for chapter 9.

Another feature of neocolonialism is its avoidance of policies fostering rapid import substitution of industrial consumer goods (in contrast with economic nationalism). We have seen that import substitution can be measured in both the domestic market and foreign exchange allocation senses. Import substitution in the foreign exchange allocation sense is shown for the four countries in diagram 8.8 of the previous chapter. For the two countries pursuing a nationalistic growth strategy, Taiwan and the Philippines, we see a rapid decline in foreign exchange allocated to imported industrial consumer goods. Malaysia's performance in this respect resembles that of Thailand, with modest fluctuations in foreign exchange allocated to imported industrial consumer goods, around a nearly constant trend.

A comparison of import substitution in the domestic market sense for the four countries is shown in the last chapter's diagram 8.7. Two features of the Malaysian case stand out when compared with the other countries. First, the domestic market share of industrial consumer goods is consistently below the other countries, even in comparison to the other neocolonial country, Thailand. This signifies that Malaysia, in its reliance upon imported sources of supply of industrial consumer goods, entered the postwar transition with a stronger colonial tradition. Malaysia shares a second feature with Thailand: although the Malaysian time series is incomplete, we see that import substitution is only a recent and slow phenomenon compared to the earlier and rapid progress in the Philippines and Taiwan.

From this statistical evidence we conclude that Malaysia resembles Thailand in exhibiting neocolonial growth characteristics. As under colonialism, exports continued to be dominated by primary product exports. There was no tendency toward the emergence of labor-intensive manufactured exports, as there was in Taiwan under export substitution. Colonial dependence upon imported industrial goods was also maintained; very little import substitution occurred because domestic manufacturing industries failed to expand rapidly enough to substitute domestic for imported supplies.

In spite of the common characteristics of neocolonialism, there are significant differences between Malaysia and Thailand. A chief

difference lies in the nature of primary product exports. Our theory
has been developed on the assumption that Thailand's primary
product exports are dominated by indigenous, unprocessed products while Malaysia's are predominantly modern and processed.
The time series for composition of Malaysia's exports are shown
in diagram 9.5. Total exports, E, are disaggregated into four cate-

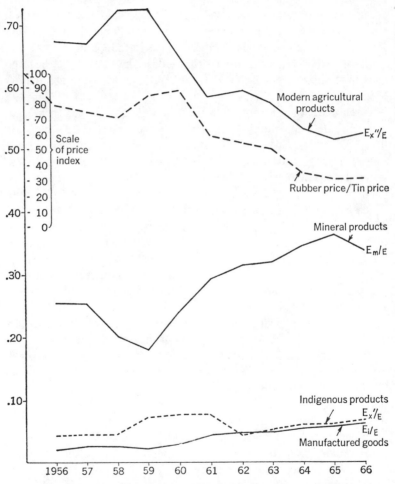

Diagram 9.5. Composition of West Malaysian Exports, 1955–66,
and Rubber/Tin Price Index

gories: (1) modern, processed agricultural products, E_x'', (e.g., rubber and palm oil); (2) mineral products, E_m, (e.g., tin); (3) indigenous, unprocessed agricultural products, E_x', and (4) manufactured products, E_i. The share of these four categories, measured as percentages of total exports, E, is shown.

Two characteristics of Malaysia's exports are emphasized by diagram 9.5. Total exports are completely dominated by modern export products (processed agricultural products, E_x'', and minerals, E_m), which together consistently account for over 90 percent of total exports. The residuals (unprocessed agricultural products, E_x', and manufactured goods E_i) remained insignificant and undeveloped during Malaysia's first decade of transition. Thus, as we assumed in our theory, Malaysia clearly represents a modern export case.

Typically, in a highly export-oriented colonial-type economy, the behavior of exports is dominated by the external force of prices as determined in the world market. Diagram 9.5 shows that a second major characteristic is compensatory movement of the two dominant components of Malaysia's exports. As mineral products gradually increase their share of total exports, the share of processed agricultural products falls. Using 1955 as a base year, the price parity between rubber and tin prices (i.e., rubber price/tin price) is shown by the dotted curve. We see that the long-run compensatory movement between the two major export categories can be explained by changes in the price parity. The long-run substitution of tin for rubber exports is caused by a deteriorating rubber price relative to tin. This price sensitivity of the composition of exports to external markets is characteristic of a highly developed colonial-type economy under a free market system.

The basic contrast between Malaysia and Thailand is brought out more sharply in diagram 9.6, which shows indigenous product exports, E_x', as a fraction of primary product exports, $J = E_x' + E_x'' + E_m$. For Thailand this ratio, E_x'/J, is reproduced from diagram 8.5 of the previous chapter. Thailand's primary product exports were consistently dominated by indigenous products (about two-thirds of the total), whereas in Malaysia, these products consistently accounted for less than 10 percent of primary product exports. This difference between the two countries reflects an un-

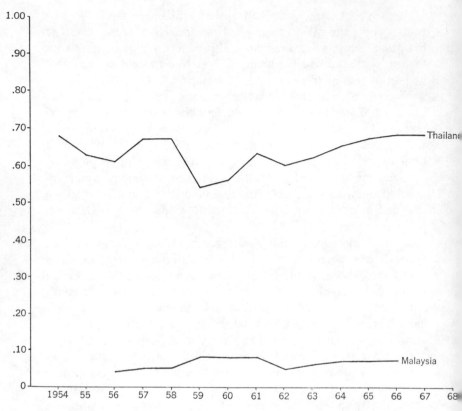

Diagram 9.6. Indigenous (Unprocessed) Products as Fraction of
Primary Product Exports (E_x'/J)

derlying contrast in factor endowments, a contrast which remained
essentially unchanged during the first generation of the transition.

Verification of theory. The Malaysian economy exhibits one of
the world's highest export ratios. In the top time series of diagram
9.7 Malaysia's export ratio (E/GDP) is shown. This series reveals
two significant features. First, the export ratio is high, fluctuating
between .42 and .51. From diagram 8.9 of the previous chapter
we see that Malaysia's export ratio is substantially above that for
the Philippines, Thailand and Taiwan. For the latter three countries the export ratios reach a maximum just over .20 which is less

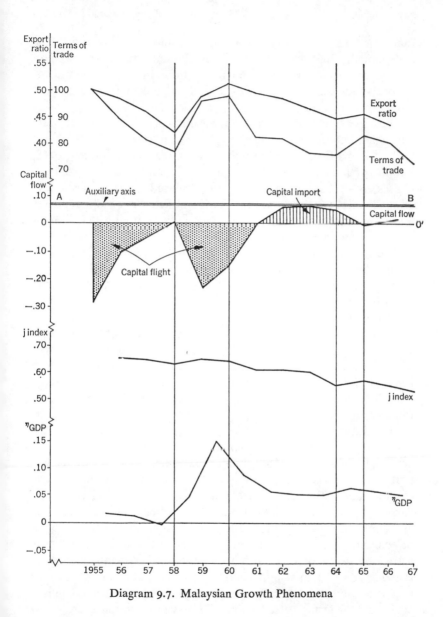

Diagram 9.7. Malaysian Growth Phenomena

than one-half of the minimum ratio exhibited by Malaysia. The exceptionally high export ratio in Malaysia renders the country extremely sensitive to short-run fluctuations in world demand for primary products, which is the second significant feature emphasized in diagram 9.7.

During the period 1955–66 the behavior of the export ratio alternated between increasing and decreasing phases. These phases are marked off by four vertical lines erected at the years 1958, 1960, 1964, and 1965. The export ratio increased in two brief phases, 1958–60 and 1964–65, and decreased in three phases covering all the remaining years. The identification of these phases assists in analyzing the short-run fluctuations in the behavior of the Malaysian economy.

The fluctuations in this highly open economy were determined mainly by variations in the international terms of trade, T. The time path of Malaysia's external terms of trade (price of exports/price of imports) is also shown in diagram 9.7. Our theory suggests that more favorable terms of trade will be associated with an increasing export ratio, and vice versa. This relationship is clearly verified by the time series for the export ratio and the terms of trade. Malaysia's export ratio increased precisely during those brief periods when the terms of trade became more favorable (1958–60 and 1964–65). In all other years, a decreasing export ratio accompanied worsening terms of trade.

Our theory has also emphasized that fluctuations in exports are associated with fluctuations in capital movements. Normally, under both colonialism and neocolonialism, a quickening of capital imports (or reduced capital outflow) may be expected during periods of more favorable terms of trade and export expansion (and vice versa). This thesis is valid when and only when political conditions are stable enough to permit capital movements solely on the basis of economic criteria. Capital inflows are shown in diagram 9.7 as a fraction of imports, A/M. The economic interpretation of A/M is the fraction of total imports financed by capital inflows. Notice that there is almost perfect symmetry between the capital inflow curve and the terms of trade curve. This symmetry, however, shows an inverse relationship between capital inflows and the terms of trade, directly contradicting the theory of capital movements under normal conditions, a contradiction that requires further elaboration.

Postwar transition growth in Malaysia has been overshadowed by decolonization and the problems of compromise among competing ethnic groups. In the climate of political uncertainty, Chinese entrepreneurs (who dominate in the control of capital) were reluctant to invest domestically, and were inclined toward capital export. This suggests the thesis of capital flight according to profit availability.

A straightforward thesis of capital flight according to profit availability may be portrayed in diagram 9.7 in the following way. Let the horizontal line, AB, be drawn as an auxiliary axis, so that the capital flow curve lies completely below AB. The capital inflow curve, A/M, now shows capital outflows throughout the period. The symmetry between the capital inflow curve and the terms of trade curve would then show an ideal case of capital flight according to profit availability. When the terms of trade improve, exports profits are larger, enabling greater capital flight. Conversely, with worsening terms of trade, the ability to transfer profits abroad is reduced.

This ideal thesis is an accurate description of reality to the extent that the auxiliary axis coincides with the actual zero axis, OO'. In other words, the thesis is an accurate description of Malaysian experience to the extent that capital export occurred in most years of the series and capital imports, when occurring, were small. The shaded areas in the diagram show that this was true. Capital imports occurred in moderate magnitude only during the brief period (1961–65) when the political compromise among ethnic groups appeared to be viable. We may conclude that for such a highly open economy as Malaysia, where reinvestment of export profits are crucial for growth, harmonious ethnic relationships are the most critical issue for viable transition growth.

A major growth performance indicator emphasized in our theory is the index of relative agricultural strength, $j = J/K$. This index, which is also shown in diagram 9.7, exhibits a clear downward trend over the period. This supports our theoretical conclusion that transition growth in this type of economy will involve an industrial orientation. The theory suggests that this is a natural outcome in an open economy with a high initial value for j and an undeveloped industrial sector—as was true in Malaysia. Our theory also predicts that this declining trend will sooner or later be arrested as the value of j approaches a long-run stationary value, j_e. However, this tendency is not yet apparent from the brief time series for Malaysia so that the present trend may be maintained for some time.

A second property of the j index is its short-run cyclical behavior. As our theory anticipated, short-run fluctuations in the value of j are superimposed upon the long-run declining trend. Diagram 9.7 shows two brief periods in which the declining trend was interrupted, 1958–60 and 1964–65. These interruptions occurred precisely during the periods when the terms of trade were improving, as predicted by our theory.

As we have noted, the long-run viability of neocolonialism is measured by the rapidity of growth. The time path of real GDP is shown in diagram 9.7 by the bottom curve, labeled η_{GDP}. The movement of the curve suggests sharp cyclical movements superimposed upon a long-run declining trend which became evident after 1960. The short-run cyclical movement is explained completely by the variations in international terms of trade. Temporary spurts in the GDP growth rate occurred precisely in those years when a noticeable improvement in the terms of trade took place (1958–60 and 1964–65).

The declining trend in the rate of growth of GDP after 1960 confirms our theory of the inevitability of the tendency toward long-run stagnation in this type of neocolonialism. If (as anticipated by our theory) this trend persists, we may expect that Malaysia will have to shift from excessive reliance upon land-based growth. The natural direction of this shift is toward the development of internally-oriented domestic industry through an import substitution strategy. Under this strategy, Malaysian entrepreneurship must be encouraged by policy measures appropriate for import substitution. Success at this strategy, however, will require ethnic harmony so that all ethnic groups may play their proper role in industrial entrepreneurship.

10

Conclusions and Policy Recommendations

Viewed from a historical perspective, the postwar growth experience of many less developed countries represents a transition process from a colonial heritage toward a modern growth epoch. In the colonial economy, growth was dominated by primary product exports, and income was mainly generated by the utilization of land-based resources in the agricultural sector. In modern economic growth, the economy's output is primarily created by human and capital resources, predominantly employed in the industrial sector. The transition process in open, dualistic economies thus involves a gradual modification of the land-based export economy through an industrialization process which involves interrelationships with the foreign sector.

Despite these common characteristics, actual transition growth experience in individual countries shows a variety of different patterns. Drastic modifications of economic structure during the transition process occur in the context of country variations in institutional, political, and economic-geographic background. These differences in initial conditions imply a need for a typological approach for analyzing postwar transition growth experience as well as for policy recommendations.

We have applied a typological approach for understanding transition growth in four Southeast Asian countries, Malaysia, the Philippines, Taiwan, and Thailand. In this chapter we first summarize the essential conclusions from this comparative approach, introducing data to assess performance under different transition growth systems. The policy implications of our findings will then be briefly considered.

1. Evaluation of Growth Performance

In order to assess growth performance of the four countries during the first generation of the transition, we employ both aggregative and disaggregative viewpoints. From the aggregate viewpoint, we use per capita real GDP to investigate the overall rapidity of growth. From the disaggregative viewpoint, we will examine the nature of structural change. In the context of open dualistic economies we examine (1) sectoral productivity change, (2) labor reallocation, and (3) the role of foreign trade. Comparison among the four countries will be emphasized, and growth performance will be interpreted with reference to transition phases identified in the preceding country chapters.

1.1. Aggregate Indicator of Growth Rapidity

The most important aggregate indicator of economic performance is real GDP per capita. Using 1955 as a base year, indices of real GDP per capita for the four countries are shown in diagram 10.1a.[1] It is immediately apparent that the performance of Taiwan

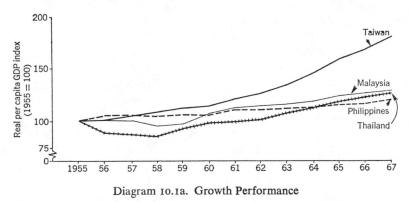

Diagram 10.1a. Growth Performance

stands apart from the other countries. Average annual growth rates over the twelve-year period 1955–67 were: Taiwan 5.1 percent, Thailand 2.0 percent, Malaysia 2.1 percent, and the

1. Data behind all diagrams in this section are presented in the Statistical Appendix, tables 22–25 for chapter 10.

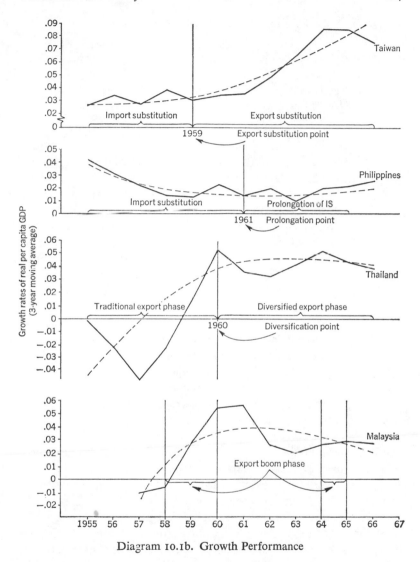

Diagram 10.1b. Growth Performance

Philippines 1.5 percent. Thus, Taiwan's growth rate was more than twice as high as the other three countries (see table 10.1).

When viewed in a long-run historical perspective of economic development, these rates of growth of real GDP per capita are

Table 10.1. Per Capita GDP Growth Rates

Country	Average annual growth rate	Decade growth rate
Taiwan	.051	.64
Malaysia	.021	.23
Thailand	.020	.22
Philippines	.015	.16

indeed quite high. They yield decade growth rates varying from a high of 64 percent for Taiwan to a low of 16 percent for the Philippines. These decade growth rates of real GDP per capita compare favorably with long period growth performance of industrially advanced countries during the epoch of modern economic growth. According to Kuznets, decade growth rates in fourteen modern growth economies were sustained at growth rates from 10 to 30 percent per decade, with "15 percent per decade as a typical low limit." [2] In these terms, the performance of Taiwan during the postwar transition period is quite remarkable. Even the Philippines, which grew least rapidly of the four countries, has performed rather well in this long-run perspective.

It may be concluded, from these performance records, that a transition to modern growth is clearly underway in these countries. The rapid growth rate in Taiwan was accompanied by a clear pattern of transformation in the economy. While a pattern of persistent structural change is not as apparent in the other three countries, it seems clear that in these countries the post–World War II period has ushered in an era in which growth has accelerated above the long-run colonial epoch trend. Although our analysis of these countries in previous chapters cited specific limitations and "failures," our overall assessment must be that there is a strong thrust toward modern economic growth.

This comparison of short-run transition growth experience with long-run growth experience of countries during the epoch of modern growth provides a historical perspective for understanding the significance of the transition growth period as a whole. In addition to a long-run historical perspective, however, we have adopted

2. Simon Kuznets, *Modern Economic Growth: Rate, Structure and Spread* (New Haven: Yale University Press, 1966), p. 67.

in this book a shorter time perspective to focus upon growth characteristics internal to the transition process. The short-run transition perspective requires an emphasis upon country diversity of growth experience, i.e., upon the typological differences which occur. We briefly recapitulate the typological conclusions from the preceding chapters.

All four countries began the transition with a primary product export economy, based upon utilization of land-based resources. Taiwan is the only country which completely altered this colonial heritage during the first generation of the transition by shifting to a labor-based export economy. A first major conclusion is that a high rate of per capita income growth (of 5-6 percent per year) requires a shift to a labor-based economy since continued reliance upon the land base yields only modest growth (about 2 percent).

The modification of economic structure which occurred in the four countries during the first generation of the transition was accomplished through a sequence of transition phases of short duration. In diagram 10.1b, the annual rates of growth (three-year moving averages) for real GDP per capita are plotted against the time axis, and short-run phases are identified for each country.

For Taiwan two distinct phases are marked off by an export substitution point in 1959. During the import substitution phase which lasted throughout the 1950 decade, domestic manufacturing industries grew rapidly. The domestic market for these goods was increasingly supplied from domestic output, freeing a growing volume of foreign exchange for importation of capital goods to spur the development of import substitution industries. During the subsequent export substitution phase, the central growth phenomenon consisted of rapid development of export capacity based upon labor-intensive manufactured goods. Among the four countries, the emergence of this labor-intensive export phase in Taiwan was a unique accomplishment enabled by the rapid growth of agricultural productivity during the preceding import substitution phase.

For the Philippines two distinct phases are marked off by the prolongation point in 1961. As in Taiwan, the transition was begun by an import substitution phase during the 1950 decade. Rapid development of import substitution industries produced market and foreign exchange substitution phenomena similar to Taiwan. In the Philippines, however, the initial import substitution phase showed termination tendencies as possibilities for further substitution became exhausted. This led to a second phase of prolongation of import substitution based on expansion of primary product exports. Export substitution did not occur because agricultural productivity remained stagnant, preventing a shift to labor-intensive manufacturing exports.

For Thailand two phases are marked off by a diversification point which occurred in 1960. During the first traditional export phase the major growth promotion force continued to be traditional indigenous export crops. During the second phase, the growth of primary product exports was accelerated mainly through diversification of indigenous export crops. Compared to Taiwan and the Philippines, the dominant growth characteristics of Thailand's postwar growth is the absence of import substitution and the retention of the colonial-type primary product export economy.

In the highly open economy of Malaysia, postwar transition growth experience was dominated by a combination of short-run cyclical and long-run growth forces. As in Thailand, a colonial primary product export base was retained as the major long-run growth force throughout the period, although in Malaysia, export products were modern goods, rather than the indigenous variety. Because of the extreme openness of the Malaysian economy, however, the transition phases were caused by fluctuations in international terms of trade, with brief phases of export boom occurring in 1958–60 and 1964–65.

The growth rates of real GDP per capita, shown for each country in diagram 10.1b, should be interpreted in the context of these transition phases. The dotted curves are fitted to the observed growth rates by freehand. Once again Taiwan's performance stands out as unique. While the growth rate was maintained at a moderately high level during the import substitution phase, marked acceleration occurred during the export substitution phase.

A comparison of the Taiwan and Philippine experience suggests that import substitution based on primary product exports has two characteristics. Initially, it provides an adequate rate of growth. Ultimately however, unless a new basis for growth is found, retardation occurs. Growth was accelerated in Taiwan only through the shift to a new growth regime. This suggests that in the case of a labor-abundant open economy, the development of labor-intensive manufactured exports offers the only feasible solution to exhaustion of import substitution growth.

Per capita growth rates for the other three countries (the Philippines, Malaysia, and Thailand) all exhibit a modest and eventually declining growth trend. Short-run improvements in primary product exports (e.g., diversification in Thailand, prolongation in the Philippines, and exogenous export booms in Malaysia) did indeed have a favorable effect on the rate of growth of per capita output. In the Philippines, the long-run declining growth trend was arrested by prolongation. In Thailand, export diversification reversed the negative growth rate occurring during the first phase, and in Malaysia, export booms produced temporary acceleration of the slow growth rate. However, in the long-run perspective these spurts were temporary phenomena which failed to produce sustained increases in the growth rate beyond the modest 1–2 percent level. This evidence emphasizes the limitations to growth under exclusive reliance upon primary product exports as the basic growth promotion force.

1.2. Sectoral Productivity Change

In diagram 10.2 the time paths of agricultural labor productivity, p, and industrial labor productivity, h, are shown, using 1955 as a base year.[3] The Philippines case stands out as unique on two counts. First, it is the only country in which the trends of labor productivity in both sectors show sharp divergence. Second, this divergence is caused by a declining trend for agricultural productivity, p, not observed in the three other countries.

Under neocolonial growth in Malaysia and Thailand, where import substitution was not pursued, gains in industrial productivity, h, were closely related to gains in agricultural productivity, p. This was true because the industrial sector merely accommodated the expansion of primary product exports. Hence, in neocolonial economies, balanced growth of industry and primary product ex-

3. Ideally, agricultural productivity should be disaggregated between export and domestic output. However, data are not available for this purpose.

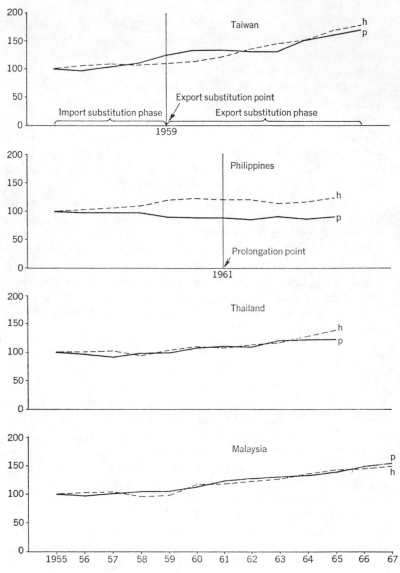

Diagram 10.2. Index of Labor Productivity in Agriculture, *p*, and Nonagriculture, *h* (1955 = 100)

ports (as analyzed earlier) is accompanied by balanced expansion of labor productivity in industry and agriculture.

In the case of Taiwan, agricultural modernization continued throughout the two phases of import substitution and export substitution, as indicated by gains in p and h of roughly the same magnitude over the entire period. Closer scrutiny of these gains between the two phases, however, reveals that agricultural productivity outpaced industrial productivity during the import substitution phase.[4] This strongly supports a thesis enunciated earlier that agricultural modernization during the import substitution phase is a precondition for successfully launching a subsequent export substitution phase. In contrast, during the export substitution phase, the gain in industrial productivity outpaced agricultural productivity.[5] Thus the rapid acceleration of growth of GDP per capita observed during the export substitution phase (diagram 10.1b) was caused mainly by a rapid expansion of labor efficiency in the industrial sector.

In the Philippines, declining agricultural productivity and a widening gap between p and h, noted earlier, occurred mainly in the import substitution phase.[6] Labor productivity in the industrial sector during this phase registered moderate gains.[7] Hence, deceleration of the rate of growth of per capita GDP during the import substitution phase (see diagram 10.1b) was caused primarily by falling agricultural productivity. This lagging growth of labor productivity in agriculture contributed to the exhaustion of the import substitution growth process. During the prolongation phase after 1961, labor productivity in both sectors remained completely stagnant. This signifies that prolongation of import substitution by promoting primary product exports is a mere holding operation, and that a new basis for progress in transition growth was needed.

Diagram 10.3 shows a comparison of agricultural productivity, p, and industrial productivity, h, among the four countries. Country

4. From 1955 to 1959, agricultural productivity rose by 24 percent, compared to 11 percent for industrial productivity.
5. From 1959 to 1966, industrial productivity gained by 60 percent, while agricultural productivity gained by 34 percent.
6. Agricultural productivity, p, in 1961 was 88 percent of the 1955 level, and remained essentially constant from 1961 to 1965.
7. From 1955 to 1961, industrial productivity grew by 18 percent.

a.

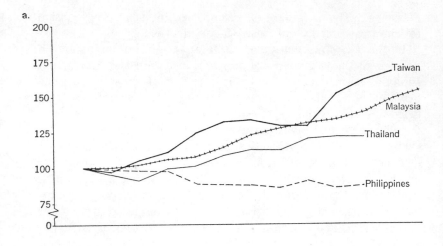

b.

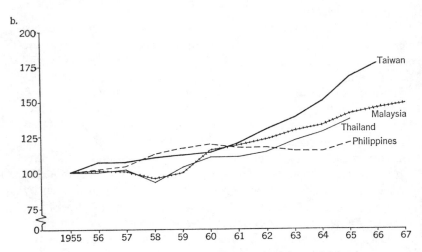

Diagram 10.3. Productivity Comparisons: Taiwan, Malaysia,
Thailand, and the Philippines
  a. Comparison of agricultural productivity, p (1955 = 100)
  b. Comparison of industrial productivity, h (1955 =100)

performance ranks are the same for labor productivity in the two sectors, the order being Taiwan, Malaysia, Thailand, and the Philippines. Quite apart from country typologies, this evidence underscores the conclusion that agricultural modernization is essential for industrial development. For the decade from 1955 to 1965, the gains in agricultural productivity were: Taiwan, 63 percent; Malaysia, 40 percent; Thailand, 21 percent; and the Philippines, −11 percent. Industrial sector gains were: Taiwan, 68 percent; Malaysia, 41 percent; Thailand, 38 percent; and the Philippines, 21 percent.

1.3. Intersectoral Labor Allocation

In the context of a dualistic economy, reallocation of labor from agriculture to nonagriculture constitutes a second major aspect of structural change[8] (in addition to sectoral productivity change, analyzed above). In diagram 10.4 the time path of the fraction, θ, of the labor force employed in the nonagricultural sector is shown for the four countries. Because of serious statistical data problems in employment data for all four countries, these data must be considered as indicative of only general tendencies rather than as precise measurements.

A casual inspection of country curves for θ shows that there has been a gain in θ in all four countries. In terms of Kuznets historical findings, this means that these countries have indeed shown a tendency toward modern growth in shifting the economy's center of gravity away from agriculture by reallocation of labor to the nonagricultural sector. The rapidity of the gains in θ may be first assessed by comparison with experience of advanced countries during the epoch of modern growth. According to Kuznets' data the United States and Japan were the two countries which showed the largest reallocation of labor from agriculture to nonagriculture.[9]

The long period change for θ in the United States and Japan is shown in table 10.2. In the United States over a period of 110

8. Simon Kuznets, chapter 3.
9. In the United States, the nonagricultural share of the labor force rose from 32 percent in 1840 to 88 percent in 1950; in Japan, the nonagriculture share rose from 15 percent in 1872 to 67 percent in 1960. Simon Kuznets, table 3.2, pp. 106–07.

a.

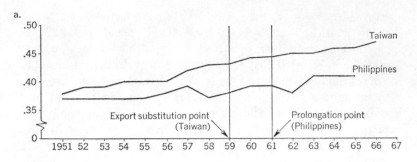

b.

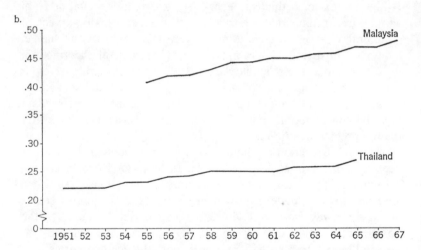

Diagram 10.4. Fraction of Labor Force Employed in Nonagriculture.
a. Import substitution countries: Taiwan, Philippines
b. Neocolonial countries: Thailand, Malaysia

years, the fraction of the labor force in nonagriculture (including both industry and services) increased from .32 to .88, a gain of 56 percentage points. Thus the per decade gain averaged 5.1 percentage points—as indicated in the last column. The corresponding figure for Japan's gain was 7 percentage points per decade. The short-run transition period changes for the four countries on which our study focuses are shown in the same table. Taiwan and Ma-

Conclusions and Policy Recommendations 237

Table 10.2. Fraction of the Labor Force in Nonagriculture, Θ:
Long-Period Change (United States and Japan)
and Short-Run Transition Change
(Other countries)

	Period	Duration (years)	Initial Θ	Terminal Θ	Gain	Gain per decade
Advanced countries						
United States	1840–50	110	.32	.88	.56	.051
Japan	1872–60	78	.15	.67	.52	.067
Import substitution countries						
Taiwan	1951–66	15	.38	.47	.09	.06
Philippines	1951–65	14	.37	.41	.04	.026
Neocolonial countries						
Malaysia	1955–67	12	.41	.48	.07	.058
Thailand	1951–65	14	.22	.27	.05	.035

Sources: For United States and Japan, Simon Kuznets, *Modern Economic Growth: Rate, Structure and Spread* (New Haven: Yale University Press, 1966), table 3.2, pp. 106-07; for other countries, see below, Statistical Appendix, table 25.

laysia registered changes per decade approaching Japan's average long-period gain; i.e., 6 percentage points in Taiwan and 5.8 in Malaysia. The Philippines and Thailand showed lower per-decade gains, i.e., 2.6 and 3.5 percentage points, respectively. Even these gains, however, compare favorably with advanced countries gains over the long period since reallocation in most countries proceeded less rapidly than in the United States and Japan.[10] This indicates that a transition to modern growth is indeed underway in all four countries.

From our typological viewpoint of transition growth, we must distinguish the import substitution countries (Taiwan and the Philippines) from the neocolonial countries (Malaysia and Thailand). Our theory suggests that in the import substitution countries, the nonagricultural sector gains were directly related to the expansion of manufacturing industries. By contrast, we would ex-

10. Examples of other per decade percentage point changes over the long-run are: Italy, .02; France, .027; Norway, .032; Sweden, .045; and Canada, .05.

pect that in the neocolonial countries, labor reallocation has been mainly to the nonagricultural services which accommodate primary product exports. These conclusions should be verified when more complete (and disaggregated) employment data become available.

The two import substitution countries, Taiwan and the Philippines, began the transition with essentially the same initial value for θ (.38 and .37, respectively). By the end of the period, however, there was a significant gap in the value of θ for the two countries (i.e., Taiwan .47; the Philippines .41). This reflects two major differences between these countries. First, the lack of agricultural productivity gains in agriculture in the Philippines prevented the agricultural sector from rapidly releasing labor. Second, labor absorption in Taiwan was accommodated by more labor-using technological adaptations than in the Philippines.

Viewing labor reallocation in the context of transition phases, it is apparent for Taiwan that much of the gain in θ occurred during the import substitution phase when θ rose from .38 to .43, a gain of 5 percentage points in eight years. This suggests that industrial development was already oriented toward labor-intensive techniques in this first transition phase, paving the way for the emergence of export substitution. In contrast, during the import substitution phase lasting ten years in the Philippines, there was a very small gain in θ, from .37 to .39. This signifies that the Philippines failed to develop labor-intensive manufactures, in turn explaining why export substitution failed to emerge. The success of Taiwan and the failure of the Philippines in shifting from land-based to labor-based growth is further confirmed by the consistent rise of θ in Taiwan and its erratic behavior in the Philippines during the period as a whole.[11]

In the neocolonial economies, Malaysia and Thailand, we first observe a large disparity in the initial values of θ.[12] This reflects the large export processing component in Malaysia's modern export economy, giving the economy a large export-oriented enclave and

---

11. In fact, in the Philippines, θ fell in 1958 and 1963.
12. In 1955 the value of θ was .23 in Thailand and .41 in Malaysia.

a very high export ratio. This contrasts with Thailand's emphasis on indigenous export products, requiring a smaller nonagricultural sector. These countries did not attempt to shift from a land-based to a labor-based economy during the first generation of the transition. We have seen that in Thailand export diversification after 1960 led to acceleration of the rate of growth of per capita GDP (diagram 10.1b). However, labor reallocation was insensitive to this acceleration of growth, as θ grew at a slow steady pace throughout the period. Malaysia exhibited the same labor reallocation phenomenon.

A question may be raised about the justification for considering the generation of postwar growth experience (1950–70) in the neocolonial countries of Malaysia and Thailand as transition growth.[13] A definitive answer to this question can perhaps be given only in long-run retrospect, for example, after a century of further growth experience. Even from our present vantage point, there is a firm basis for believing that transition growth has begun. Income acceleration has occurred based upon balanced expansion of both industrial and agricultural productivity. Moreover, in very recent years (since 1965), unmistakable tendencies toward import substitution policies have emerged. Finally, these economic changes have been accompanied by a marked rise in aspirations, providing the hope for continued momentum toward modern growth.

1.4. The Role of Foreign Trade

In an ex-colonial less developed country, the basic structure of the economy combines domestic dualism between agriculture and nonagriculture with a high degree of openness (foreign trade orientation) inherited from economic colonialism. The transition growth process involves interaction between the dualistic sectors and foreign trade as modernization occurs.

Under neocolonial transition growth, a high degree of external orientation is maintained since primary product exports remain as the basic vehicle for growth. Import substitution growth under economic nationalism precipitates a shift toward an internal growth

13. This question was raised by Professor Simon Kuznets.

orientation, although primary product exports are relied upon to provide the imported capital goods and domestic markets for launching this growth process. Under export substitution, domestic manufactures are produced for foreign markets and the economy adopts an external orientation. We have verified these differences in foreign trade orientation under the contrasting growth regimes in the four countries. Variations in export ratios were used to measure these differences in diagram 8.9 of chapter 8.

Our typology of transition growth is also based upon the composition of exports. Primary product exports continue to dominate total exports under both neocolonial and import substitution growth regimes. Only export substitution produces a sharp break from this colonial heritage as manufactured exports become dominant. These observations were verified by data in diagram 8.4 of chapter 8.

Finally, alternative patterns of transition growth produce significant differences in the composition of imports. Under import substitution, a rapid shift away from imports of consumer goods occurs as producer goods (capital and intermediate goods) come to dominate the import account. In neocolonial transition growth, however, this shift is much less perceptible. These differences were clearly shown from actual data for the four countries in diagram 8.8 of chapter 8.

2. Development Strategy and Policy Conclusions

The analysis of the transition in open dualistic economies has important strategy and policy implications for a large number of less developed countries. Our conclusions permeate three levels of government decision-making activities related to development. The most basic level involves the identification of development strategy to highlight the dominant growth issues over a specified time horizon. At the second level, planning for policy is needed to select policy instruments appropriate to the major growth issues implicit in a particular development strategy. Finally, policies may be supported by a third level of activities having to do with planning for resources, which involves using planning models to provide guidelines for allocation of resources.

2.1. Historical Perspective

When development policy is viewed in the historical perspective of transition growth (which is emphasized throughout this book), policy implications are mainly pertinent to the first two levels, overall development strategy and planning for consistent policy instruments.[14] In this historical perspective, two major guidelines to development policy emerge: typology and the evolutionary nature of transition growth.

Need for a typological approach. We have seen that transition growth involves pervasive economic change within a brief time horizon of one generation. Two characteristics of this process have been observed: (1) diversity of transition experience among different countries and (2) the phenomenon of sequences of brief transition phases (lasting approximately one decade) in individual countries. These typological features of transition growth have been verified by data from four countries in the first part of this chapter.

Although these short-run typological differences may seem less significant from the long-run view of transition growth,[15] they are of paramount importance in adapting development strategy and policy to conditions in individual countries. The essence of transition strategy is to identify and overcome by proper policies those crucial short-run bottlenecks which impede smooth transition growth.

Transition growth as an evolutionary process. Transition growth has been interpreted as an evolutionary process in which an economy traverses a sequence of phases that simultaneously transform its structure and its mode of operation. Successful transition growth requires a succession of phases in which progressively more advanced functions are acquired by the society, but the emergence of each phase is conditioned by the growth accomplishments in the

14. While we do not investigate "planning for resources" in this section, it is our view that planning of this type should be guided by and subordinate to strategy formulation and policy planning.

15. An example of the long-run historical perspective is found in the pioneering work of Simon Kuznets, in which development experience was viewed over a time horizon of 100–150 years.

preceding phase. Realistic development strategy must, therefore, be formulated in terms of alternatives based upon a particular society's heritage from immediately preceding transition phases. This evolutionary conception of transition growth provides a natural framework for emphasizing two types of policy implications from our study. On the one hand, we may evaluate the past transition experience of the four countries in retrospect as strategy lessons from growth accomplishments. On the other hand, a more forward-looking perspective is needed to consider the emergence of new growth phases in the future.

Development policy conclusions will be presented in the context of this typological and evolutionary perspective of postwar transition growth. Major policy conclusions are listed as S 1–S 20 ("S" standing for "summary conclusions" 1–20). In section 2.2 we concentrate upon lessons from past experience (S 1–S 8), while section 2.3 is concerned with conclusions (S 9–S 20) derived from a forward-looking perspective.

2.2. Lessons from Past Experience

Labor-surplus economies. At the end of the first generation of postwar transition growth (about 1970), the bulk of population living in less developed countries was concentrated in Asia.[16] A predominant characteristic of countries in the Asian region is the existence of labor-surplus economies. Among Asian countries, only a few clear exceptions may be noted, i.e., Burma, Malaysia, and Thailand.

Development of labor-surplus economies requires a special type of development strategy, focusing upon transformation of a land-based to a labor-based economy to provide employment and productive use of the economy's surplus labor. In applying this general strategy, a first distinction must be made between large and small labor-surplus countries. In the handful of large labor-surplus countries (e.g., China and India in Asia), employment opportunities must be primarily created by internally-oriented investment

16. Roughly speaking, population in less developed countries was distributed as follows: Asia, 1,700 million (of which China and India contained 1,250 million); Latin America, 245 million; Africa and the Middle East, 360 million.

(e.g., large-scale labor-intensive projects such as construction and irrigation). Smaller economies, however, have an alternative (not available to large countries) in view of their inherited openness to foreign trade. This opportunity consists of producing labor-intensive manufactures for the world market, providing import capacity for promoting development through acquisition of capital and intermediate goods which cannot yet be produced domestically.

Among the countries covered in this study, the Philippines and Taiwan represent small labor-surplus economies. The lessons from their transition experience are applicable to other countries in Asia and elsewhere which have begun the transition to modern growth. The experience of Taiwan, as presented in chapter 6, portrays successful pursuit of the strategy of shifting to labor-based manufactures for export. This experience leads to our first policy conclusion:

S 1: *In the case of a small, labor-surplus economy, the achievement of export substitution is an important and feasible initial goal of transition growth.*

In Taiwan, export substitution has offered more than a decade of unusually rapid growth, and this success is further confirmed by similar experience in South Korea. Hence, the strategy of export substitution may indeed facilitate a shift to a labor-based economy, providing rapid growth of output and employment, during the first generation of transition growth.

In the conclusions in this section, the experience of the Philippines and Taiwan will be emphasized, while the contrasting experience of Malaysia and Thailand will be considered in the next section.

The timing of export substitution growth. Export substitution is viewed as the basic strategy to enable the small labor-surplus economy to utilize its unemployed labor force efficiently. Our study suggests, however, that export substitution growth will not emerge as a direct outgrowth from the inherited colonial economy. An initial phase of import substitution growth is an essential precondition. This sequence was clearly shown in the chapter on Taiwan, and it is confirmed by South Korea's experience, where export substitution also emerged. This leads to our second development policy conclusion:

S 2: *For small, labor-surplus economies, export substitution growth must be preceded by a phase of import substitution growth. This preparatory phase lasts about ten years and export substitution will emerge if and only if growth accomplishments are favorable.*

This conclusion involves two evolutionary issues: (1) the necessity for an import substitution phase to precede export substitution, and (2) the conditions under which import substitution will terminate in export substitution rather than an alternative growth phase. These issues are discussed in order.

The import substitution strategy. The colonial economic heritage left two structural characteristics: (1) compartmentalization of growth between a relatively modern enclave and a large, backward agricultural sector and (2) domination of the enclave by primary product exports, with little or no manufacturing activities. This leads to identification of two major development tasks: integration of the economy through agricultural modernization, and industrialization. Small labor-surplus economies usually find it easier to initiate transition growth by concentrating on the second task, i.e., industrialization, achieved by pursuing an import substitution strategy.

In the colonial economy, the primary product producing enclave provided the source of the economy's export profits. After decolonization, utilization of this existing surplus to promote industrialization by indigenous entrepreneurs is facilitated by an import substitution strategy. Our earlier analysis produced several conclusions about this strategy which may be summarized here.

S 3: *The essence of an import substitution strategy is to transfer primary product export profits to industrial entrepreneurs. This strategy is carried out through several foreign trade-related policies.*

The policies typically employed are (1) overvaluation of domestic currency by an official exchange rate, (2) protective tariffs, (3) domestic price inflation, and (4) concessionary interest rates and other ancillary policies. In our detailed examination of these policies in chapter 3 it was shown that a set of these policies are mutually consistent to transfer export profits, and that they foster industrialization for the domestic market by invoking a supply of inexperienced indigenous entrepreneurs. The necessity to spark entrepreneurship and the export profit base employed for the purpose are both products of the colonial heritage.

Given the inherited trade orientation, these policies are administratively simple and they have powerful inducement effects. The appeal of the strategy is obvious; there is no need to adopt policies which pose greater institutional demands or which require venturing into unfamiliar tasks. Political feasibility is assured by the fact that the strategy favors a nascent indigenous entrepreneurial class at the expense of alien entrepreneurs (who dominated the colonial enclave). There is thus a natural tendency for indigenous industrialists to accede to political power, often in cooperation with military or other elite groups in the postindependence climate.

From the viewpoint of resource endowments, the import substitution strategy is a natural response to depletion of resources for expansion of primary product exports. In labor-surplus economies, where land resources are increasingly absorbed by traditional agriculture because of population pressure, a new direction in transition growth to replace the colonial primary product export orientation is imperative.

These background conditions leading to the common emergence of import substitution to initiate transition growth may be summarized:

S 4: *The import substitution strategy is a natural outgrowth of nationalism expressed in the displacement of alien entrepreneurs in favor of indigenous industrialists, and this tendency is reinforced by population pressure on land.*

These conditions are the general case in less developed countries. Where exceptions occur, as in Malaysia and Thailand, these typical background factors do not exert similar pressures toward adoption of the import substitution strategy.

Evolutionary significance of the import substitution phase. Adoption of an import substitution strategy typically offers very tangible results in rapid growth of industrial sector output (see diagram 6.6 of chapter 6 and diagram 7.12 of chapter 7). This performance, however, affects only the enclave, inherited from colonialism, leaving the second major task of transition growth, modernization of

traditional agriculture, untouched. In fact, the inherited compartmentalization of economy may be accentuated by the very nature
of import substitution growth.

Failure to integrate the large and backward agricultural sector
into the transition growth process is manifested in deceleration of
import substitution growth and its eventual termination, as we saw
in chapter 7. More significant from the viewpoint of evolutionary
transition growth, however, this deficiency prevents the emergence
of export substitution growth—a lesson brought out by comparison
between Taiwan and the Philippines. This leads to an important
strategy conclusion:

S 5: *Under normal circumstances, integration of the economy
through modernization of traditional agriculture is a prerequisite
for the emergence of export substitution growth.*

Agricultural modernization is needed, first, as a condition to enable the release of surplus labor for transfer to the industrial sector,
to be employed for production of labor-intensive exports. There is,
however, a second, and more basic, sense in which agricultural
productivity gains from modernization contribute to export substitution growth. Agricultural productivity gains permit the release
of labor to be accompanied by real savings from the agricultural
sector, in the form of food. This avoids diverting foreign exchange
to food imports, a phenomenon which appeared in the Philippines.
The difference in agricultural savings capacities in the Taiwan and
the Philippines are fundamental in explaining the emergence of
export substitution in Taiwan and its failure to appear in the Philippines.

The postwar transition experience of South Korea offers a quali-
fication to the generalization in S 5. Export substitution followed
an initial phase of import substitution growth without extensive
modernization of traditional agriculture. The explanation lies in the
fact that the acceleration of the domestic savings rate required for
export substitution growth was brought about by a massive inflow
of foreign capital. This fortuitous circumstance allowed 70 to 80
percent of domestic industrial investment to be financed from
foreign sources (rather than by mobilization of real savings from
agriculture).

In our evolutionary view of transition growth, import substitution has been regarded as a preparatory phase for the emergence of export substitution. Protection is provided to evoke a first wave of indigenous entrepreneurship in import-replacing industries. A shift to labor-intensive industrial growth, however, eventually depends upon the introduction of labor-using (capital-saving) technology in the industrial sector. It is only through such innovations that labor-intensive exports can emerge to replace primary product exports.

The policy measures associated with the import substitution strategy, however, typically involve a capital-using (labor-saving) bias. Overvalued domestic currency, tariff protection, and other instruments converge to perpetuate importation of capital-intensive technology. Where this tendency proceeds undiminished by government policy, industrial sector growth fails to absorb the economy's labor surplus. This conclusion may be summarized as follows:

S 6: *The import substitution strategy involves a labor-saving bias and where it is not mitigated in the IS phase impedes the emergence of export substitution.*

A comparison of labor reallocation to the industrial sector during the IS phase confirms the relevance of this conclusion. Utilization of the economy's surplus labor progressed during the IS phase in Taiwan while it remained sluggish in the Philippines (see diagram 10.4 of this chapter).

To sum up, the evolutionary significance of the IS phase is that with proper government policy, it lays the foundation for emergence of a phase of export substitution, which constitutes a shift to labor-based transition growth. The IS phase offers a temporary growth regime during which the more difficult task of agricultural modernization may be begun and it provides opportunities (through learning-by-doing) for entrepreneurs to shift to labor-using technology. When these two conditions are fulfilled, export substitution growth is likely to emerge and offer a relatively long phase of rapid income growth.

Liberalization and stabilization. Import substitution is a phase of transition growth during which the economy has a marked internal orientation, supported by policies which encourage production for the domestic market and discourage exports. When termination tendencies appear, there is a perceptible shift toward an external orientation. This shift occurred in both the Philippines and Taiwan, as seen from the rising export ratio after the import substitution phase (see diagram 8.9 of chapter 8). The composition of expanding exports which produced this common result, however, was very different in the two countries.

The similarity in the shift to export promotion after import substitution implies that development strategy takes on a distinctly different character, regardless of the nature of the subsequent growth phase. The essence of the change is relaxation of the control measures associated with the import substitution strategy, in particular reflected in adoption of a more realistic official exchange rate and restraint of domestic price inflation. Briefly this policy reorientation may be summarized under the two concepts of liberalization and stabilization. This conclusion may be stated:

S 7: *As import substitution shows termination tendencies, development policy shifts toward simultaneous liberalization and stabilization, both of which have clear-cut export expansion effects.*

In the Philippine case, export promotion policies were adopted because termination tendencies in import substitution growth produced marked retardation effects throughout the economy. The control measures of the IS phase had sharply discriminating effects against primary product exports, and these exports had remained sluggish throughout that phase. Liberalization and stabilization were undertaken to prolong import substitution by giving a new stimulus to primary product export expansion. The effectiveness of the export promotion policies can be seen from the data cited in chapter 7. A comparison of the closing gap between the official exchange rate, r, and the free market rate, b (diagram 7.14), and the growth of primary product exports (diagram 7.8) shows a dramatic export response to this liberalization policy.[17] This comparison also shows that during the retardation phase in the Philippines, falling primary product exports were associated with a growing squeeze on exports (increasing disparity between r and b). The policy change was effective in reversing this trend.

17. A similar reversal in Thailand in 1955, ending the early phase of bureaucratic industrialization, had similarly dramatic effects in accelerating primary product export expansion (see chapter 8).

The experience of Taiwan, as reviewed in chapter 6, shows that a similar combination of liberalization and stabilization policies produced a vigorous response in terms of export expansion. In Taiwan, however, the export response took the form of rapid expansion of manufactured goods exports, shifting the composition of exports from primary products toward industrial goods. Thus, we may conclude that liberalization and stabilization appear to be generally effective in promoting exports,[18] but that the shifting composition is attributable to other causes. In short:

S 8: *Liberalization and stabilization are effective policy devices to promote export expansion. In spite of this general effectiveness, however, they have limited significance in inducing evolutionary transition growth, i.e., in bringing about a shift from land-based to labor-based industrial exports.*

The transformation from a colonial land-based export economy to a labor-based export economy cannot be accomplished by mere trade-related policies. The root causes of this basic shift lie in modernization of agriculture and technological innovations in the industrial sector that emphasize labor-using techniques. These fundamental changes must be initiated during the IS phase if export substitution is to emerge upon the termination of import substitution growth.

2.3. *The Future Prognosis*

The usefulness of a typological approach to development strategy lies not only in its relevance for interpreting past transition growth experience but also in providing a framework to identify development strategy issues pertinent to future transition growth. In this section the latter forward-looking perspective will be applied to the four countries (Taiwan, the Philippines, Thailand, and Malaysia) whose transition growth experience has been analyzed in this study.

Taiwan: strategy beyond export substitution growth. Taiwan has already experienced more than a decade of export substitution growth. This phase has produced a historic shift from a land-based primary product export economy to an economy based on labor-

18. Similar policies adopted in South Korea also produced rapid export expansion.

intensive exports. This shift has induced rapid reallocation of surplus labor from the agricultural sector to industrial employment, causing a tendency toward termination of the initial labor-surplus condition. Taiwan is now approaching a transition phase in which labor scarcity will emerge as a dominant force in future transition growth. This tendency has been verified in chapter 6 (see diagram 6.11).

In the development literature, the exhaustion of an economy's labor surplus is referred to as the *commercialization point*.[19] The implications of this historic event in an economy's transition may be summarized as follows:

S 9: *With the termination of the labor-surplus condition, the industrial real wage increase will accelerate and be sustained at a higher level. This basic change will produce several consequences*: (1) a more rapid shift in income distribution favoring the labor class; (2) expansion of the domestic market; (3) a shift toward an internal orientation for the economy; (4) relative decline of property income and savings; (5) income deceleration (caused by item 4).

The fact that the industrial real wage will increase and be sustained at a higher level is a direct result of the termination of the labor-surplus condition. This signifies that the economy has escaped from its inherited land-based growth and traversed a period of labor-based growth. When this occurs, income distribution will shift toward labor (the high consumption group). The income shares of the high savings class (the industrial property class) will fall. This will cause a decline in the economy's savings rate and arrest the rapid income acceleration observed in the export substitution phase.

19. This point was first recognized by W. Arthur Lewis in his famous article, "Economic Development with Unlimited Supplies of Labor," *The Manchester School* 22 (May 1954). Lewis referred to this point as the "turning point" to signal the sharp increase in the industrial real wages associated with termination of the unlimited supply of labor. It was relabeled "commercialization point" to emphasize that the appearance of labor scarcity in agriculture produces, for the first time, equality between the agricultural real wage and labor's marginal productivity, so that the labor force will be henceforth used on a commercial basis. In our application of this concept to Taiwan, we view a "turning range," covering the period 1970–75. See also John C. H. Fei and Gustav Ranis, *Development of the Labor Surplus Economy* (Homewood, Illinois: Richard D. Irwin, Inc., 1964).

The rising share of wages will lead to an expansion of the domestic market, which in turn leads to rapid growth of expenditures on consumer durables (e.g., automobiles, refrigerators, air conditioners), and induces a shift from the external orientation of the export substitution phase toward the domestic market. We should therefore anticipate the earlier tendency toward rapid increase in the economy's export ratio to be arrested.

These changes will be accompanied by an underlying shift from a crude labor base to an economy whose growth emphasizes skilled labor and capital intensity. Development strategy must therefore be oriented toward preparation for this basic shift in the economy's productive factors. This preparatory strategy will be manifested in objectives in three crucial areas, agriculture, industry, and human resources. We may note that this conforms to our evolutionary view of development strategy and illustrates the principle of adapting policies to the emergence of a new transition growth phase.

In the agricultural sector, the exodus of labor during the export substitution phase and the appearance of the commercialization point will lead to substitution of capital for labor:

S 10: *Rising real wages in agriculture will induce a policy emphasis upon labor-saving innovation to prolong the export substitution phase.*

During the import substitution phase, agricultural development strategy focuses upon institutional programs (e.g., land reform, agricultural extension), modern inputs (e.g., fertilizer), and agricultural infrastructure (e.g., irrigation) to increase agricultural productivity in the context of labor-using objectives. With the appearance of labor scarcity during the export substitution phase, the objective of strategy is reversed to emphasize release of labor by adoption of labor-saving innovations. Government policies will now encourage land consolidation, mechanization, and long-term credit to promote the growth of larger scale commercial enterprise.

There are also implications for foreign trade policy:

S 11: *Foreign trade policy in the late export substitution phase will focus upon selective use of tariff protection to protect new industries engaged in backward-linkage import substitution (capital and industrial intermediate goods) and production of durable consumer goods.*

While the liberalization policies which accommodated the rise of export substitution must be continued in the market-oriented economy after the commercialization point, protective tariffs must be employed to protect infant industries engaged in introducing new technology for backward linkage and more sophisticated consumer goods. Japanese experience confirms the feasibility of this compromise between advancing consumer welfare and tariff adjustments consistent with dynamic changes in labor scarcity, capital abundance, and technological advance.

Growing reliance upon continuous acquisition of labor skills is imperative:

S 12: *Qualitative development of the labor force requires a strategy to promote technical and professional education.*

Educational policies will shift from emphasis upon mere literacy programs to specialized education for more advanced economic and social functions. An important objective in this connection is overcoming traditional preference for general education and degree status. Industrial and technological occupations must be elevated in status at the expense of generalists and civil servants. This educational emphasis will no doubt be an important vehicle for closing the education and technical gaps between the recent immigrants from the mainland and the Taiwanese (the earlier immigrants). This will enhance opportunities for political participation by the latter group.

The specific policies embraced by S 10 through S 12 are relevant to a strategy which offers new growth opportunities when the appearance of the commercialization point begins to terminate the labor-intensive growth system under export substitution. Increasing real wages will induce market adjustments to favor these changes in accord with shifts in factor endowments. Government policies may thus be viewed as facilitating the natural market response to the underlying transition forces operating in the economy.

The Philippines: strategy beyond prolonged import substitution growth. The Philippines' transition experience is common to many contemporary less developed countries. As described, the Philippines have had prolonged import substitution growth, which has not led to the more advanced phase of export substitution growth, as in Taiwan.

Import substitution growth has been emphasized by the organizational system in the Philippines throughout the postwar period. After six to seven years of effective growth under this system (1950–56), serious problems were encountered. Since the late 1950s the country's growth has been stalled by the near exhaustion of import substitution. Neither the emphasis on reviving primary product export promotion nor the rice production program contributed to solving this basic problem, although they did serve as palliatives to take the edge off emerging crises. As Philippine economists are well aware,[20] the major bottleneck is the failure of the industrial sector to penetrate export markets. In short:

S 13: *The crucial need for Philippine transition growth is to move into the next phase of export substitution.*

Two major policy areas are involved in overcoming the present stagnation of transition growth. First, and foremost, at both the public and private levels, a major reorientation toward productive efficiency in the industrial sector is needed to promote competitiveness of labor-intensive manufactures in foreign markets. Specifically, this means that Philippine industrial entrepreneurs must learn to dispense with the high levels of protection and subsidization and to abandon the capital-intensive technology that has marked the postwar era.

Second, emphasis upon general agricultural modernization is needed to provide a cheap labor supply and domestic raw materials as a basis for exports of manufactured goods. This effort imposes special requirements on the public sector to provide infrastructure investment for agricultural modernization (e.g., irrigation, marketing facilities, land reform, and improved transport). These preparatory conditions may be summarized as:

S 14: *To promote the emergence of a new phase of export substitution growth, priority in development strategy should be given to: (1) a stronger emphasis on stabilization and liberalization policies to correct the labor-saving industrial sector bias inherited from the IS phase, and (2) an aggressive program of public infrastructure investment to modernize traditional agriculture.*

20. See, for example, Gerardo P. Sicat, "A Design for Export-Oriented Industrial Development," Discussion Paper no. 67-5, mimeographed (University of the Philippines, School of Economics, June 20, 1967).

Thus, the fostering of political leadership to prod the society toward thoroughgoing agricultural modernization and industrial efficiency is the most general and crucial strategy issue. The deficiency in transition growth is traceable more to public leadership than to the response of private entrepreneurs.

Malaysia and Thailand: strategy beyond export promotion growth. Among the less developed countries in Asia, Malaysia and Thailand stand out as relatively unique in inheriting land-surplus economies from colonialism. While both countries have a low density of population, Malaysia has the additional advantage of a diversified natural resource base, making possible primary product export diversification. Because of the land-surplus condition, these countries have been able to continue to rely upon primary product export promotion during the first generation of transition growth.

This initial phase of transition growth under export promotion has brought moderate success, although a tendency toward long-run deceleration of income growth was observed in both countries (see diagram 10.1b of this chapter). Further, this tendency was predicted in our theory of transition growth as applied to both countries.[21] This suggests that the key issue in forward-looking development strategy is the duration of the present land-based export growth system:

S 15: *The crucial development strategy issue for countries pursuing neocolonial export promotion growth is the duration of this growth phase.*

Fundamental to assessment of growth prospects under this system is the potential supply of land-based resources for primary product export expansion. There is also a political issue, however, since the modest and declining growth rate is likely to generate pressures for a more promising transition growth system.

The Malaysian and Thailand land-surplus condition resembles the land abundance of several Latin American countries.[22] Transition experience in that area began in the 1930s and we have

21. For Thailand, see chapter 8, diagram 8.7 and for Malaysia, see chapter 9, pp. 10–12.
22. See Albert O. Hirschman, "The Political Economy of Import-Substituting Industrialization in Latin America," *Quarterly Journal of Economics* 82, no. 1 (February 1968).

observed several decades of import substitution growth superimposed on a primary product export base. This Latin American model is likely to emerge as the next transition phase in Malaysia and Thailand:

S 16: *Immediate development strategy issues in Malaysia and Thailand focus upon the emergence of an import substitution process superimposed upon a strong primary product export base.*

While the analysis of Latin American growth experience lies outside the scope of this book, several characteristics of that experience may be cited as relevant to future transition growth in Malaysia and Thailand. First, the growth phase combining import substitution and primary product export expansion is likely to be of relatively long duration (twenty to thirty years rather than one decade) because of the land-surplus condition. Second, the composition of exports is likely to undergo little change. Specifically, the phenomenon of a shift to labor-intensive exports (so conspicuous in the case of Taiwan) is not anticipated. Third, we expect a drastic shift in the structure of imports to complement the growth of industrial capital and technological capacity. Fourth, modernization of traditional agriculture is likely to proceed slowly because of emphasis on the agricultural export sector. This may be expected to produce a food-deficit situation, impeding the import substitution process — a phenomenon common to Latin American experience.

A prolonged phase of import substitution growth, mixed with primary product export promotion, will tend to cause subphases in the import substitution process, as the process works itself backward from consumer goods to capital and industrial intermediate goods. The notion of "backward-linkage import substitution," in fact, has been derived from observation of Latin America's postwar growth experience.

We may conclude that this pattern of prolonged import substitution is appropriate to the land-surplus condition in Malaysia and Thailand. Tendencies toward superimposition of import substitution on the initial postwar export promotion growth system are apparent in both countries. Thus:

S 17: *Development strategy in Malaysia and Thailand should be adapted to an emerging growth phase, of anticipated duration*

of twenty to thirty years, during which: (1) exports will continue
to consist of land-based primary products; (2) imports will undergo an import substitution process proceeding through several
categories, i.e., industrial consumer goods, industrial intermediate
goods, and capital and durable consumer goods.

The sequential order of this series of import substitution processes cannot be predicated in advance. The entire process may,
however, be dampened by the appearance of food deficits, causing
diversion of foreign exchange resources from import substitution
activities.

Transition from the inherited colonial economy toward a modern growth economy requires industrialization for the domestic
market. A phase of import substitution growth is a first step in this
direction, and this step requires a redirection of imports to accommodate industrial capital formation. This redirection involves profit
transfer from primary product exports to indigenous industrial entrepreneurs. If this strategy is to be implemented, political power
must shift in favor of industrialists. Antagonism against alien ethnic
minorities who dominate entrepreneurship in both countries is
clearly an obstacle to evolution of import substitution growth:

S 18: *Aggressive fostering of import substitution growth is impeded by political conditions which militate against employing the
profit transfer mechanism.*

As Kuznets has pointed out, nationalism is a prerequisite for
modern economic growth.[23] Expressed internally, nationalism implies the willingness to sacrifice particular group interests for the
advancement of society as a whole. This, in fact, is the heart of
the development strategy issue confronting Thailand and Malaysia,
especially the latter. This problem implies that profit transfer policies to accommodate evolution of the next transition growth phase
cannot be pursued aggressively at the outset. They will become
more feasible only as greater racial harmony is achieved.

The experience of Latin America teaches us that the Latin
American model of prolonged import substitution may involve
serious drawbacks. Aggressive profit transfer policies have caused
persistent inflation, food deficits, and balance of payments problems

23. Simon Kuznets, pp. 12–15.

almost universally. These symptoms have interfered with the efficiency of markets in stimulating technological improvements and moving toward export substitution. Failure to modernize traditional agriculture has intensified these difficulties. This experience suggests two final policy lessons which differ from the aggressive import substitution policies pursued in the labor surplus countries of the Philippines and Taiwan. These lessons are relevant for the emerging phase in Malaysia and Thailand:

S 19: *Import substitution should proceed in the context of maintenance of price and foreign exchange stability. Tariff protection should be selectively employed and profit transfers restrained to minimize disincentive effects on exports.*

S 20: *Profit transfers from primary product exports should not focus exclusively upon private entrepreneurs. Revenues should also be made available to the government to finance infrastructure investment in the traditional agricultural sector.*

3. POSTSCRIPT ON RESEARCH METHODOLOGY

Our study has emphasized a particular research methodology applied to development of contemporary less developed countries. In adopting a historical approach, typological differences among countries have been stressed in our research design. These two major strains in methodology have been woven together in our focus upon transition growth during the brief postwar time horizon (1950–70).

The historical approach is reflected in the very concept of transition growth as a process of change from the colonial economy epoch to a modern growth epoch. Because of the brevity of observed transition growth (roughly one generation), country experience exhibits a variety of alternative growth paths, accompanied by different sequences of short transition growth phases. The diversity of this transition growth experience underlines the importance of adapting development strategy and policy to the particular process of evolutionary transition growth occurring in a society.

Although the study has concentrated on open, dualistic economies and our empirical case studies have been confined to Southeast Asia, the research methodology we have advocated appears to be appropriate to further investigation of this and other types of developing economies throughout the less developed world. We recognize that more general application may uncover transition growth types (and sequences of phases) not found in our own geographically limited empirical coverage.

The typological approach, exemplified in this book, involves four steps in research procedure, which were, in fact, followed in the preparation of this study. We conclude by briefly recapitulating these steps used for the design of a typological approach to development research.

Step one consists of the identification of typological characteristics by scrutiny of inductive evidence. This first task emphasizes examination of country time series covering the relevant economic data mainly organized within a national income accounting framework appropriate to the general type of economy under investigation (in our case, open dualism).[24] Identification of finer typological differences among economies within this broad group requires comparison among countries, rather than examination of country series in isolation. This first step provides a rough sense of country classification as significant differences appear in the time series data.

The second step consists of constructing theories of transition growth for each individual country (or subgroups in the classification). At this stage, theorizing of the conventional type (involving concentration upon economic variables and neglecting institutional factors) is appropriate to explain the economic phenomena in the individual country behavior patterns. Examples in our study include the specific models constructed for Taiwan, the Philippines, Thailand, and Malaysia.

Step three is devoted to typological theorizing proper, explaining why individual countries exhibit variations in initial and subsequent transition growth phases. Relevant questions from our study include, for example, (1) why did the neocolonial countries (Thailand and Malaysia) initiate transition growth by primary product export promotion rather than import substitution; and (2) why did an initial phase of import substitution give rise to a subsequent phase of export substitution in Taiwan and not in the

24. Data includes aggregate and sectoral outputs, inputs, imports, exports, investment, savings, labor force etc.

Philippines? In our view the answers to these typological questions must be found in background institutional and resource factors, essentially in the resource endowments and the political and entrepreneurial heritage left by colonialism. Specifically, these factors are handled separately from the more formal economic theory used in the second step.

In the fourth and final step, development strategy and policy conclusions are deduced from the typological and economic theorizing. This step involves an evolutionary view of transition growth, applied to both strategy and policy lessons from past experience and future prognostication. This outlook emphasizes that conscious strategy and policy choices cannot be arbitrary if they are to promote development. Feasible policy alternatives are sharply limited by a country's growth accomplishments in previous transition growth phases.

These four steps emphasize analysis of economic aspects of transition growth, a process which has broader political, social, and cultural implications. A broader approach is particularly relevant to government strategy and policy. Analysis of policy issues in the past and future policy alternatives should both be examined in terms of their impact on different interest groups in the society. We have briefly considered some of these issues (e.g., the ethnic problems in Malaysia and Thailand and the political background of Philippine import substitution strategy). It is hoped that the present study will encourage interdisciplinary research for more penetrating analysis of these broader policy questions.

Statistical Appendix

This appendix presents actual data and sources behind diagrams employed in the text. Relevance of tables in the appendix to specific chapters and to specific diagrams is shown below:

For chapter 6: tables 1 and 2
For chapter 7: tables 3–10
    Table 3: diagram 7.8
    Table 4: diagram 7.9
    Table 5: diagram 7.10
    Table 6: diagram 7.11
    Table 7: diagram 7.12
    Table 8: diagram 7.13
    Table 9: diagram 7.14
    Table 10: diagram 7.15
For chapter 8: tables 11–17
    Table 11: diagram 8.3
    Table 12: diagram 8.4
    Table 13: diagram 8.6
    Table 14: diagram 8.7
    Table 15: diagram 8.8
    Table 16: diagram 8.9
    Table 17: diagram 8.10
For chapter 9: tables 18–21
    Table 18: diagram 9.4
    Table 19a: diagram 9.5
    Table 19b: diagram 9.5
    Table 20: diagram 9.6
    Table 21: diagram 9.7
For chapter 10: tables 22–25
    Table 22: diagram 10.1a
    Table 23: diagram 10.1b
    Table 24: diagrams 10.2, 10.3
    Table 25: diagram 10.4

Table 1. Time Series for Taiwan, Product and Employment
(Product in million constant 1964 N.T. dollars; employment in thousands)

Year	GDP	Y	X	I	R	W	F	h	p	w_i (1952 = 100)
1952	41,117	27,999	13,118	865	6,818	1,144	1,792	24,475	7,320	100.0
1953	44,426	29,319	15,307	1,292	7,770	1,133	1,812	25,877	8,448	106.3
1954	48,116	34,736	13,380	1,445	9,210	1,189	1,811	29,214	7,388	118.6
1955	51,828	36,896	14,932	1,072	9,661	1,214	1,812	30,392	8,241	119.0
1956	54,488	38,935	15,553	1,466	10,985	1,199	1,806	32,473	8,612	111.3
1957	58,574	42,725	15,849	1,802	12,420	1,300	1,810	32,865	8,756	105.5
1958	62,798	46,037	16,761	1,766	13,211	1,365	1,813	33,727	9,245	105.2
1959	67,375	49,698	17,677	1,824	15,735	1,419	1,853	35,023	9,540	99.6
1960	71,576	52,193	19,383	2,368	23,107	1,467	1,877	35,578	10,327	106.4
1961	77,073	55,957	21,116	2,639	24,867	1,517	1,912	36,887	11,044	122.8
1962	82,237	61,682	20,555	2,558	26,163	1,568	1,936	39,338	10,617	123.4
1963	91,092	69,970	21,112	3,145	26,280	1,645	1,972	42,535	10,706	126.7
1964	103,288	78,106	25,182	4,604	34,694	1,700	2,010	45,945	12,528	131.7
1965	115,541	89,534	26,007	5,591	39,992	1,738	2,017	51,516	12,894	146.6
1966	126,358	99,226	27,132	7,020	34,448	1,820	2,050	54,520	13,235	158.7
1967	138,911	110,447	28,464	9,794	42,116	2,087	2,043	52,921	13,932	166.2

Sources: *GDP* and components from Directorate-General of Budgets, Accounts and Statistics, *National Income of the Republic of China*, various issues.

Employment by sector from Department of Civil Affairs, Taiwan Provincial Government, *Household Registration Statistics of Taiwan, Republic of China*.

Wage index from Directorate-General of Budgets, Accounts and Statistics, *Statistical Abstract of the Republic of China*; and Department of Reconstruction, Taiwan Provincial Government, *Report of Taiwan Labor Statistics*.

R and *I* from Input-Output table for 1955, compiled by T. H. Lee, S. C. Shieh, and Y. C. Wang, 1961; Input-Output tables for 1964 and 1966, compiled by the Council for International Economic Cooperation and Development, Taipei, Taiwan.

Note: Definition of symbols.

GDP:	Gross domestic product	*W:*	Employment in nonagricultural sector
Y:	Nonagricultural value added	*F:*	Employment in agricultural sector
X:	Agricultural value added	*h:*	Labor productivity in nonagricultural sector
I:	Domestically produced capital goods	*p:*	Labor productivity in agricultural sector
R:	Domestically produced raw materials	w_i:	Industrial real wage

Table 2. Time Series for Taiwan, Foreign Trade

(All foreign trade flows in million constant N.T. dollars; exchange rates in actual current N.T. dollars)

Year	M	M_y	M_z	M_p	M_i	M_R	E	E_x	E_y	A	r	b
1952	7,077	2,251	775	4,051	795	3,256	4,640	4,354	286	2,437	12.30	23.11
1953	7,358	1,597	714	5,047	907	4,140	5,618	5,251	367	1,740	15.02	26.49
1954	7,397	1,294	1,042	5,061	948	4,113	4,207	3,610	597	3,190	15.55	30.31
1955	6,427	945	610	4,872	870	4,002	5,085	4,358	727	1,369	23.35	39.84
1956	8,002	1,313	783	5,906	1,388	4,518	5,384	4,364	1,020	2,618	23.35	38.53
1957	8,478	1,166	626	6,686	1,536	5,150	5,885	4,950	935	2,593	23.35	38.40
1958	9,836	1,132	958	7,746	1,837	5,909	7,057	5,636	1,421	2,779	36.85	46.58
1959	10,164	1,246	697	8,221	2,191	6,030	7,808	5,212	2,596	2,356	39.70	45.26
1960	10,940	1,349	970	8,621	2,615	6,006	8,769	5,052	3,717	2,171	39.85	42.26
1961	12,453	1,295	1,274	9,884	2,844	7,040	9,933	4,589	5,344	4,720	40.03	43.89
1962	13,794	1,777	1,347	10,670	2,516	8,154	10,915	3,645	7,270	2,879	40.03	47.00
1963	14,106	2,095	1,994	10,017	2,230	7,787	14,168	6,176	7,992	— 62	40.03	42.50
1964	16,936	2,640	1,549	12,747	3,038	9,709	17,879	7,983	9,896	— 943	40.03	45.80
1965	21,452	3,261	1,514	16,677	5,170	11,507	21,633	7,987	13,646	— 181	40.03	41.63
1966	22,559	4,103	1,482	16,974	5,392	11,582	24,672	6,758	17,914	−2,113	40.03	41.00
1967	27,924	3,574	1,815	22,535	7,439	15,096	29,271	5,722	23,549	−1,347	40.03	41.50

Sources: Foreign trade flows from Chinese Maritime Customs, Statistical Department, Inspectorate General of Customs, *The Trade of China,* Statistical series no. 1.

Exchange rates: *b*, from The Central Bank of China; *r* is the official export rate found in International Monetary Fund, *International Financial Statistics,* various issues.

Note: Definition of symbols.

M: Total imports
M_y: Imports of industrial consumer goods
M_z: Imports of agricultural consumer goods
M_p: Imports of producer goods
M_i: Imports of capital goods
M_R: Imports of raw materials

E: Total exports
E_z: Agricultural exports
E_y: Industrial exports
A: Import surplus (equals capital inflow)
r: Official exchange rate
b: Free market exchange rate

Table 3. Export Series
(Million pesos, constant 1955 prices)

Merchandise exports

Year	E_x	E_m	$E_x + E_m$	E_i	E^a	E/GDP^a	E_m/E_x
1950	730	58	788	19	807	.204	.079
1951	897	108	1,005	24	1,029	.222	.120
1952	856	164	1,020	29	1,049	.214	.192
1953	794	162	956	34	990	.208	.204
1954	912	207	1,119	24	1,143	.209	.227
1955	993	266	1,259	31	1,290	.210	.268
1956	1,091	343	1,434	32	1,466	.212	.314
1957	1,093	342	1,435	35	1,470	.203	.313
1958	965	334	1,299	41	1,340	.175	.346
1959	953	350	1,303	63	1,366	.170	.367
1960	1,085	430	1,515	54	1,569	.182	.396
1961	1,082	497	1,579	69	1,648	.176	.459
1962	1,128	516	1,644	88	1,732	.175	.457
1963	1,233	579	1,812	99	1,911	.178	.470
1964	1,332	561	1,893	135	2,028	.187	.421
1965	1,286	642	1,928	131	2,059	.197	.499

Source: Basic data for exports and components are obtained from George L. Hicks and Geoffrey McNicoll, *Trade and Growth in the Philippines: An Open, Dual Economy* (Ithaca: Cornell University Press, 1971), table 5, p. 49.

Note: Definition of symbols.
E_x: Agricultural exports
E_m: Extractive exports
E_i: Industrial exports
E: Total exports

   a. Total exports here includes all foreign exchange earnings from merchandise and service exports. See Douglas S. Paauw, "The Philippines: Estimates of Flows in the Open, Dualistic Economy Framework, 1949–1965," NPA, mimeographed (February 1968), p. 39.

Table 4. Comparison: Taiwan and Philippines

	Labor productivity in agriculture (1952 = 1.00)		Ratio of industrial exports to total exports, E_i/E	
Year	Taiwan	Philippines	Taiwan	Philippines
1952	1.00	1.00	.062	.028
1953	1.15	1.09	.065	.034
1954	1.01	1.11	.142	.021
1955	1.13	1.12	.143	.024
1956	1.18	1.10	.189	.022
1957	1.20	1.10	.159	.024
1958	1.26	1.10	.201	.031
1959	1.30	1.00	.332	.046
1960	1.41	.99	.424	.034
1961	1.51	.99	.538	.042
1962	1.45	.95	.666	.051
1963	1.46	1.01	.564	.052
1964	1.71	.96	.553	.067
1965	1.76	.99	.631	.064

Sources:

Agricultural Productivity: For Taiwan, agricultural product derived from Directorate-General of Budgets, Accounts and Statistics, *National Income of the Republic of China*, various issues. Agricultural employment from Department of Civil Affairs, Taiwan Provincial Government, *Household Registration Statistics of Taiwan.* For the Philippines, agricultural product from D. S. Paauw, "The Philippines: Estimates of Flows in the Open, Dualistic Economy Framework, 1949–1965," NPA, mimeographed (February, 1968), p. 101. Employment data from Bureau of Census and Statistics, *Philippine Survey of Households Bulletin* and Central Bank of the Philippines, *Statistical Bulletin.*

E_i/E: For Taiwan, export disaggregation from Chinese Maritime Customs, Statistical Department, Inspectorate General of Customs, *The Trade of China*, statistical series no. 1. For the Philippines, see Statistical Appendix, above, table 3.

Note: For definition of symbols, see table 3.

Table 5. Import Substitution, Domestic Market Sense

Year	M_y	y	M_y/y	$\eta_{M_v/y}$ (annual growth)	$\eta_{M_v/y}$ (3-year average)
1949	764	557	1.372		
1950	476	634	.751	−.453	
1951	645	737	.875	.166	−.126
1952	590	741	.796	−.090	−.028
1953	558	834	.669	−.159	−.077
1954	655	962	.681	.018	−.091
1955	710	1,200	.592	−.131	−.080
1956	642	1,241	.517	−.126	−.077
1957	733	1,381	.531	.026	−.094
1958	621	1,429	.435	−.181	−.125
1959	526	1,552	.339	−.220	−.130
1960	561	1,637	.343	.011	−.131
1961	479	1,712	.280	−.184	−.079
1962	480	1,832	.262	−.064	−.092
1963	495	1,944	.255	−.028	−.017
1964	535	2,019	.265	.041	.024
1965	564	2,009	.281	.059	

Sources and method: M_y and other import components from D. S. Paauw, "The Philippines: Estimates of Flows in the Open, Dualistic Economy Framework, 1949–1965," NPA, mimeographed (February 1968), pp. 52–66.

Domestic production was derived by adjusting value added estimates on the basis of annual ratios of value added/domestic production as developed in D. S. Paauw, "The Philippines."

Value added estimates were taken from the National Economic Council, "The National Accounts of the Philippines, CY 1946 to CY 1967," *The Statistical Reporter* 13, no. 1 (January–March 1969).

Note: Definition of symbols.

M_y: Imports of industrial consumer goods

y: Domestic output of industrial consumer goods

$\eta_{M_v/y}$: Growth rate: ratio of imports of industrial consumer goods to domestic output of industrial consumer goods

Table 6. Import Substitution, Foreign Exchange Allocation Sense
(Million pesos, constant 1955 prices)

Year	M_x	M_x/M	M_y	M_y/M	M_p	M_p/M	$\eta_{M_p/M}$ (3-year average)	M
1949	220.8	.120	763.8	.417	849.4	.463		1,834.0
1950	91.9	.076	475.6	.390	649.5	.534		1,217.0
1951	129.4	.083	645.3	.413	787.3	.504	.059	1,562.0
1952	93.4	.062	589.8	.394	812.8	.544	.033	1,496.0
1953	106.8	.067	557.8	.348	936.4	.585	.047	1,601.0
1954	120.3	.066	655.2	.357	1,058.5	.577	.034	1,834.0
1955	145.7	.068	710.2	.332	1,283.1	.600	.025	2,139.0
1956	153.7	.072	641.8	.299	1,279.5	.629	.036	2,145.0
1957	169.4	.067	733.4	.291	1,621.2	.642	.011	2,524.0
1958	151.1	.075	621.1	.306	1,256.8	.619	.028	2,029.0
1959	102.1	.052	526.1	.268	1,332.8	.680	.031	1,961.0
1960	115.0	.052	560.5	.253	1,539.5	.700	.041	2,215.0
1961	231.4	.099	478.8	.205	1,630.8	.696	.023	2,341.0
1962	130.4	.058	480.1	.215	1,624.5	.727	−.008	2,235.0
1963	254.1	.108	494.7	.211	1,599.2	.681	.000	2,348.0
1964	284.6	.107	534.7	.200	1,846.7	.693	−.027	2,666.0
1965	386.3	.135	564.4	.197	1,912.3	.668		2,863.0

Source: D. S. Paauw, "The Philippines: Estimates of Flows in the Open, Dualistic Economy Framework, 1949–1965," NPA, mimeographed (February 1968), p. 62. See pp. 52–66 for discussion of method.

Note: Definition of symbols.

M_x: Imports of agricultural consumer goods
M: Total imports
M_y: Imports of industrial consumer goods
M_p: Imports of producer goods
$\eta_{M_p/M}$: Growth rate: ratio of producer goods imports to total imports

Table 7. Manufacturing Value Added: Annual Growth Rates
(Constant 1955 pesos)

Year

1950–51	.173
1951–52	.052
1952–53	.131
1953–54	.124
1954–55	.126
1955–56	.134
1956–57	.058
1957–58	.084
1958–59	.090
1959–60	.021
1960–61	.041
1961–62	.053
1962–63	.081
1963–64	.017
1964–65	.009
1950–1965	.080
1951–1956	.123
1957–1959	.077
1960–1965	.037

Source: National Economic
Council, "The National Ac-
counts of the Philippines,
CY 1946–1967," *The Sta-
tistical Reporter* 13, no. 1
(January–March 1969).

Table 8. Exports, Imports, and Import Surplus
(Constant prices, million 1955 pesos)

Year	E	M	A
1950	1,279	1,217	−62
1951	1,455	1,562	107
1952	1,507	1,496	−11
1953	1,587	1,601	14
1954	1,708	1,834	126
1955	1,833	2,139	306
1956	2,006	2,145	139
1957	1,991	2,524	533
1958	1,755	2,029	274
1959	1,802	1,961	159
1960	1,978	2,215	237
1961	2,049	2,341	292
1962	2,098	2,235	137
1963	2,250	2,348	98
1964	2,429	2,666	237
1965	2,724	2,868	144

Source: D. S. Paauw, "The Philippines: Estimates of Flows in the Open, Dualistic Economy Framework, 1949–1965," NPA, mimeographed (February 1968), p. 36. See pp. 26–37 for discussion of method.

Note: Unlike table 3 of the Statistical Appendix, estimates of *E* in this table include all receipts, merchandise as well as services.

Definition of symbols.

E: Total exports
M: Total imports
A: Import surplus (equals capital inflow)

Table 9. Exchange Rates: Free Market, *b*, and Official Export, *r*
(Pesos per U.S. $1.00)

Year	b	r
1950	2.87	2.00
1951	3.00	2.00
1952	2.70	2.00
1953	2.82	2.00
1954	2.96	2.00
1955	2.85	2.00
1956	3.21	2.00
1957	3.49	2.00
1958	3.21	2.00
1959	4.30	2.00
1960	3.81	2.50
1961	3.76	2.75
1962	3.93	3.51
1963	3.94	3.51
1964	3.90	3.51
1965	4.15	3.90
1966	3.98	3.89
1967	3.97	3.90

Sources:
b: Midyear quotations from Franz
Pick, *Pick's Currency Yearbook* (New
York: Pick Publishing Corporation,
various years).
r: Official Export rate from *International Financial Statistics*, various
issues.

Table 10. Agricultural Shortfall and Components
(As fraction of total imports)

Year	M_x/M	M_x'/M	F/M
1950	.076	.125	.201
1951	.083	.113	.196
1952	.062	.134	.196
1953	.067	.119	.186
1954	.066	.113	.181
1955	.068	.138	.206
1956	.072	.130	.202
1957	.067	.142	.209
1958	.075	.180	.255
1959	.052	.139	.191
1960	.052	.148	.200
1961	.099	.132	.231
1962	.058	.167	.225
1963	.108	.143	.251
1964	.107	.174	.281
1965	.135	.182	.317

Sources: Estimates of M_x and M_x' were calculated from Central Bank, *Statistical Bulletin*, Bureau of Census and Statistics, *Foreign Trade Statistics of the Philippines*, and from worksheets made available by the Central Bank.

Note: Definition of symbols.
M_x: Imports of agricultural consumer goods
M_x': Imports of agricultural raw materials
M: Total imports
$F (= M_x + M_x')$: Total agricultural shortfall

Table 11. Foreign Trade and Product Series: Thailand
(Million baht, 1962 constant prices)

Year	E	J E_x'	J E_x''	J E_m	J Total	J E_i	M	M_y	A	GDP	Real per capita GDP (Constant 1962 baht)
1951	6,015	5,436	1,885	628	7,949		3,786	1,325	−2,229	37,549	1,993
1952	8,553	5,422	2,459	686	8,567		6,000	2,154	−2,553	39,348	2,050
1953	8,569	5,274	2,523	808	8,605		6,788	2,247	−1,781	42,998	2,199
1954	8,054	6,198	2,300	827	9,325	105	6,942	2,458	−1,112	42,732	2,145
1955	8,689	5,408	2,257	410	8,075	122	7,805	2,771	−884	46,251	2,278
1956	8,790	4,718	3,424	603	8,745	185	8,024	2,912	−766	47,301	2,012
1957	9,506	5,366	3,610	696	9,672	181	8,896	3,203	−610	48,195	1,992
1958	8,206	6,610	3,097	745	10,452	131	9,176	3,358	970	48,576	1,953
1959	8,869	6,405	3,284	921	10,610	124	9,904	3,506	1,035	53,626	2,093
1960	9,809	6,822	3,225	984	11,031	137	10,572	3,774	763	59,347	2,249
1961	10,644	8,986	3,516	1,294	13,796	192	10,546	3,428	−98	61,875	2,274
1962	10,838	9,941	3,192	1,763	14,896	228	12,194	4,122	1,356	65,209	2,324
1963	11,314	12,208	3,562	2,111	17,881	283	13,683	4,474	2,369	71,637	2,477
1964	14,063	13,481	3,699	2,547	19,727	267	15,276	4,583	1,213	76,713	2,573
1965	15,200					304	16,477	5,718	1,277	82,834	2,694
1966	18,358					477	20,044	7,717	1,686	89,190	2,814
1967	20,212					485	24,290		4,078	94,109	2,880

Sources:

E, M, A, M_y: From Thailand, Department of Customs, Annual Statement of Foreign Trade, various years. Export and Import Deflators are taken from IMF, International Financial Statistics.

$J = E_x' + E_x'' + E_m$, and E_i: Ratios for disaggregating E from data in U.N., Yearbook of International Trade Statistics, various years.

Real GDP and Real Per Capita GDP: GDP, with adjustments from National Economic Development Board, National Income of Thailand, various issues. Population series from U.N., Demographic Yearbook.

Note: Definition of symbols.

E:	Total exports	E_i:	Industrial exports
E_x':	Indigenous product exports	M:	Total imports
E_x'':	Processed agricultural product exports	M_y:	Imports of industrial consumer goods
E_m:	Mineral exports	A:	Import surplus (equals capital inflow)
J:	Primary product exports	GDP:	Gross domestic product

Table 12. Primary Product Exports, *J*, as Percentage of Total Exports,
E: Malaysia, Philippines, Taiwan, Thailand, 1954–67

Year	Malaysia	Philippines	Taiwan	Thailand
1954		97.9	85.8	98.7
1955		97.6	85.7	98.6
1956	97.7	97.8	81.1	97.9
1957	97.2	97.6	84.1	98.1
1958	97.2	96.9	79.9	98.4
1959	97.8	95.4	66.8	98.6
1960	97.2	96.6	57.6	98.6
1961	95.6	95.8	46.2	98.2
1962	95.4	94.9	33.4	97.9
1963	94.8	94.8	43.6	97.5
1964	94.2	93.3	44.7	98.1
1965	94.0	93.6	36.9	98.0
1966	93.4		27.4	97.4
1967			19.6	97.6

Sources:
  Malaysia: Statistical Appendix, table 18.
  Philippines: Statistical Appendix, table 3 where $J = E_x + E_m$.
  Taiwan: Statistical Appendix (table 2, Foreign Trade Series), where $J = E_x$.
  Thailand: Statistical Appendix, table 11.

Table 13. Primary Product Exports, *J*, as Percentage of Nonagricultural Value Added, *Y*: Thailand, 1954–67

Year	J	Y	J/Y (%)
1954	7,949.3	24,466	32.49
1955	8,567.3	23,849	35.92
1956	8,605.4	25,296	34.01
1957	9,325.4	26,870	34.70
1958	8,074.7	25,186	32.06
1959	8,744.8	30,055	29.10
1960	9,671.7	30,869	31.33
1961	10,452.4	33,001	31.67
1962	10,610.4	35,899	29.55
1963	11,031.1	38,798	28.43
1964	13,795.8	42,870	32.18
1965	14,896.0	47,378	31.44
1966	17,880.7	53,197	33.61
1967	19,726.9	59,538	33.13

Sources:
   J: Statistical Appendix, table 11.
   Y (nonagricultural value added): Same as source given for
GDP in Statistical Appendix, table 11.

Table 14. Import Substitution, Domestic Market Sense, $y/(y + M_y)$:
Malaysia, Philippines, Taiwan, Thailand

Year	Malaysia	Philippines	Taiwan	Thailand
1950		0.596		
1951		0.560	0.623	0.685
1952		0.595	0.690	0.599
1953		0.637	0.777	0.630
1954		0.627	0.834	0.624
1955		0.636	0.871	0.616
1956		0.686	0.834	0.626
1957		0.670	0.875	0.613
1958		0.722	0.862	0.603
1959		0.769	0.859	0.613
1960	0.410	0.761	0.868	0.603
1961	0.390	0.796	0.882	0.642
1962	0.350	0.804	0.857	0.634
1963	0.370	0.811	0.866	0.636
1964	0.410	0.801	0.866	0.653
1965	0.440	0.794	0.837	0.638
1966	0.470		0.815	0.608
1967	0.530			0.702

Sources:

Malaysia: y (value added in manufacturing) from Department of Statistics, *National Accounts of West Malaysia* (1960–1967). M_y from United Nations, *Yearbook of International Trade Statistics*, various issues.

Philippines: y from National Economic Council, *The Statistical Reporter* (April–June 1969), table 10, p. 52. M_y from Statistical Appendix, table 5.

Taiwan: y from source for *GDP* and components given in Statistical Appendix (table 1, Product and Employment). M_y from Statistical Appendix (table 2, Foreign Trade Series).

Thailand: y from United Nations, *Yearbook of National Account Statistics*, various issues; and National Economic Development Board, *National Income of Thailand*, various issues. M_y from Statistical Appendix, table 11.

Note: Definition of symbols.
y: Domestic output of industrial consumer goods
M_y: Imports of industrial consumer goods

Table 15. Import Substitution, Foreign Exchange Allocation Sense, M_y/M

Year	Taiwan	Philippines	Thailand	Malaysia
1950		.390		
1951		.413	.350	
1952	.318	.394	.359	
1953	.217	.348	.331	
1954	.175	.357	.354	
1955	.147	.332	.355	
1956	.164	.299	.355	
1957	.138	.291	.360	.319
1958	.115	.306	.366	.316
1959	.123	.268	.354	.309
1960	.123	.253	.357	.299
1961	.104	.205	.325	.325
1962	.129	.215	.338	.351
1963	.149	.211	.327	.361
1964	.156	.200	.300	.366
1965	.152	.197	.347	.357
1966	.182	.195	.385	.331
1967	.128	.194		.310
1968		.205		
1969		.194		
1970		.184		

Sources:
   Taiwan: Statistical Appendix, tables 1 and 2.
   Philippines: Statistical Appendix, table 6.
   Thailand: Statistical Appendix, table 11.
   Malaysia: United Nations, Yearbook of International Trade Statistics, various issues.

Note: Definition of symbols.
M_y: Imports of industrial consumer goods
M: Total imports

Table 16. Export Ratios, E/GDP

Year	Taiwan	Philippines	Thailand
1950		.204	
1951		.222	.160
1952	.113	.214	.217
1953	.126	.208	.199
1954	.087	.209	.188
1955	.098	.210	.188
1956	.099	.211	.186
1957	.100	.203	.197
1958	.112	.175	.169
1959	.116	.170	.165
1960	.123	.182	.175
1961	.129	.176	.180
1962	.133	.175	.170
1963	.156	.178	.164
1964	.173	.187	.191
1965	.187	.197	.191
1966	.195	.203	.206
1967	.204	.210	.215

Sources:
  Taiwan: Statistical Appendix, tables 1 and 2.
  Philippines: Statistical Appendix, table 3.
  Thailand: Statistical Appendix, table 11.

Note: Definition of symbols.
E: Total exports
GDP: Gross domestic product

Table 17. Capital Inflow, 3-Year Moving Average
(Million U.S. dollars)

Year	Taiwan	Philippines	Thailand
1952		12.1	−105.0
1953	61.4	14.3	− 87.1
1954	52.5	49.6	− 60.4
1955	59.8	63.5	− 44.2
1956	54.8	108.7	− 36.2
1957	66.5	108.4	− 19.6
1958	64.4	110.8	22.3
1959	60.8	77.9	44.3
1960	77.0	91.9	27.2
1961	81.3	89.4	32.3
1962	62.8	77.8	58.0
1963	15.5	53.3	79.0
1964	− 9.9	51.6	77.7
1965	−27.0		66.8
1966	−30.3		112.6

Sources and method:

Taiwan: Statistical Appendix (table 2, Foreign Trade Series). N.T. dollar estimates converted to U.S. dollars using exchange rate of N.T. $40.03 = U.S. $1.00, which is 1964 rate given in International Monetary Fund, *International Financial Statistics.*

Philippines: Same source as given for Table 8 in Statistical Appendix.

Thailand: Statistical Appendix, table 11, source given for *A.* Baht estimates converted to U.S. dollars using exchange rate of baht 20.84 = U.S. $1.00, which is 1962 rate given in International Monetary Fund, *International Financial Statistics.*

Table 18. West Malaysia: Composition of Exports[a]
(Million Malaysian dollars)

Year	$J = E_x + E_m$	J		E_i	$E = J + E_i$
		E_x	E_m		
1956	2,144.7	1,582.9	561.8	50.0	2,194.7
1957	2,057.4	1,516.5	540.9	59.5	2,116.9
1958	1,763.5	1 400.2	363.3	51.0	1,814.5
1959	2,338.1	1,909.9	428.2	53.6	2,391.7
1960	2,746.2	2,071.7	674.5	78.9	2,825.1
1961	2,412.2	1,669.9	742.3	110.2	2,522.4
1962	2,456.8	1,645.3	811.5	118.3	2,575.1
1963	2,522.3	1,670.1	852.2	138.5	2,660.8
1964	2,577.8	1,621.9	955.9	159.0	2,736.8
1965	2,868.3	1,758.5	1,109.8	182.0	3,050.3
1966	2,877.2	1,833.8	1,043.4	202.2	3,079.4
1967	2,650.6	1,676.2	974.4	201.9	2,852.6

Source: United Nations, *Yearbook of International Trade Statistics*, various issues.

Note: Definition of symbols.

J: Primary product exports
E_x: Agricultural exports
E_m: Mineral exports
E_i: Industrial exports
E: Total merchandise exports

a. Total exports and components refer only to merchandise exports (i.e., service exports are not included).

Table 19a. West Malaysia: Composition of Exports, 1956–66
(By type, as fraction of total)

Year	Unprocessed agricultural products E_x'/E	Processed agricultural products E_x''/E	Mineral products E_m/E	Manufactured products E_i/E
1956	.044	.677	.256	.023
1957	.045	.671	.256	.028
1958	.048	.724	.200	.028
1959	.073	.726	.179	.022
1960	.080	.653	.239	.028
1961	.079	.583	.294	.044
1962	.045	.594	.315	.046
1963	.053	.575	.320	.052
1964	.061	.532	.349	.058
1965	.062	.514	.364	.060
1966	.068	.527	.339	.066

Source: Basic data from United Nations, *Yearbook of International Trade Statistics*, various issues.

Note: See Table 19b for definition of symbols.

Table 19b. West Malaysia: Tin and Rubber Prices

Year	Tin	Rubber	P rubber/P tin	Index
1955	740	114	.154	100
1956	787	96	.122	79
1957	754	88	.117	76
1958	734	80	.109	71
1959	785	101	.129	84
1960	796	108	.136	88
1961	888	83	.093	60
1962	896	78	.087	56
1963	909	72	.079	51
1964	1,239	68	.055	36
1965	1,413	70	.050	33
1966	1,296	65	.050	33

Source: Department of Statistics, West Malaysia, *Statistical Bulletin of West Malaysia*, various issues.

Note: Definition of symbols (for tables 19a and b):

E_x': Unprocessed agricultural product exports
E_x'': Processed agricultural product exports
E_m: Mineral product exports
E_i: Industrial exports
E: Total merchandise exports
P: Export price

Table 20. Indigenous (Unprocessed) Products as Fraction of
Primary Product Exports, E_x'/J: Malaysia, Thailand

Year	Malaysia	Thailand
1954		0.68
1955		0.63
1956	0.04	0.61
1957	0.05	0.67
1958	0.05	0.67
1959	0.08	0.54
1960	0.08	0.56
1961	0.08	0.63
1962	0.05	0.60
1963	0.06	0.62
1964	0.07	0.65
1965	0.07	0.67
1966	0.07	0.68
1967		0.68

Source: Basic data from United Nations, *Year-book of International Trade Statistics,* various issues.

Table 21. Malaysia: Export Ratio, Terms of Trade,
Capital Flow, J-Index, GDP Growth Rate

Year	Export ratio (1)	Terms of trade (2)	Capital flow (3)	J-Index (4)	GDP growth rate, η_{GDP} (5)
1955	0.50	100.0	-0.297		
1956	0.48	89.0	-0.104	0.66	0.034
1957	0.46	81.0	-0.052	0.65	0.025
1958	0.42	76.4	0.006	0.63	-0.007
1959	0.48	95.2	-0.235	0.65	0.047
1960	0.51	97.0	-0.153	0.64	0.142
1961	0.49	82.0	-0.006	0.61	0.071
1962	0.48	81.5	0.064	0.61	0.058
1963	0.46	75.6	0.069	0.60	0.050
1964	0.44	75.5	0.046	0.55	0.047
1965	0.45	82.8	-0.011	0.57	0.071
1966	0.43	79.6	0.011	0.55	0.056
1967		72.3			0.049

Sources and methods:

Column 1: Basic data from Statistical Appendix, table 18; and Malaysia, Department of Statistics, *National Accounts of West Malaysia,* various issues.

Column 2: Economic Commission for Asia and the Far East, *Economic Survey of Asia and the Far East,* various issues.

Column 3: Malaysia, Department of Statistics, *National Accounts of West Malaysia* (1966); and United Nations, *Yearbook of National Accounts Statistics,* various issues.

Column 4: $J = J/Y$ where J is primary product exports and Y is nonagricultural value added. J from Statistical Appendix, table 18, and Y from Department of Statistics, Malaysia, *National Accounts of West Malaysia,* various issues.

Column 5: GDP in constant 1964 prices estimated from source immediately above.

Table 22. Index of Real Per Capita GDP (1955 = 100.0): West Malaysia,
Philippines, Taiwan, Thailand

Year	West Malaysia	Philippines	Taiwan	Thailand
1955	100.0	100.0	100.0	100.0
1956	100.5	104.8	100.5	88.4
1957	100.0	105.7	105.5	87.4
1958	95.9	104.8	109.0	85.7
1959	97.4	107.6	112.7	91.9
1960	107.8	107.2	115.4	98.7
1961	111.7	110.9	120.5	99.8
1962	114.4	110.7	125.0	102.0
1963	116.4	112.8	133.1	108.7
1964	118.7	112.0	146.4	112.9
1965	123.6	115.2	159.9	118.3
1966	126.4	117.7	169.8	123.5
1967	128.2	120.1	181.7	126.4

Sources:

West Malaysia: Statistical Appendix, table 21; United Nations, *Demographic Yearbook*, various issues.

Philippines: National Economic Council, *The Statistical Reporter*, various issues.

Taiwan: Statistical Appendix, table 1; United Nations, *Demographic Yearbook*, various issues.

Thailand: Statistical Appendix, table 11.

Statistical Appendix   285

Table 23. Growth Rates of Real Per Capita GDP (3-Year moving averages):
Malaysia, Philippines, Taiwan, Thailand

Year	Malaysia	Philippines	Taiwan	Thailand
1955		.042	.028	−.001
1956		.031	.034	−.021
1957	−.010	.021	.029	−.048
1958	−.007	.014	.039	−.022
1959	.027	.013	.031	−.014
1960	.053	.022	.034	.052
1961	.056	.014	.035	.036
1962	.026	.019	.049	.033
1963	.020	.010	.067	.042
1964	.026	.019	.086	.051
1965	.028	.020	.085	.043
1966	.026	.025	.075	.038
AVERAGE	.021	.015	.055	.020

Sources: Same as for table 22 in Statistical Appendix.

Table 24. Indexes of Labor Productivity in Agriculture, *p*, and
Nonagriculture, *h* (1955 = 100.0)

Year	Taiwan		Philippines		Thailand		Malaysia	
	p	*h*	*p*	*h*	*p*	*h*	*p*	*h*
1955	100.0	100.0	100.0	100.0	100.0	100.0	100.0	100.0
1956	97.7	107.4	98.7	103.8	96.3	101.8	99.7	102.4
1957	105.4	107.9	98.3	105.0	91.0	103.6	102.0	102.2
1958	111.3	110.5	98.3	112.3	99.4	93.4	105.3	96.9
1959	124.7	111.3	89.5	117.4	100.3	104.8	107.8	99.9
1960	132.1	114.1	88.7	120.7	109.1	111.6	114.1	115.1
1961	133.9	121.1	88.6	118.7	113.0	111.5	123.8	119.4
1962	129.1	130.1	85.2	118.2	112.7	115.2	127.3	124.6
1963	129.2	139.5	90.6	115.3	120.1	122.5	130.0	129.4
1964	151.8	150.4	86.0	116.9	121.6	128.9	133.2	133.6
1965	162.7	168.1	88.5	121.2	121.0	138.0	139.8	141.0
1966	167.4	177.8					148.3	145.2
1967							154.3	149.2

Sources:

Taiwan: Statistical Appendix, table 1.

Philippines: D. S. Paauw, "The Philippines: Estimates of the Flows in the Open Dualistic Framework, 1949–1965," mimeographed (February 1968).

Thailand: Product estimates from National Economic Development Board, *National Income of Thailand*, various issues; employment estimates from National Statistical Office, *1960 Census* and later surveys.

Malaysia: Product estimates same source as Statistical Appendix, table 21; employment estimates from International Labor Office, *Yearbook of Labor Statistics* and Malaysian data.

Table 25. Fraction of Labor Force Employed in Nonagriculture, θ

Year	Taiwan	Philippines	Thailand	Malaysia
1951	.38	.37	.22	
1952	.39	.37	.22	
1953	.39	.37	.22	
1954	.40	.37	.23	
1955	.40	.37	.23	.41
1956	.40	.38	.24	.42
1957	.42	.39	.24	.42
1958	.43	.37	.25	.43
1959	.43	.38	.25	.44
1960	.44	.39	.25	.44
1961	.44	.39	.25	.45
1962	.45	.38	.26	.45
1963	.45	.41	.26	.46
1964	.46	.41	.26	.46
1965	.46	.41	.27	.47
1966	.47			.47
1967				.48

Sources: Same as for table 24 in Statistical Appendix.

Index

Agricultural export sector: commercialized, in colonial economy, 4, 5; interaction with industry, 14–16, 196–97; under import substitution growth, 19, 55, 131; discriminated against by tariffs, 44–45; under neocolonialism, 70, 166; under indigenous export-led growth, 172; in Malaysia, 196–97, 211
Agricultural gap: large, defined, 136; critical, 136, 138; increasing, 136, 138–40, 147; small, 136, 139; constant, 136–38; effects on import substitution growth, 136–40; phases of, 140; under prolonged import substitution growth, 147. *See also* Agricultural shortfall
Agricultural orientation, index of: defined, 166; behavior of, 170–74; in Thailand, 184–85, 190, 191; in Malaysia, 223–24
Agricultural sector, traditional, 10, 87; under colonialism, 4, 7, 8, 11; modernization during transition growth, 7, 14, 23, 33, 55, 86, 87, 93–94, 113–15, 124–25, 126, 128–30, 146, 154, 164, 197, 210–11, 233, 235, 245–47, 249, 253–54, 255, 257; as basis for industrialization, 14–17; changing role in transitional economy, 16–17; interaction with industry, 16–17, 24, 31–32, 77, 112, 115–16, 117–20, 122, 126, 128, 198–200; under import substitution growth, 24, 25, 55, 126, 128, 129, 130, 147, 148, 245–46, 247; labor migration from, to industry, 24, 113–16, 126, 128;

under export substitution growth, 31–32, 120, 121; and emergence of export substitution growth, 33, 113–15, 164, 233, 246–47, 249; under economic nationalism, 38–41, 79, 84; and inflation, 42; in Taiwan, 55–56, 86, 93–94, 112, 114–15, 117–20, 122, 229; in the Philippines, 55–56, 124–26, 128–29, 140, 151 53, 154, 158, 164, 230, 233, 238, 246, 253–54; under neocolonialism, 57, 59, 60, 61, 78, 85; productivity during transition, 59, 77, 116, 120–22, 158, 229, 230, 233, 238; in open dualistic economies, 77, 83; and typology of transition growth, 85–86; in Thailand, 87, 177–78; and industrial sector, productivity compared during export substitution growth, 120, 121; affected by entrepreneurial deficiency, 124–25; backwardness, and prolonged import substitution growth, 126–28, 141, 146, 151; and the modern enclave, 126, 193–94, 244; during retardation phase of import substitution growth, 130, 158; inputs from industry, during prolonged import substitution growth, 141–43; during export promotion growth, 166; and primary product export expansion, 167–69; in Malaysia, 193–95, 197, 204, 205, 208, 209, 210–11; under modern export-led growth, 198–200; under combined import substitution/export promotion growth, 255

289

Entrepreneurship, 7, 8, 14; and export substitution growth, 33, 73n, 112, 113, 115–16, 253; under import substitution growth, 35, 51–52, 53, 54, 73n, 77, 78, 79, 98, 113, 124, 133, 147–48, 244–45; availability, and investment finance, 47; and termination of import substitution growth, 55–56, 79, 124–25, 134; and investment demand function, under neocolonialism, 65; and import competition, under neocolonialism, 73n, 75; in the Philippines and Taiwan, contrasted, 86–87; in Taiwan, 93–94, 113, 115, 153; and backward-linkage import substitution, 97; and rate of industrialization, 120, 122; in the Philippines, 125, 128, 129, 151, 153, 164, 253; and prolonged import substitution, 141, 146; in Hong Kong, 153; in Thailand, 176–77, 179; in Malaysia, 223, 224

Epoch: economic, defined, 3

Ethnic groups: and politics of neocolonialism, 58–59, 71, 72, 84–85; in Malaysia and Thailand, compared, 71, 84–85; empirical measurement of composition, 87–88; nondiscriminatory policy toward, in Thailand, 178–79; economic specialization of, in Malaysia, 193, 194, 205, 209; access to export sector, in Malaysia, 211–12; and future growth in Malaysia, 223, 224. *See also* Aliens; Entrepreneurs

Evans, Hans-Dieter, 176n

Evolution: economic, during transition growth, 8–9, 249

Exchange Equalization Fund, 176

Exchange, foreign: provided by primary product exports, 15, 23, 126, 127, 177; use under import substitution growth, 96, 97, 126; and agricultural shortfall, 128, 140; utilization under prolonged import substitution, 143; use in Taiwan, 153, 229

Exchange rate: under export promo-

tion growth, 29, 53; free market and official, 38–39, 40; effect of overvaluation on industrial sector, 40–41; and inflation, 43; under import substitution growth, 50, 99, 141, 173; system, in Taiwan, 108–10; in the Philippines, 159–61; system, in Thailand, 176–77; realistic, as liberalization policy, 248
— policy: analytical model of, 38–41; under import substitution growth, 38–42; and profit transfer, 38–42, 244; and tariff policy, 43–45; impact on investment, 45–47

Export capacity: in Taiwan, 108–09

Export growth: under colonialism, 5–6, 15, 17–18, 28–29, 36, 173; under export promotion growth, 25–28, 29; under neocolonialism, 58, 61, 62, 68–70, 71; under import substitution growth, 72, 79, 83, 85, 140–48, 166–67, 240; under prolonged import substitution, 79, 124, 141, 143–45, 146, 148, 161–62; in the Philippines, 160–61, 230; in Thailand, 165, 177–79, 180–83, 190–91; and real cost of export production, 166; indigenous export-led, 166, 167–74; modern export-led, 166–67, 195–204; in Malaysia, 192, 195, 196–98, 206; use of liberalization policies for, 248–49. *See also* Export promotion growth; Export substitution growth; Growth rate; Import substitution growth

Export promotion growth, 13, 50; under neocolonialism, 13, 57, 58, 59, 77–78, 166; defined, 17–18; operation in free market system, 18, 61–67; as alternative to import substitution growth, 24–25; major features of, 24–25, 28–30; analytical model of, 25–28; mathematical model of, 27; contrasted with import substitution growth, 28–30; combined with import substitution growth, 30–31, 52–53, 255–56; and natural resource endowments, 60, 83, 124; duration of, 80; political determinants of, 85, 176;

Economic Growth Center Book Publications

*Werner Baer, *Industrialization and Economic Development in Brazil* (1965).

Werner Baer and Isaac Kerstenetzky, eds., *Inflation and Growth in Latin America* (1964).

*Bela A. Balassa, *Trade Prospects for Developing Countries* (1964).

Carlos F. Díaz Alejandro, *Essays on the Economic History of the Argentine Republic* (1970).

*John C. H. Fei and Gustav Ranis, *Development of Labor Surplus Economy: Theory and Policy* (1964).

*Gerald K. Helleiner, *Peasant Agriculture, Government, and Economic Growth in Nigeria* (1966).

*Lawrence R. Klein and Kazushi Ohkawa, eds., *Economic Growth: The Japanese Experience since the Meiji Era* (1968)

*A. Lamfalussy, *The United Kingdom and the Six* (1963).

*Markos J. Mamalakis and Clark W. Reynolds, *Essays on the Chilean Economy* (1965).

*Donald C. Mead, *Growth and Structural Change in the Egyptian Economy* (1967).

*Richard Moorsteen and Raymond P. Powell, *The Soviet Capital Stock* (1966).

Howard Pack, *Structural Change and Economic Policy in Israel* (1971).

*Frederick L. Pryor, *Public Expenditures in Communist and Capitalist Nations* (1968).

Gustav Ranis, ed., *Government and Economic Development* (1971).

Clark W. Reynolds, *The Mexican Economy: Twentieth-Century Structure and Growth* (1970).

*Lloyd G. Reynolds and Peter Gregory, *Wages, Productivity, and Industrialization in Puerto Rico* (1965).

*Donald R. Snodgrass, *Ceylon: An Export Economy in Transition* (1966).

* Available from Richard D. Irwin, Inc., 1818 Ridge Rd., Homewood, Ill. 60430.